1972

By William James

THE VARIETIES OF RELIGIOUS EXPERIENCE: A STUDY IN HU-MAN NATURE. Gifford Lectures delivered at Edinburgh University. 8vo. New York, London, Bombay, and Calcutta: Longmans, Green & Co.

PRAGMATISM: A NEW NAME FOR SOME OLD WAYS OF THINK-ING together with FOUR RELATED ESSAYS SELECTED FROM THE MEANING OF TRUTH. 8vo. New York, London, Bombay, and Calcutta: Longmans, Green & Co.

THE MEANING OF TRUTH: A SEQUEL TO "PRAGMATISM." 8vo. New York, London, Bombay, and Calcutta: Longmans, Green & Co.

SOME PROBLEMS OF PHILOSOPHY: A BEGINNING OF AN IN-TRODUCTION TO PHILOSOPHY. 8vo. New York, London, Bom-bay, and Calcutta: Longmans, Green & Co.

ESSAYS IN RADICAL EMPIRICISM and A PLURALISTIC UNI-VERSE (in one volume). 8vo. New York, London, Bombay, and Cal-cutta: Longmans, Green & Co.

ESSAYS ON FAITH AND MORALS (selected from volumes originally entitled THE WILL TO BELIEVE AND OTHER ESSAYS IN POPU-LAR PHILOSOPHY, TALKS TO TEACHERS, and MEMORIES AND STUDIES). 12mo. New York, London, Bombay, and Calcutta: Longmans, Green & Co.

THE PRINCIPLES OF PSYCHOLOGY. 2 vols., 8vo. New York: Henry Holt & Co. London: Macmillan & Co.

PSYCHOLOGY: BRIEFER COURSE. 12mo. New York: Henry Holt & Co. London: Macmillan & Co.

TALKS TO TEACHERS ON PSYCHOLOGY: AND TO STUDENTS ON SOME OF LIFE'S IDEALS. 12mo. New York: Henry Holt & Co. London, Bombay, and Calcutta: Longmans, Green & Co.

COLLECTED ESSAYS AND REVIEWS. Edited by R. B. Perry. 8vo. New York, London, Bombay, and Calcutta: Longmans, Green & Co.

ON VITAL RESERVES. Reprint of "The Energies of Men" and the "Gospel of Relaxation." 16mo. New York: Henry Holt & Co.

ON SOME OF LIFE'S IDEALS. Reprint of "On a Certain Blindness in Human Beings" and "What Makes a Life Significant." 16mo. New York: Henry Holt & Co.

LETTERS OF WILLIAM JAMES. Selected and edited with Biographical Introduction and Notes by his son Henry James. 2 vols., 8vo. Boston: Little, Brown & Co.

ESSAYS IN
RADICAL EMPIRICISM

A PLURALISTIC
UNIVERSE

By WILLIAM JAMES

GLOUCESTER, MASS.

PETER SMITH

1967

EDITOR'S PREFACE

THE present volume is composed of two previously published volumes, *Essays in Radical Empiricism*, originally published in 1912, and *A Pluralistic Universe*, originally published in 1909. Although the *Essays in Radical Empiricism* was not published until after James's death, the several essays had appeared in the years 1905–1907 and were collected and bound under the above title by James himself in the latter year. He considered them as forming a connected whole. For a summary statement of the doctrine the reader is referred to the Preface of *The Meaning of Truth*, reprinted in the new edition of *Pragmatism*. Four essays which appeared in the earlier edition of *Essays in Radical Empiricism* are here omitted — IX, X, and XI because they are primarily controversial in character, and XII because it dates from earlier years before the doctrine of Radical Empiricism had been matured. *A Plural-*

EDITOR'S PREFACE

istic Universe is reprinted without change other than the omission of Appendices A and B, which here appear as parts of the *Essays in Radical Empiricism*. Except for the above omissions and the consolidation of the indexes, the paging of the original volumes is preserved. The present edition makes available within a single volume the most important of James's metaphysical writings.

RALPH BARTON PERRY

CAMBRIDGE, MASSACHUSETTS
September 1, 1942

CONTENTS

VOLUME I. ESSAYS IN RADICAL EMPIRICISM

VOLUME II. A PLURALISTIC UNIVERSE

LECTURE I

Our age is growing philosophical again, 3. Change of tone since 1860, 4. Empiricism and Rationalism defined, 7. The process of Philosophizing: Philosophers choose some part of the world to interpret the whole by, 8. They seek to make it seem less strange, 11. Their temperamental differences, 12. Their systems must be reasoned out, 13. Their tendency to over-technicality, 15. Excess of this in Germany, 17. The type of vision is the important thing in a philosopher, 20. Primitive thought, 21. Spiritualism and Materialism: Spiritualism shows two types, 23. Theism and Pantheism, 24. Theism makes a duality of Man and God, and leaves Man an outsider, 25. Pantheism identifies Man with God, 29. The con-

CONTENTS

CONTENTS

CONTENTS

CONTENTS

CONTENTS

VOLUME I

ESSAYS IN RADICAL EMPIRICISM

I

DOES 'CONSCIOUSNESS' EXIST?[1]

'THOUGHTS' and 'things' are names for two
sorts of object, which common sense will always find contrasted and will always practically oppose to each other. Philosophy, reflecting on the contrast, has varied in the
past in her explanations of it, and may be
expected to vary in the future. At first,
'spirit and matter,' 'soul and body,' stood for
a pair of equipollent substances quite on a par
in weight and interest. But one day Kant undermined the soul and brought in the transcendental ego, and ever since then the bipolar
relation has been very much off its balance.
The transcendental ego seems nowadays in
rationalist quarters to stand for everything, in
empiricist quarters for almost nothing. In the
hands of such writers as Schuppe, Rehmke,
Natorp, Münsterberg — at any rate in his

[1] [Reprinted from the *Journal of Philosophy, Psychology and Scientific Methods*, vol. I, No. 18, September 1, 1904. For the relation between this essay and those which follow, cf. below, pp. 53–54. ED.]

1

earlier writings, Schubert-Soldern and others, the spiritual principle attenuates itself to a thoroughly ghostly condition, being only a name for the fact that the 'content' of experience *is known*. It loses personal form and activity — these passing over to the content — and becomes a bare *Bewusstheit* or *Bewusstsein überhaupt*, of which in its own right absolutely nothing can be said.

I believe that 'consciousness,' when once it has evaporated to this estate of pure diaphaneity, is on the point of disappearing altogether. It is the name of a nonentity, and has no right to a place among first principles. Those who still cling to it are clinging to a mere echo, the faint rumor left behind by the disappearing 'soul' upon the air of philosophy. During the past year, I have read a number of articles whose authors seemed just on the point of abandoning the notion of consciousness,[1] and substituting for it that of an absolute experience not due to two factors. But they were not

[1] Articles by Baldwin, Ward, Bawden, King, Alexander and others. Dr. Perry is frankly over the border.

quite radical enough, not quite daring enough in their negations. For twenty years past I have mistrusted 'consciousness' as an entity; for seven or eight years past I have suggested its non-existence to my students, and tried to give them its pragmatic equivalent in realities of experience. It seems to me that the hour is ripe for it to be openly and universally discarded.

To deny plumply that 'consciousness' exists seems so absurd on the face of it — for undeniably 'thoughts' do exist — that I fear some readers will follow me no farther. Let me then immediately explain that I mean only to deny that the word stands for an entity, but to insist most emphatically that it does stand for a function. There is, I mean, no aboriginal stuff or quality of being,[1] contrasted with that of which material objects are made, out of which our thoughts of them are made; but there is a function in experience which thoughts perform, and for the performance of which this

---

[1] [Similarly, there is no "activity of 'consciousness' as such." See below, pp. 170 ff., note. Ed.]

quality of being is invoked. That function is *knowing*. 'Consciousness' is supposed necessary to explain the fact that things not only are, but get reported, are known. Whoever blots out the notion of consciousness from his list of first principles must still provide in some way for that function's being carried on.

I

My thesis is that if we start with the supposition that there is only one primal stuff or material in the world, a stuff of which everything is composed, and if we call that stuff 'pure experience,' then knowing can easily be explained as a particular sort of relation towards one another into which portions of pure experience may enter. The relation itself is a part of pure experience; one of its 'terms' becomes the subject or bearer of the knowledge, the knower,[1] the other becomes the object known. This will need much explanation before it can be understood. The best way to

---

[1] In my *Psychology* I have tried to show that we need no knower other than the 'passing thought.' [*Principles of Psychology*, vol. I, pp. 338 ff.]

get it understood is to contrast it with the alternative view; and for that we may take the recentest alternative, that in which the evaporation of the definite soul-substance has proceeded as far as it can go without being yet complete. If neo-Kantism has expelled earlier forms of dualism, we shall have expelled all forms if we are able to expel neo-Kantism in its turn.

For the thinkers I call neo-Kantian, the word consciousness to-day does no more than signalize the fact that experience is indefeasibly dualistic in structure. It means that not subject, not object, but object-plus-subject is the minimum that can actually be. The subject-object distinction meanwhile is entirely different from that between mind and matter, from that between body and soul. Souls were detachable, had separate destinies; things could happen to them. To consciousness as such nothing can happen, for, timeless itself, it is only a witness of happenings in time, in which it plays no part. It is, in a word, but the logical correlative of 'content' in an Experience of which the peculiarity is that *fact comes to light* in it, that *awareness of content* takes place. Consciousness as such is entirely impersonal — 'self' and its activities belong to the content. To say that I am self-conscious, or conscious of putting forth volition, means only that certain contents, for which 'self' and 'effort of will' are the names, are not without witness as they occur.

Thus, for these belated drinkers at the Kantian spring, we should have to admit consciousness as an 'epistemological' necessity, even if we had no direct evidence of its being there.

But in addition to this, we are supposed by almost every one to have an immediate consciousness of consciousness itself. When the world of outer fact ceases to be materially present, and we merely recall it in memory, or fancy it, the consciousness is believed to stand out and to be felt as a kind of impalpable inner flowing, which, once known in this sort of experience, may equally be detected in presentations of the outer world. "The moment we try to fix our attention upon consciousness and to see *what*, distinctly, it is," says a recent writer,

6

"it seems to vanish. It seems as if we had before us a mere emptiness. When we try to in-
trospect the sensation of blue, all we can see is
the blue; the other element is as if it were dia-
phanous. Yet it *can* be distinguished, if we
look attentively enough, and know that there
is something to look for." [1] "Consciousness"
(Bewusstheit), says another philosopher, "is
inexplicable and hardly describable, yet all conscious experiences have this in common that
what we call their content has this peculiar reference to a centre for which 'self' is the name,
in virtue of which reference alone the content
is subjectively given, or appears. . . . While
in this way consciousness, or reference to a
self, is the only thing which distinguishes a conscious content from any sort of being that
might be there with no one conscious of it, yet
this only ground of the distinction defies all
closer explanations. The existence of consciousness, although it is the fundamental fact of
psychology, can indeed be laid down as certain, can be brought out by analysis, but can

[1] G. E. Moore: *Mind*, vol. xii, N. S., [1903], p. 450.

neither be defined nor deduced from anything but itself." [1]

'Can be brought out by analysis,' this author says. This supposes that the consciousness is one element, moment, factor — call it what you like — of an experience of essentially dualistic inner constitution, from which, if you abstract the content, the consciousness will remain revealed to its own eye. Experience, at this rate, would be much like a paint of which the world pictures were made. Paint has a dual constitution, involving, as it does, a menstruum [2] (oil, size or what not) and a mass of content in the form of pigment suspended therein. We can get the pure menstruum by letting the pigment settle, and the pure pigment by pouring off the size or oil. We operate here by physical subtraction; and the usual view is, that by mental subtraction we can separate the two factors of experience in an

---

[1] Paul Natorp: *Einleitung in die Psychologie*, 1888, pp. 14, 112.

[2] "Figuratively speaking, consciousness may be said to be the one universal solvent, or menstruum, in which the different concrete kinds of psychic acts and facts are contained, whether in concealed or in obvious form." G. T. Ladd: *Psychology, Descriptive and Explanatory*, 1894, p. 30.

analogous way — not isolating them entirely, but distinguishing them enough to know that they are two.

II

Now my contention is exactly the reverse of this. *Experience, I believe, has no such inner duplicity; and the separation of it into consciousness and content comes, not by way of subtraction, but by way of addition* — the addition, to a given concrete piece of it, of other sets of experiences, in connection with which severally its use or function may be of two different kinds. The paint will also serve here as an illustration. In a pot in a paint-shop, along with other paints, it serves in its entirety as so much saleable matter. Spread on a canvas, with other paints around it, it represents, on the contrary, a feature in a picture and performs a spiritual function. Just so, I maintain, does a given undivided portion of experience, taken in one context of associates, play the part of a knower, of a state of mind, of 'consciousness'; while in a different context the same undivided bit of experience plays the part of a thing known, of an objective 'content.' In a word, in one group it figures as a thought, in another group as a thing. And, since it can figure in both groups simultaneously we have every right to speak of it as subjective and objective both at once. The dualism connoted by such double-barrelled terms as 'experience,' 'phenomenon,' 'datum,' '*Vorfindung*' — terms which, in philosophy at any rate, tend more and more to replace the single-barrelled terms of 'thought' and 'thing' — that dualism, I say, is still preserved in this account, but reinterpreted, so that, instead of being mysterious and elusive, it becomes verifiable and concrete. It is an affair of relations, it falls outside, not inside, the single experience considered, and can always be particularized and defined.

The entering wedge for this more concrete way of understanding the dualism was fashioned by Locke when he made the word 'idea' stand indifferently for thing and thought, and by Berkeley when he said that what common sense means by realities is exactly what the philosopher means by ideas. Neither Locke nor Berkeley thought his truth out into perfect clearness, but it seems to me that the conception I am defending does little more than consistently carry out the 'pragmatic' method which they were the first to use.

If the reader will take his own experiences, he will see what I mean. Let him begin with a perceptual experience, the 'presentation,' so called, of a physical object, his actual field of vision, the room he sits in, with the book he is reading as its centre; and let him for the present treat this complex object in the common-sense way as being 'really' what it seems to be, namely, a collection of physical things cut out from an environing world of other physical things with which these physical things have actual or potential relations. Now at the same time it is just *those self-same things* which his mind, as we say, perceives; and the whole philosophy of perception from Democritus's time downwards has been just one long wrangle over the paradox that what is evidently one reality should be in two places at once, both in outer space and in a person's mind. 'Represent-

11

ative' theories of perception avoid the logical paradox, but on the other hand they violate the reader's sense of life, which knows no intervening mental image but seems to see the room and the book immediately just as they physically exist.

The puzzle of how the one identical room can be in two places is at bottom just the puzzle of how one identical point can be on two lines. It can, if it be situated at their intersection; and similarly, if the 'pure experience' of the room were a place of intersection of two processes, which connected it with different groups of associates respectively, it could be counted twice over, as belonging to either group, and spoken of loosely as existing in two places, although it would remain all the time a numerically single thing.

Well, the experience is a member of diverse processes that can be followed away from it along entirely different lines. The one self-identical thing has so many relations to the rest of experience that you can take it in disparate systems of association, and treat it as belonging with opposite contexts.[1] In one of these contexts it is your 'field of consciousness'; in another it is 'the room in which you sit,' and it enters both contexts in its wholeness, giving no pretext for being said to attach itself to consciousness by one of its parts or aspects, and to outer reality by another. What are the two processes, now, into which the room-experience simultaneously enters in this way?

One of them is the reader's personal biography, the other is the history of the house of which the room is part. The presentation, the experience, the *that* in short (for until we have decided *what* it is it must be a mere *that*) is the last term of a train of sensations, emotions, decisions, movements, classifications, expectations, etc., ending in the present, and the first term of a series of similar 'inner' operations extending into the future, on the reader's part. On the other hand, the very same *that* is the *terminus ad quem* of a lot of previous

---

[1] [For a parallel statement of this view, cf. the author's *Meaning of Truth*, p. 49, note. Cf. also below, pp. 196–197. ED.]

physical operations, carpentering, papering, furnishing, warming, etc., and the *terminus a quo* of a lot of future ones, in which it will be concerned when undergoing the destiny of a physical room. The physical and the mental operations form curiously incompatible groups. As a room, the experience has occupied that spot and had that environment for thirty years. As your field of consciousness it may never have existed until now. As a room, attention will go on to discover endless new details in it. As your mental state merely, few new ones will emerge under attention's eye. As a room, it will take an earthquake, or a gang of men, and in any case a certain amount of time, to destroy it. As your subjective state, the closing of your eyes, or any instantaneous play of your fancy will suffice. In the real world, fire will consume it. In your mind, you can let fire play over it without effect. As an outer object, you must pay so much a month to inhabit it. As an inner content, you may occupy it for any length of time rent-free. If, in short, you follow it in the mental direction, taking it along with events of personal biography solely, all sorts of things are true of it which are false, and false of it which are true if you treat it as a real thing experienced, follow it in the physical direction, and relate it to associates in the outer world.

III

So far, all seems plain sailing, but my thesis will probably grow less plausible to the reader when I pass from percepts to concepts, or from the case of things presented to that of things remote. I believe, nevertheless, that here also the same law holds good. If we take conceptual manifolds, or memories, or fancies, they also are in their first intention mere bits of pure experience, and, as such, are single *thats* which act in one context as objects, and in another context figure as mental states. By taking them in their first intention, I mean ignoring their relation to possible perceptual experiences with which they may be connected, which they may lead to and terminate in, and which then they may be supposed to 'repre-

15

sent.' Taking them in this way first, we confine the problem to a world merely 'thought-
of' and not directly felt or seen.[1] This world,
just like the world of percepts, comes to us at
first as a chaos of experiences, but lines of order
soon get traced. We find that any bit of it
which we may cut out as an example is connected with distinct groups of associates, just
as our perceptual experiences are, that these
associates link themselves with it by different
relations,[2] and that one forms the inner history
of a person, while the other acts as an impersonal 'objective' world, either spatial and temporal, or else merely logical or mathematical,
or otherwise 'ideal.'

The first obstacle on the part of the reader to
seeing that these non-perceptual experiences

[1] [For the author's recognition of "concepts as a co-ordinate
realm" of reality, cf. his *Meaning of Truth*, pp. 42, 195, note; *A Pluralistic Universe*, pp. 339–340; *Some Problems of Philosophy*, pp. 50–57.
67–70; and below, p. 16, note. Giving this view the name 'logical
realism,' he remarks elsewhere that his philosophy "may be regarded
as somewhat eccentric in its attempt to combine logical realism with
an otherwise empiricist mode of thought" (*Some Problems of Philosophy*, p. 106). ED.]

[2] Here as elsewhere the relations are of course *experienced* relations, members of the same originally chaotic manifold of non-
perceptual experience of which the related terms themselves are
parts. [Cf. below, p. 42.]

have objectivity as well as subjectivity will probably be due to the intrusion into his mind of *percepts*, that third group of associates with which the non-perceptual experiences have relations, and which, as a whole, they 'represent,' standing to them as thoughts to things. This important function of the non-perceptual experiences complicates the question and confuses it; for, so used are we to treat percepts as the sole genuine realities that, unless we keep them out of the discussion, we tend altogether to overlook the objectivity that lies in non-perceptual experiences by themselves. We treat them, 'knowing' percepts as they do, as through and through subjective, and say that they are wholly constituted of the stuff called consciousness, using this term now for a kind of entity, after the fashion which I am seeking to refute.[1]

Abstracting, then, from percepts altogether, what I maintain is, that any single non-per-

[1] Of the representative function of non-perceptual experience as a whole, I will say a word in a subsequent article: it leads too far into the general theory of knowledge for much to be said about it in a short paper like this. [Cf. below, pp. 52 ff.]

ceptual experience tends to get counted twice over, just as a perceptual experience does, figuring in one context as an object or field of objects, in another as a state of mind: and all this without the least internal self-diremption on its own part into consciousness and content. It is all consciousness in one taking; and, in the other, all content.

I find this objectivity of non-perceptual experiences, this complete parallelism in point of reality between the presently felt and the remotely thought, so well set forth in a page of Münsterberg's *Grundzüge*, that I will quote it as it stands.

"I may only think of my objects," says Professor Münsterberg; "yet, in my living thought they stand before me exactly as perceived objects would do, no matter how different the two ways of apprehending them may be in their genesis. The book here lying on the table before me, and the book in the next room of which I think and which I mean to get, are both in the same sense given realities for me, realities which I acknowledge and of which I take account. If you agree that the perceptual object is not an idea within me, but that percept and thing, as indistinguishably one, are really experienced *there, outside*, you ought not to believe that the merely thought-of object is hid away inside of the thinking subject. The object of which I think, and of whose existence I take cognizance without letting it now work upon my senses, occupies its definite place in the outer world as much as does the object which I directly see."

"What is true of the here and the there, is also true of the now and the then. I know of the thing which is present and perceived, but I know also of the thing which yesterday was but is no more, and which I only remember. Both can determine my present conduct, both are parts of the reality of which I keep account. It is true that of much of the past I am uncertain, just as I am uncertain of much of what is present if it be but dimly perceived. But the interval of time does not in principle alter my relation to the object, does not transform it from an object known into a mental state. . . .

The things in the room here which I survey, and those in my distant home of which I think, the things of this minute and those of my long-vanished boyhood, influence and decide me alike, with a reality which my experience of them directly feels. They both make up my real world, they make it directly, they do not have first to be introduced to me and mediated by ideas which now and here arise within me. . . . This not-me character of my recollections and expectations does not imply that the external objects of which I am aware in those experiences should necessarily be there also for others. The objects of dreamers and hallucinated persons are wholly without general validity. But even were they centaurs and golden mountains, they still would be 'off there,' in fairy land, and not 'inside' of ourselves." [1]

This certainly is the immediate, primary, naïf, or practical way of taking our thought-of world. Were there no perceptual world to serve as its 'reductive,' in Taine's sense, by

[1] Münsterberg: *Grundzüge der Psychologie*, vol. I, p. 48.

being 'stronger' and more genuinely 'outer' (so that the whole merely thought-of world seems weak and inner in comparison), our world of thought would be the only world, and would enjoy complete reality in our belief. This actually happens in our dreams, and in our day-dreams so long as percepts do not interrupt them.

And yet, just as the seen room (to go back to our late example) is *also* a field of consciousness, so the conceived or recollected room is *also* a state of mind; and the doubling-up of the experience has in both cases similar grounds.

The room thought-of, namely, has many thought-of couplings with many thought-of things. Some of these couplings are inconstant, others are stable. In the reader's personal history the room occupies a single date — he saw it only once perhaps, a year ago. Of the house's history, on the other hand, it forms a permanent ingredient. Some couplings have the curious stubbornness, to borrow Royce's term, of fact; others show the fluidity of fancy — we let them come and go as we please. Grouped with the rest of its house, with the name of its town, of its owner, builder, value, decorative plan, the room maintains a definite foothold, to which, if we try to loosen it, it tends to return, and to reassert itself with force.[1] With these associates, in a word, it coheres, while to other houses, other towns, other owners, etc., it shows no tendency to cohere at all. The two collections, first of its cohesive, and, second, of its loose associates, inevitably come to be contrasted. We call the first collection the system of external realities, in the midst of which the room, as 'real,' exists; the other we call the stream of our internal thinking, in which, as a 'mental image,' it for a moment floats.[2] The room thus again gets counted twice over. It plays two different rôles, being *Gedanke* and *Gedachtes*, the thought-of-an-object, and the object-thought-of, both in one; and all this without paradox or mystery, just as the same

[1] Cf. A. L. Hodder: *The Adversaries of the Sceptic*, pp. 94–99.

[2] For simplicity's sake I confine my exposition to 'external' reality. But there is also the system of ideal reality in which the room plays its part. Relations of comparison, of classification, serial order, value, also are stubborn, assign a definite place to the room, unlike the incoherence of its places in the mere rhapsody of our successive thoughts. [Cf. above, p. 16.]

material thing may be both low and high, or small and great, or bad and good, because of its relations to opposite parts of an environing world.

As 'subjective' we say that the experience represents; as 'objective' it is represented. What represents and what is represented is here numerically the same; but we must remember that no dualism of being represented and representing resides in the experience *per se*. In its pure state, or when isolated, there is no self-splitting of it into consciousness and what the consciousness is 'of.' Its subjectivity and objectivity are functional attributes solely, realized only when the experience is 'taken,' *i. e.*, talked-of, twice, considered along with its two differing contexts respectively, by a new retrospective experience, of which that whole past complication now forms the fresh content.

The instant field of the present is at all times what I call the 'pure' experience. It is only virtually or potentially either object or subject as yet. For the time being, it is plain, unqualified actuality, or existence, a simple *that*. In this *naïf* immediacy it is of course *valid;* it is *there,* we *act* upon it; and the doubling of it in retrospection into a state of mind and a reality intended thereby, is just one of the acts. The 'state of mind,' first treated explicitly as such in retrospection, will stand corrected or confirmed, and the retrospective experience in its turn will get a similar treatment; but the immediate experience in its passing is always 'truth,' [1] practical truth, *something to act on,* at its own movement. If the world were then and there to go out like a candle, it would remain truth absolute and objective, for it would be 'the last word,' would have no critic, and no one would ever oppose the thought in it to the reality intended. [2]

I think I may now claim to have made my

[1] Note the ambiguity of this term, which is taken sometimes objectively and sometimes subjectively.

[2] In the *Psychological Review* for July [1904], Dr. R. B. Perry has published a view of Consciousness which comes nearer to mine than any other with which I am acquainted. At present, Dr. Perry thinks, every field of experience is so much 'fact.' It becomes 'opinion' or 'thought' only in retrospection, when a fresh experience, thinking the same object, alters and corrects it. But the corrective experience becomes itself in turn corrected, and thus experience as a whole is a process in which what is objective originally forever turns subjective, turns into our apprehension of the object. I strongly recommend Dr. Perry's admirable article to my readers.

24

thesis clear. Consciousness connotes a kind of external relation, and does not denote a special stuff or way of being. *The peculiarity of our experiences, that they not only are, but are known, which their 'conscious' quality is invoked to explain, is better explained by their relations — these relations themselves being experiences — to one another.*

IV

Were I now to go on to treat of the knowing of perceptual by conceptual experiences, it would again prove to be an affair of external relations. One experience would be the knower, the other the reality known; and I could perfectly well define, without the notion of 'consciousness,' what the knowing actually and practically amounts to — leading-towards, namely, and terminating-in percepts, through a series of transitional experiences which the world supplies. But I will not treat of this, space being insufficient.[1] I will rather consider

[1] I have given a partial account of the matter in *Mind*, vol. x, p. 27, 1885 [reprinted in *The Meaning of Truth*, pp. 1–42], and in the *Psychological Review*, vol. ii, p. 105, 1895 [partly reprinted in *The Meaning of Truth*, pp. 43–50]. See also C. A. Strong's article in the

a few objections that are sure to be urged against the entire theory as it stands.

V

First of all, this will be asked: "If experience has not 'conscious' existence, if it be not partly made of 'consciousness,' of what then is it made? Matter we know, and thought we know, and conscious content we know, but neutral and simple 'pure experience' is something we know not at all. Say *what* it consists of — for it must consist of something — or be willing to give it up!"

To this challenge the reply is easy. Although for fluency's sake I myself spoke early in this article of a stuff of pure experience, I have now to say that there is no *general* stuff of which experience at large is made. There are as many stuffs as there are 'natures' in the things experienced. If you ask what any one bit of pure experience is made of, the answer is always the

Journal of Philosophy, Psychology and Scientific Methods, vol. 1, p. 253, May 12, 1904. I hope myself very soon to recur to the matter. [See below, pp. 52 ff.]

26

same: "It is made of *that*, of just what appears, of space, of intensity, of flatness, brownness, heaviness, or what not." Shadworth Hodgson's analysis here leaves nothing to be desired.[1] Experience is only a collective name for all these sensible natures, and save for time and space (and, if you like, for 'being') there appears no universal element of which all things are made.

VI

The next objection is more formidable, in fact it sounds quite crushing when one hears it first.

"If it be the self-same piece of pure experience, taken twice over, that serves now as thought and now as thing" — so the objection runs — "how comes it that its attributes should differ so fundamentally in the two takings. As thing, the experience is extended; as thought, it occupies no space or place. As thing, it is red, hard, heavy; but who ever heard

---

[1] [Cf. Shadworth Hodgson: *The Metaphysic of Experience*, vol. I, *passim*; *The Philosophy of Reflection*, bk. II, ch. IV, § 3. ED.]

of a red, hard or heavy thought? Yet even now you said that an experience is made of just what appears, and what appears is just such adjectives. How can the one experience in its thing-function be made of them, consist of them, carry them as its own attributes, while in its thought-function it disowns them and attributes them elsewhere. There is a self-contradiction here from which the radical dualism of thought and thing is the only truth that can save us. Only if the thought is one kind of being can the adjectives exist in it 'intentionally' (to use the scholastic term); only if the thing is another kind, can they exist in it constitutively and energetically. No simple subject can take the same adjectives and at one time be qualified by it, and at another time be merely 'of' it, as of something only meant or known."

The solution insisted on by this objector, like many other common-sense solutions, grows the less satisfactory the more one turns it in one's mind. To begin with, *are* thought and thing as heterogeneous as is commonly said?

No one denies that they have some categories in common. Their relations to time are identical. Both, moreover, may have parts (for psychologists in general treat thoughts as having them); and both may be complex or simple. Both are of kinds, can be compared, added and subtracted and arranged in serial orders. All sorts of adjectives qualify our thoughts which appear incompatible with consciousness, being as such a bare diaphaneity. For instance, they are natural and easy, or laborious. They are beautiful, happy, intense, interesting, wise, idiotic, focal, marginal, insipid, confused, vague, precise, rational, casual, general, particular, and many things besides. Moreover, the chapters on 'Perception' in the psychology-books are full of facts that make for the essential homogeneity of thought with thing. How, if 'subject' and 'object' were separated 'by the whole diameter of being,' and had no attributes in common, could it be so hard to tell, in a presented and recognized material object, what part comes in through the sense-organs and what part comes 'out of one's own head'? Sensations and apperceptive ideas fuse here so intimately that you can no more tell where one begins and the other ends, than you can tell, in those cunning circular panoramas that have lately been exhibited, where the real foreground and the painted canvas join together.[1]

Descartes for the first time defined thought as the absolutely unextended, and later philosophers have accepted the description as correct. But what possible meaning has it to say that, when we think of a foot-rule or a square yard, extension is not attributable to our thought? Of every extended object the *adequate* mental picture must have all the extension of the object itself. The difference between objective and subjective extension is one of relation to a context solely. In the mind the various extents maintain no necessarily stubborn order relatively to each other, while

[1] Spencer's proof of his 'Transfigured Realism' (his doctrine that there is an absolutely non-mental reality) comes to mind as a splendid instance of the impossibility of establishing radical heterogeneity between thought and thing. All his painfully accumulated points of difference run gradually into their opposites, and are full of exceptions. [Cf. Spencer: *Principles of Psychology*, part VII, ch. XIX.]

in the physical world they bound each other
stably, and, added together, make the great
enveloping Unit which we believe in and call
real Space. As 'outer,' they carry themselves
adversely, so to speak, to one another, exclude
one another and maintain their distances;
while, as 'inner,' their order is loose, and they
form a *durcheinander* in which unity is lost.[1]
But to argue from this that inner experience is
absolutely inextensive seems to me little short
of absurd. The two worlds differ, not by the
presence or absence of extension, but by the
relations of the extensions which in both
worlds exist.

Does not this case of extension now put us
on the track of truth in the case of other qualities? It does; and I am surprised that the facts
should not have been noticed long ago. Why,
for example, do we call a fire hot, and water
wet, and yet refuse to say that our mental
state, when it is 'of' these objects, is either wet
or hot? 'Intentionally,' at any rate, and when

---

[1] I speak here of the complete inner life in which the mind plays
freely with its materials. Of course the mind's free play is restricted
when it seeks to copy real things in real space.

the mental state is a vivid image, hotness and wetness are in it just as much as they are in the physical experience. The reason is this, that, as the general chaos of all our experiences gets sifted, we find that there are some fires that will always burn sticks and always warm our bodies, and that there are some waters that will always put out fires; while there are other fires and waters that will not act at all. The general group of experiences that *act*, that do not only possess their natures intrinsically, but wear them adjectively and energetically, turning them against one another, comes inevitably to be contrasted with the group whose members, having identically the same natures, fail to manifest them in the 'energetic' way.[1] I make for myself now an experience of blazing fire; I place it near my body; but it does not warm me in the least. I lay a stick upon it, and the stick either burns or remains green, as I please. I call up water, and pour it on the fire, and absolutely no difference ensues. I account

---

[1] [But there are also "mental activity trains," in which thoughts do "work on each other." Cf. below, p. 184, note. ED.]

for all such facts by calling this whole train of experiences unreal, a mental train. Mental fire is what won't burn real sticks; mental water is what won't necessarily (though of course it may) put out even a mental fire. Mental knives may be sharp, but they won't cut real wood. Mental triangles are pointed, but their points won't wound. With 'real' objects, on the contrary, consequences always accrue; and thus the real experiences get sifted from the mental ones, the things from our thoughts of them, fanciful or true, and precipitated together as the stable part of the whole experience-chaos, under the name of the physical world. Of this our perceptual experiences are the nucleus, they being the originally *strong* experiences. We add a lot of conceptual experiences to them, making these strong also in imagination, and building out the remoter parts of the physical world by their means; and around this core of reality the world of laxly connected fancies and mere rhapsodical objects floats like a bank of clouds. In the clouds, all sorts of rules are violated which in the core are kept. Extensions there can be indefinitely located; motion there obeys no Newton's laws.

VII

There is a peculiar class of experiences to which, whether we take them as subjective or as objective, we *assign* their several natures as attributes, because in both contexts they affect their associates actively, though in neither quite as 'strongly' or as sharply as things affect one another by their physical energies. I refer here to *appreciations*, which form an ambiguous sphere of being, belonging with emotion on the one hand, and having objective 'value' on the other, yet seeming not quite inner nor quite outer, as if a diremption had begun but had not made itself complete.[1]

Experiences of painful objects, for example, are usually also painful experiences; perceptions of loveliness, of ugliness, tend to pass muster as lovely or as ugly perceptions; intuitions of the morally lofty are lofty intuitions.

[1] [This topic is resumed below, pp. 137 ff. Ed.]

Sometimes the adjective wanders as if uncertain where to fix itself. Shall we speak of seductive visions or of visions of seductive things? Of wicked desires or of desires for wickedness? Of healthy thoughts or of thoughts of healthy objects? Of good impulses, or of impulses towards the good? Of feelings of anger, or of angry feelings? Both in the mind and in the thing, these natures modify their context, exclude certain associates and determine others, have their mates and incompatibles. Yet not as stubbornly as in the case of physical qualities, for beauty and ugliness, love and hatred, pleasant and painful can, in certain complex experiences, coexist.

If one were to make an evolutionary construction of how a lot of originally chaotic pure experiences became gradually differentiated into an orderly inner and outer world, the whole theory would turn upon one's success in explaining how or why the quality of an experience, once active, could become less so, and, from being an energetic attribute in some cases, elsewhere lapse into the status of an inert or merely internal 'nature.' This would be the 'evolution' of the psychical from the bosom of the physical, in which the esthetic, moral and otherwise emotional experiences would represent a halfway stage.

VIII

But a last cry of *non possumus* will probably go up from many readers. "All very pretty as a piece of ingenuity," they will say, "but our consciousness itself intuitively contradicts you. We, for our part, *know* that we are conscious. We *feel* our thought, flowing as a life within us, in absolute contrast with the objects which it so unremittingly escorts. We can not be faithless to this immediate intuition. The dualism is a fundamental *datum:* Let no man join what God has put asunder."

My reply to this is my last word, and I greatly grieve that to many it will sound materialistic. I can not help that, however, for I, too, have my intuitions and I must obey them. Let the case be what it may in others, I am as confident as I am of anything that, in myself, the stream of thinking (which I recognize emphatically as a phenomenon) is only a careless name for what, when scrutinized, reveals itself to consist chiefly of the stream of my breathing. The 'I think' which Kant said must be able to accompany all my objects, is the 'I breathe' which actually does accompany them. There are other internal facts besides breathing (intracephalic muscular adjustments, etc., of which I have said a word in my larger Psychology), and these increase the assets of 'consciousness,' so far as the latter is subject to immediate perception; [1] but breath, which was ever the original of 'spirit,' breath moving outwards, between the glottis and the nostrils, is, I am persuaded, the essence out of which philosophers have constructed the entity known to them as consciousness. *That entity is fictitious, while thoughts in the concrete are fully real. But thoughts in the concrete are made of the same stuff as things are.*

I wish I might believe myself to have made

---

[1] [*Principles of Psychology*, vol. I, pp. 299–305. Cf. below, pp. 169–171 (note).]

that plausible in this article. In another article
I shall try to make the general notion of a
world composed of pure experiences still more
clear.

II

A WORLD OF PURE EXPERI-
ENCE[1]

I⊤ is difficult not to notice a curious unrest in the philosophic atmosphere of the time, a loosening of old landmarks, a softening of oppositions, a mutual borrowing from one another on the part of systems anciently closed, and an interest in new suggestions, however vague, as if the one thing sure were the inadequacy of the extant school-solutions. The dissatisfaction with these seems due for the most part to a feeling that they are too abstract and academic. Life is confused and superabundant, and what the younger generation appears to crave is more of the temperament of life in its philosophy, even though it were at some cost of logical rigor and of formal purity. Tran-

---

[1] [Reprinted from the *Journal of Philosophy, Psychology and Scientific Methods*, vol. I, 1904, No. 20, September 29, and No. 21, October 13. Pp. 52–76 have also been reprinted, with some omissions, alterations and additions, in *The Meaning of Truth*, pp. 102–120. The alterations have been adopted in the present text. This essay is referred to in *A Pluralistic Universe*, p. 280, note 5. ED.]

scendental idealism is inclining to let the world
wag incomprehensibly, in spite of its Absolute
Subject and his unity of purpose. Berkeleyan
idealism is abandoning the principle of parsi-
mony and dabbling in panpsychic speculations. Empiricism flirts with teleology; and,
strangest of all, natural realism, so long de-
cently buried, raises its head above the turf,
and finds glad hands outstretched from the
most unlikely quarters to help it to its feet
again. We are all biased by our personal feelings, I know, and I am personally discontented
with extant solutions; so I seem to read the
signs of a great unsettlement, as if the up-
heaval of more real conceptions and more fruitful methods were imminent, as if a true landscape might result, less clipped, straight-edged
and artificial.

If philosophy be really on the eve of any considerable rearrangement, the time should be
propitious for any one who has suggestions of
his own to bring forward. For many years past
my mind has been growing into a certain type
of *Weltanschauung*. Rightly or wrongly, I have

got to the point where I can hardly see things in any other pattern. I propose, therefore, to describe the pattern as clearly as I can consistently with great brevity, and to throw my description into the bubbling vat of publicity where, jostled by rivals and torn by critics, it will eventually either disappear from notice, or else, if better luck befall it, quietly subside to the profundities, and serve as a possible ferment of new growths or a nucleus of new crystallization.

I. RADICAL EMPIRICISM

I give the name of 'radical empiricism' to my *Weltanschauung*. Empiricism is known as the opposite of rationalism. Rationalism tends to emphasize universals and to make wholes prior to parts in the order of logic as well as in that of being. Empiricism, on the contrary, lays the explanatory stress upon the part, the element, the individual, and treats the whole as a collection and the universal as an abstraction. My description of things, accordingly, starts with the parts and makes of the whole a being of the second order. It is essentially a mosaic philosophy, a philosophy of plural facts, like that of Hume and his descendants, who refer these facts neither to Substances in which they inhere nor to an Absolute Mind that creates them as its objects. But it differs from the Humian type of empiricism in one particular which makes me add the epithet radical.

To be radical, an empiricism must neither admit into its constructions any element that is not directly experienced, nor exclude from them any element that is directly experienced. For such a philosophy, *the relations that connect experiences must themselves be experienced relations, and any kind of relation experienced must be accounted as 'real' as anything else in the system.* Elements may indeed be redistributed, the original placing of things getting corrected, but a real place must be found for every kind of thing experienced, whether term or relation, in the final philosophic arrangement.

Now, ordinary empiricism, in spite of the fact that conjunctive and disjunctive relations present themselves as being fully co-ordinate parts of experience, has always shown a tendency to do away with the connections of things, and to insist most on the disjunctions. Berkeley's nominalism, Hume's statement that whatever things we distinguish are as 'loose and separate' as if they had 'no manner of connection,' James Mill's denial that similars have anything 'really' in common, the resolution of the causal tie into habitual sequence, John Mill's account of both physical things and selves as composed of discontinuous possibilities, and the general pulverization of all Experience by association and the mind-dust theory, are examples of what I mean.[1]

The natural result of such a world-picture has been the efforts of rationalism to correct its incoherencies by the addition of transexperiential agents of unification, substances, intellectual categories and powers, or Selves;

[1] [Cf. Berkeley: *Principles of Human Knowledge*, Introduction; Hume: *An Enquiry Concerning Human Understanding*, sect. VII, part II (Selby-Bigge's edition, p. 74); James Mill: *Analysis of the Phenomena of the Human Mind*, ch. VIII; J. S. Mill: *An Examination of Sir William Hamilton's Philosophy*, ch. XI, XII; W. K. Clifford: *Lectures and Essays*, pp. 274 ff.]

whereas, if empiricism had only been radical
and taken everything that comes without dis-
favor, conjunction as well as separation, each
at its face value, the results would have called
for no such artificial correction. *Radical empiricism*, as I understand it, *does full justice to
conjunctive relations*, without, however, treating them as rationalism always tends to treat
them, as being true in some supernal way, as if
the unity of things and their variety belonged
to different orders of truth and vitality altogether.

II. Conjunctive Relations

Relations are of different degrees of intimacy. Merely to be 'with' one another in a
universe of discourse is the most external relation that terms can have, and seems to involve
nothing whatever as to farther consequences.
Simultaneity and time-interval come next, and
then space-adjacency and distance. After
them, similarity and difference, carrying the
possibility of many inferences. Then relations
of activity, tying terms into series involving

change, tendency, resistance, and the causal order generally. Finally, the relation experienced between terms that form states of mind, and are immediately conscious of continuing each other. The organization of the Self as a system of memories, purposes, strivings, fulfilments or disappointments, is incidental to this most intimate of all relations, the terms of which seem in many cases actually to compenetrate and suffuse each other's being.[1]

Philosophy has always turned on grammatical particles. With, near, next, like, from, towards, against, because, for, through, my — these words designate types of conjunctive relation arranged in a roughly ascending order of intimacy and inclusiveness. *A priori*, we can imagine a universe of withness but no nextness; or one of nextness but no likeness, or of likeness with no activity, or of activity with no purpose, or of purpose with no ego. These would be universes, each with its own grade of unity. The universe of human experience is, by one or another of its parts, of each and all these grades.

[1] [See "The Experience of Activity," below, pp. 155–189.]

Whether or not it possibly enjoys some still more absolute grade of union does not appear upon the surface.

Taken as it does appear, our universe is to a large extent chaotic. No one single type of connection runs through all the experiences that compose it. If we take space-relations, they fail to connect minds into any regular system. Causes and purposes obtain only among special series of facts. The self-relation seems extremely limited and does not link two different selves together. *Prima facie*, if you should liken the universe of absolute idealism to an aquarium, a crystal globe in which goldfish are swimming, you would have to compare the empiricist universe to something more like one of those dried human heads with which the Dyaks of Borneo deck their lodges. The skull forms a solid nucleus; but innumerable feathers, leaves, strings, beads, and loose appendices of every description float and dangle from it, and, save that they terminate in it, seem to have nothing to do with one another. Even so my experiences and yours float and dangle, terminating, it is true, in a nucleus of common perception, but for the most part out of sight and irrelevant and unimaginable to one another. This imperfect intimacy, this bare relation of *withness* between some parts of the sum total of experience and other parts, is the fact that ordinary empiricism over-emphasizes against rationalism, the latter always tending to ignore it unduly. Radical empiricism, on the contrary, is fair to both the unity and the disconnection. It finds no reason for treating either as illusory. It allots to each its definite sphere of description, and agrees that there appear to be actual forces at work which tend, as time goes on, to make the unity greater.

The conjunctive relation that has given most trouble to philosophy is *the co-conscious transition*, so to call it, by which one experience passes into another when both belong to the same self. About the facts there is no question. My experiences and your experiences are 'with' each other in various external ways, but mine pass into mine, and yours pass into yours in a way in which yours and mine never pass into one another. Within each of our personal histories, subject, object, interest and purpose *are continuous or may be continuous.*[1] Personal histories are processes of change in time, and *the change itself is one of the things immediately experienced.* 'Change' in this case means continuous as opposed to discontinuous transition. But continuous transition is one sort of a conjunctive relation; and to be a radical empiricist means to hold fast to this conjunctive relation of all others, for this is the strategic point, the position through which, if a hole be made, all the corruptions of dialectics and all the metaphysical fictions pour into our philosophy. The holding fast to this relation means taking it at its face value, neither less nor more; and to take it at its face value means first of all to take it just as we feel it, and not to confuse ourselves with abstract talk *about* it, involving words that drive us to invent secondary conceptions in order to neutralize their

---

[1] The psychology books have of late described the facts here with approximate adequacy. I may refer to the chapters on 'The Stream of Thought' and on the Self in my own *Principles of Psychology*, as well as to S. H. Hodgson's *Metaphysic of Experience*, vol. I, ch. VII and VIII.

suggestions and to make our actual experience again seem rationally possible.

What I do feel simply when a later moment of my experience succeeds an earlier one is that though they are two moments, the transition from the one to the other is *continuous*. Continuity here is a definite sort of experience; just as definite as is the *discontinuity-experience* which I find it impossible to avoid when I seek to make the transition from an experience of my own to one of yours. In this latter case I have to get on and off again, to pass from a thing lived to another thing only conceived, and the break is positively experienced and noted. Though the functions exerted by my experience and by yours may be the same (*e. g.*, the same objects known and the same purposes followed), yet the sameness has in this case to be ascertained expressly (and often with difficulty and uncertainty) after the break has been felt; whereas in passing from one of my own moments to another the sameness of object and interest is unbroken, and both the earlier and the later experience are of things directly lived.

There is no other *nature*, no other whatness than this absence of break and this sense of continuity in that most intimate of all conjunctive relations, the passing of one experience into another when they belong to the same self. And this whatness is real empirical 'content,' just as the whatness of separation and discontinuity is real content in the contrasted case. Practically to experience one's personal continuum in this living way is to know the originals of the ideas of continuity and of sameness, to know what the words stand for concretely, to own all that they can ever mean. But all experiences have their conditions; and over-subtle intellects, thinking about the facts here, and asking how they are possible, have ended by substituting a lot of static objects of conception for the direct perceptual experiences. "Sameness," they have said, "must be a stark numerical identity; it can't run on from next to next. Continuity can't mean mere absence of gap; for if you say two things are in immediate contact, *at* the contact how can they be two? If, on the other hand, you put a relation of transition between them, that itself is a third thing, and needs to be related or hitched to its terms. An infinite series is involved," and so on. The result is that from difficulty to difficulty, the plain conjunctive experience has been discredited by both schools, the empiricists leaving things permanently disjoined, and the rationalist remedying the looseness by their Absolutes or Substances, or whatever other fictitious agencies of union they may have employed.[1] From all which artificiality we can be saved by a couple of simple reflections: first, that conjunctions and separations are, at all events, co-ordinate phenomena which, if we take experiences at their face value, must be accounted equally real; and second, that if we insist on treating things as really separate when they are given as continuously joined, invoking, when union is required, transcendental principles to overcome the separateness we have assumed, then we ought to stand ready to perform the converse act. We ought to invoke higher principles of *dis*union, also, to

[1] [See "The Thing and its Relations," below, pp. 92–122.]

make our merely experienced *dis*junctions more truly real. Failing thus, we ought to let the originally given continuities stand on their own bottom. We have no right to be lopsided or to blow capriciously hot and cold.

III. THE COGNITIVE RELATION

The first great pitfall from which such a radical standing by experience will save us is an artificial conception of the *relations between knower and known*. Throughout the history of philosophy the subject and its object have been treated as absolutely discontinuous entities; and thereupon the presence of the latter to the former, or the 'apprehension' by the former of the latter, has assumed a paradoxical character which all sorts of theories had to be invented to overcome. Representative theories put a mental 'representation,' 'image,' or 'content' into the gap, as a sort of intermediary. Common-sense theories left the gap untouched, declaring our mind able to clear it by a self-transcending leap. Transcendentalist theories left it impossible to traverse by finite knowers, and brought an Absolute in to perform the saltatory act. All the while, in the very bosom of the finite experience, every conjunction required to make the relation intelligible is given in full. Either the knower and the known are:

(1) the self-same piece of experience taken twice over in different contexts; or they are

(2) two pieces of *actual* experience belonging to the same subject, with definite tracts of conjunctive transitional experience between them; or

(3) the known is a *possible* experience either of that subject or another, to which the said conjunctive transitions *would* lead, if sufficiently prolonged.

To discuss all the ways in which one experience may function as the knower of another, would be incompatible with the limits of this essay.[1] I have just treated of type 1, the

---

[1] For brevity's sake I altogether omit mention of the type constituted by knowledge of the truth of general propositions. This type has been thoroughly and, so far as I can see, satisfactorily, elucidated in Dewey's *Studies in Logical Theory*. Such propositions are reducible to the S-is-P form; and the 'terminus' that verifies and fulfils is the SP in combination. Of course percepts may be involved in the medi-

kind of knowledge called perception.[1] This is the type of case in which the mind enjoys direct 'acquaintance' with a present object. In the other types the mind has 'knowledge-about' an object not immediately there. Of type 2, the simplest sort of conceptual knowledge, I have given some account in two [earlier] articles.[2] Type 3 can always formally and hypothetically be reduced to type 2, so that a brief description of that type will put the present reader sufficiently at my point of view, and make him see what the actual meanings of the mysterious cognitive relation may be.

Suppose me to be sitting here in my library

ating experiences, or in the 'satisfactoriness' of the P in its new position.

[1] [See above, pp. 9–15.]

[2] ["On the Function of Cognition," *Mind*, vol. x, 1885, and "The Knowing of Things Together," *Psychological Review*, vol. ii, 1895. These articles are reprinted, the former in full, the latter in part, in *The Meaning of Truth*, pp. 1–50. ED.] These articles and their doctrine, unnoticed apparently by any one else, have lately gained favorable comment from Professor Strong. ["A Naturalistic Theory of the Reference of Thought to Reality," *Journal of Philosophy, Psychology and Scientific Methods*, vol. i, 1904.] Dr. Dickinson S. Miller has independently thought out the same results ["The Meaning of Truth and Error," *Philosophical Review*, vol. ii, 1893; "The Confusion of Function and Content in Mental Analysis," *Psychological Review*, vol. ii, 1895], which Strong accordingly dubs the James-Miller theory of cognition.

at Cambridge, at ten minutes' walk from 'Memorial Hall,' and to be thinking truly of the latter object. My mind may have before it only the name, or it may have a clear image, or it may have a very dim image of the hall, but such intrinsic differences in the image make no difference in its cognitive function. Certain *extrinsic* phenomena, special experiences of conjunction, are what impart to the image, be it what it may, its knowing office.

For instance, if you ask me what hall I mean by my image, and I can tell you nothing; or if I fail to point or lead you towards the Harvard Delta; or if, being led by you, I am uncertain whether the Hall I see be what I had in mind or not; you would rightly deny that I had 'meant' that particular hall at all, even though my mental image might to some degree have resembled it. The resemblance would count in that case as coincidental merely, for all sorts of things of a kind resemble one another in this world without being held for that reason to take cognizance of one another.

On the other hand, if I can lead you to the

hall, and tell you of its history and present uses; if in its presence I feel my idea, however imperfect it may have been, to have led hither and to be now *terminated;* if the associates of the image and of the felt hall run parallel, so that each term of the one context corresponds serially, as I walk, with an answering term of the others; why then my soul was prophetic, and my idea must be, and by common consent would be, called cognizant of reality. That percept was what I *meant*, for into it my idea has passed by conjunctive experiences of sameness and fulfilled intention. Nowhere is there jar, but every later moment continues and corroborates an earlier one.

In this continuing and corroborating, taken in no transcendental sense, but denoting definitely felt transitions, *lies all that the knowing of a percept by an idea can possibly contain or signify.* Wherever such transitions are felt, the first experience *knows* the last one. Where they do not, or where even as possibles they can not, intervene, there can be no pretence of knowing. In this latter case the extremes will be connected, if connected at all, by inferior relations — bare likeness or succession, or by 'withness' alone. Knowledge of sensible realities thus comes to life inside the tissue of experience. It is *made;* and made by relations that unroll themselves in time. Whenever certain intermediaries are given, such that, as they develop towards their terminus, there is experience from point to point of one direction followed, and finally of one process fulfilled, the result is that *their starting-point thereby becomes a knower and their terminus an object meant or known.* That is all that knowing (in the simple case considered) can be known-as, that is the whole of its nature, put into experiential terms. Whenever such is the sequence of our experiences we may freely say that we had the terminal object 'in mind' from the outset, even although *at* the outset nothing was there in us but a flat piece of substantive experience like any other, with no self-transcendency about it, and no mystery save the mystery of coming into existence and of being gradually followed by other pieces of substantive experience, with

conjunctively transitional experiences between.
That is what we *mean* here by the object's
being 'in mind.' Of any deeper more real way
of being in mind we have no positive conception, and we have no right to discredit our
actual experience by talking of such a way
at all.

I know that many a reader will rebel at this.
"Mere intermediaries," he will say, "even
though they be feelings of continuously growing fulfilment, only *separate* the knower from
the known, whereas what we have in knowledge
is a kind of immediate touch of the one by the
other, an 'apprehension' in the etymological
sense of the word, a leaping of the chasm as by
lightning, an act by which two terms are smit-
ten into one, over the head of their distinctness. All these dead intermediaries of yours
are out of each other, and outside of their
termini still."

But do not such dialectic difficulties remind
us of the dog dropping his bone and snapping
at its image in the water? If we knew any more
real kind of union *aliunde*, we might be entitled

to brand all our empirical unions as a sham. But unions by continuous transition are the only ones we know of, whether in this matter of a knowledge-about that terminates in an acquaintance, whether in personal identity, in logical predication through the copula 'is,' or elsewhere. If anywhere there were more absolute unions realized, they could only reveal themselves to us by just such conjunctive results. These are what the unions are *worth*, these are all that *we can ever practically mean* by union, by continuity. Is it not time to repeat what Lotze said of substances, that to *act like* one is to *be* one? [1] Should we not say here that to be experienced as continuous is to be really continuous, in a world where experience and reality come to the same thing? In a picture gallery a painted hook will serve to hang a painted chain by, a painted cable will hold a painted ship. In a world where both the terms and their distinctions are affairs of experience, conjunctions that are experienced must be at least as real as anything else. They

[1] [Cf. H. Lotze: *Metaphysik*, §§ 37–39, 97, 98, 243.]

will be 'absolutely' real conjunctions, if we have no transphenomenal Absolute ready, to derealize the whole experienced world by, at a stroke. If, on the other hand, we had such an Absolute, not one of our opponents' theories of knowledge could remain standing any better than ours could; for the distinctions as well as the conjunctions of experience would impartially fall its prey. The whole question of how 'one' thing can know 'another' would cease to be a real one at all in a world where otherness itself was an illusion.[1]

So much for the essentials of the cognitive relation, where the knowledge is conceptual in type, or forms knowledge 'about' an object. It consists in intermediary experiences (possible, if not actual) of continuously developing progress, and, finally, of fulfilment, when the sensible percept, which is the object, is reached. The percept here not only *verifies* the concept, proves its function of knowing that percept to

[1] Mr. Bradley, not professing to know his absolute *aliunde*, nevertheless derealizes Experience by alleging it to be everywhere infected with self-contradiction. His arguments seem almost purely verbal, but this is no place for arguing that point out. [Cf. F. H. Bradley; *Appearance and Reality, passim;* and below, pp. 106–122.]

be true, but the percept's existence as the terminus of the chain of intermediaries *creates* the function. Whatever terminates that chain was, because it now proves itself to be, what the concept 'had in mind.'

The towering importance for human life of this kind of knowing lies in the fact that an experience that knows another can figure as its *representative*, not in any quasi-miraculous 'epistemological' sense, but in the definite practical sense of being its *substitute* in various operations, sometimes physical and sometimes mental, which lead us to its associates and results. By experimenting on our ideas of reality, we may save ourselves the trouble of experimenting on the real experiences which they severally mean. The ideas form related systems, corresponding point for point to the systems which the realities form; and by letting an ideal term call up its associates systematically, we may be led to a terminus which the corresponding real term would have led to in case we had operated on the real world. And this brings us to the general question of substitution.

IV. SUBSTITUTION

In Taine's brilliant book on 'Intelligence,' substitution was for the first time named as a cardinal logical function, though of course the facts had always been familiar enough. What, exactly, in a system of experiences, does the 'substitution' of one of them for another mean?

According to my view, experience as a whole is a process in time, whereby innumerable particular terms lapse and are superseded by others that follow upon them by transitions which, whether disjunctive or conjunctive in content, are themselves experiences, and must in general be accounted at least as real as the terms which they relate. What the nature of the event called 'superseding' signifies, depends altogether on the kind of transition that obtains. Some experiences simply abolish their predecessors without continuing them in any way. Others are felt to increase or to enlarge their meaning, to carry out their purpose, or to bring us nearer to their goal. They 'represent' them, and may fulfil their function better than they fulfilled it themselves. But to 'fulfil a function' in a world of pure experience can be conceived and defined in only one possible way. In such a world transitions and arrivals (or terminations) are the only events that happen, though they happen by so many sorts of path. The only function that one experience can perform is to lead into another experience; and the only fulfilment we can speak of is the reaching of a certain experienced end. When one experience leads to (or can lead to) the same end as another, they agree in function. But the whole system of experiences as they are immediately given presents itself as a quasi-chaos through which one can pass out of an initial term in many directions and yet end in the same terminus, moving from next to next by a great many possible paths.

Either one of these paths might be a functional substitute for another, and to follow one rather than another might on occasion be an advantageous thing to do. As a matter of fact, and in a general way, the paths that run through conceptual experiences, that is, through 'thoughts' or 'ideas' that 'know' the things in which they terminate, are highly advantageous paths to follow. Not only do they yield inconceivably rapid transitions; but, owing to the 'universal' character [1] which they frequently possess, and to their capacity for association with one another in great systems, they outstrip the tardy consecutions of the things themselves, and sweep us on towards our ultimate termini in a far more labor-saving way than the following of trains of sensible perception ever could. Wonderful are the new cuts and the short-circuits which the thought-paths make. Most thought-paths, it is true, are substitutes for nothing actual; they end outside the real world altogether, in wayward fancies, utopias, fictions or mistakes. But where they do re-enter reality and terminate therein, we substitute them always; and with

[1] Of which all that need be said in this essay is that it also can be conceived as functional, and defined in terms of transitions, or of the possibility of such. [Cf. *Principles of Psychology*, vol. I, pp. 473–480, vol. II, pp. 337–340; *Pragmatism*, p. 265; *Some Problems of Philosophy*, pp. 63–74; *Meaning of Truth*, pp. 246–247, etc. ED.]

these substitutes we pass the greater number of our hours.

This is why I called our experiences, taken all together, a quasi-chaos. There is vastly more discontinuity in the sum total of experiences than we commonly suppose. The objective nucleus of every man's experience, his own body, is, it is true, a continuous percept; and equally continuous as a percept (though we may be inattentive to it) is the material environment of that body, changing by gradual transition when the body moves. But the distant parts of the physical world are at all times absent from us, and form conceptual objects merely, into the perceptual reality of which our life inserts itself at points discrete and relatively rare. Round their several objective nuclei, partly shared and common and partly discrete, of the real physical world, innumerable thinkers, pursuing their several lines of physically true cogitation, trace paths that intersect one another only at discontinuous perceptual points, and the rest of the time are quite incongruent; and around all the nuclei of shared 'reality,' as around the Dyak's head of my late metaphor, floats the vast cloud of experiences that are wholly subjective, that are non-substitutional, that find not even an eventual ending for themselves in the perceptual world — the mere day - dreams and joys and sufferings and wishes of the individual minds. These exist *with* one another, indeed, and with the objective nuclei, but out of them it is probable that to all eternity no interrelated system of any kind will ever be made.

This notion of the purely substitutional or conceptual physical world brings us to the most critical of all the steps in the development of a philosophy of pure experience. The paradox of self-transcendency in knowledge comes back upon us here, but I think that our notions of pure experience and of substitution, and our radically empirical view of conjunctive transitions, are *Denkmittel* that will carry us safely through the pass.

V. What Objective Reference Is.

Whosoever feels his experience to be something substitutional even while he has it, may be said to have an experience that reaches beyond itself. From inside of its own entity it says 'more,' and postulates reality existing elsewhere. For the transcendentalist, who holds knowing to consist in a *salto mortale* across an 'epistemological chasm,' such an idea presents no difficulty; but it seems at first sight as if it might be inconsistent with an empiricism like our own. Have we not explained that conceptual knowledge is made such wholly by the existence of things that fall outside of the knowing experience itself — by intermediary experiences and by a terminus that fulfils? Can the knowledge be there before these elements that constitute its being have come? And, if knowledge be not there, how can objective reference occur?

The key to this difficulty lies in the distinction between knowing as verified and completed, and the same knowing as in transit and on its way. To recur to the Memorial Hall example lately used, it is only when our idea of the Hall has actually terminated in the percept that we know 'for certain' that from the beginning it was truly cognitive of *that*. Until established by the end of the process, its quality of knowing that, or indeed of knowing anything, could still be doubted; and yet the knowing really was there, as the result now shows. We were *virtual* knowers of the Hall long before we were certified to have been its actual knowers, by the percept's retroactive validating power. Just so we are 'mortal' all the time, by reason of the virtuality of the inevitable event which will make us so when it shall have come.

Now the immensely greater part of all our knowing never gets beyond this virtual stage. It never is completed or nailed down. I speak not merely of our ideas of imperceptibles like ether-waves or dissociated 'ions,' or of 'ejects' like the contents of our neighbors' minds; I speak also of ideas which we might verify if we would take the trouble, but which we hold for true although unterminated perceptually, because nothing says 'no' to us, and there is no contradicting truth in sight. *To continue thinking unchallenged is, ninety-nine times out of a hundred, our practical substitute for knowing in the completed sense.* As each experience runs by cognitive transition into the next one, and we nowhere feel a collision with what we elsewhere count as truth or fact, we commit ourselves to the current as if the port were sure. We live, as it were, upon the front edge of an advancing wave-crest, and our sense of a determinate direction in falling forward is all we cover of the future of our path. It is as if a differential quotient should be conscious and treat itself as an adequate substitute for a traced-out curve. Our experience, *inter alia*, is of variations of rate and of direction, and lives in these transitions more than in the journey's end. The experiences of tendency are sufficient to act upon — what more could we have *done* at those moments even if the later verification comes complete?

This is what, as a radical empiricist, I say to

the charge that the objective reference which is so flagrant a character of our experiences involves a chasm and a mortal leap. A positively conjunctive transition involves neither chasm nor leap. Being the very original of what we mean by continuity, it makes a continuum wherever it appears. I know full well that such brief words as these will leave the hardened transcendentalist unshaken. Conjunctive experiences *separate* their terms, he will still say: they are third things interposed, that have themselves to be conjoined by new links, and to invoke them makes our trouble infinitely worse. To 'feel' our motion forward is impossible. Motion implies terminus; and how can terminus be felt before we have arrived? The barest start and sally forwards, the barest tendency to leave the instant, involves the chasm and the leap. Conjunctive transitions are the most superficial of appearances, illusions of our sensibility which philosophical reflection pulverizes at a touch. Conception is our only trustworthy instrument, conception and the Absolute working hand in hand. Conception disintegrates experience utterly, but its disjunctions are easily overcome again when the Absolute takes up the task.

Such transcendentalists I must leave, provisionally at least, in full possession of their creed.[1] I have no space for polemics in this article, so I shall simply formulate the empiricist doctrine as my hypothesis, leaving it to work or not work as it may.

Objective reference, I say then, is an incident of the fact that so much of our experience comes as an insufficient and consists of process and transition. Our fields of experience have no more definite boundaries than have our fields of view. Both are fringed forever by a *more* that continuously develops, and that continuously supersedes them as life proceeds. The relations, generally speaking, are as real here as the terms are, and the only complaint of the transcendentalist's with which I could at all sympathize would be his charge that, by first making knowledge to consist in external relations as I have done, and by then confess-

---

[1] [Cf. below, pp. 93 ff.]

ing that nine-tenths of the time these are not actually but only virtually there, I have knocked the solid bottom out of the whole business, and palmed off a substitute of knowledge for the genuine thing. Only the admission, such a critic might say, that our ideas are self-transcendent and 'true' already, in advance of the experiences that are to terminate them, can bring solidity back to knowledge in a world like this, in which transitions and terminations are only by exception fulfilled.

This seems to me an excellent place for applying the pragmatic method. When a dispute arises, that method consists in auguring what practical consequences would be different if one side rather than the other were true. If no difference can be thought of, the dispute is a quarrel over words. What then would the self-transcendency affirmed to exist in advance of all experiential mediation or termination, be *known-as*? What would it practically result in for *us*, were it true?

It could only result in our orientation, in the turning of our expectations and practical tendencies into the right path; and the right path here, so long as we and the object are not yet face to face (or can never get face to face, as in the case of ejects), would be the path that led us into the object's nearest neighborhood. Where direct acquaintance is lacking, 'knowledge about' is the next best thing, and an acquaintance with what actually lies about the object, and is most closely related to it, puts such knowledge within our grasp. Ether-waves and your anger, for example, are things in which my thoughts will never *perceptually* terminate, but my concepts of them lead me to their very brink, to the chromatic fringes and to the hurtful words and deeds which are their really next effects.

Even if our ideas did in themselves carry the postulated self-transcendency, it would still remain true that their putting us into possession of such effects *would be the sole cash-value of the self-transcendency for us.* And this cash-value, it is needless to say, is *verbatim et literatim* what our empiricist account pays in. On pragmatist principles therefore, a dispute over self-transcendency is a pure logomachy. Call our concepts of ejective things self-transcendent or the reverse, it makes no difference, so long as we don't differ about the nature of that exalted virtue's fruits — fruits for us, of course, humanistic fruits. If an Absolute were proved to exist for other reasons, it might well appear that *his* knowledge is terminated in innumerable cases where ours is still incomplete. That, however, would be a fact indifferent to our knowledge. The latter would grow neither worse nor better, whether we acknowledged such an Absolute or left him out.

So the notion of a knowledge still *in transitu* and on its way joins hands here with that notion of a 'pure experience' which I tried to explain in my [essay] entitled 'Does Consciousness Exist?' The instant field of the present is always experience in its 'pure' state, plain unqualified actuality, a simple *that*, as yet undifferentiated into thing and thought, and only virtually classifiable as objective fact or as some one's opinion about fact. This is as true when the field is conceptual as when it is perceptual. 'Memorial Hall' is 'there' in my idea as much as when I stand before it. I proceed to act on its account in either case. Only in the later experience that supersedes the present one is this *naïf* immediacy retrospectively split into two parts, a 'consciousness' and its 'content,' and the content corrected or confirmed. While still pure, or present, any experience — mine, for example, of what I write about in these very lines — passes for 'truth.' The morrow may reduce it to 'opinion.' The transcendentalist in all his particular knowledges is as liable to this reduction as I am: his Absolute does not save him. Why, then, need he quarrel with an account of knowing that merely leaves it liable to this inevitable condition? Why insist that knowing is a static relation out of time when it practically seems so much a function of our active life? For a thing to be valid, says Lotze, is the same as to make itself valid. When the whole universe seems only to be making itself valid and to be still incomplete (else why its ceaseless changing?) why, of all things, should knowing be exempt? Why should it not be making itself valid like everything else? That some parts of it may be already valid or verified beyond dispute, the empirical philosopher, of course, like any one else, may always hope.

VI. THE CONTERMINOUSNESS OF DIFFERENT MINDS [1]

With transition and prospect thus enthroned in pure experience, it is impossible to subscribe to the idealism of the English school. Radical empiricism has, in fact, more affinities with natural realism than with the views of Berkeley or of Mill, and this can be easily shown.

For the Berkeleyan school, ideas (the verbal equivalent of what I term experiences) are discontinuous. The content of each is wholly immanent, and there are no transitions with which they are consubstantial and through which their beings may unite. Your Memorial Hall and mine, even when both are percepts, are wholly out of connection with each other.

[1] [Cf. "How Two Minds Can Know One Thing," below, pp. 123–136.]

Our lives are a congeries of solipsisms, out of
which in strict logic only a God could compose
a universe even of discourse. No dynamic
currents run between my objects and your
objects. Never can our minds meet in the
same.

The incredibility of such a philosophy is
flagrant. It is 'cold, strained, and unnatural'
in a supreme degree; and it may be doubted
whether even Berkeley himself, who took it
so religiously, really believed, when walking
through the streets of London, that his spirit
and the spirits of his fellow wayfarers had
absolutely different towns in view.

To me the decisive reason in favor of our
minds meeting in *some* common objects at least
is that, unless I make that supposition, I have
no motive for assuming that your mind exists
at all. Why do I postulate your mind? Because I see your body acting in a certain way.
Its gestures, facial movements, words and conduct generally, are 'expressive,' so I deem it
actuated as my own is, by an inner life like
mine. This argument from analogy is my *rea-*

son, whether an instinctive belief runs before it or not. But what is 'your body' here but a percept in *my* field ? It is only as animating *that* object, *my* object, that I have any occasion to think of you at all. If the body that you actuate be not the very body that I see there, but some duplicate body of your own with which that has nothing to do, we belong to different universes, you and I, and for me to speak of you is folly. Myriads of such universes even now may coexist, irrelevant to one another; my concern is solely with the universe with which my own life is connected.

In that perceptual part of *my* universe which I call *your* body, your mind and my mind meet and may be called conterminous. Your mind actuates that body and mine sees it ; my thoughts pass into it as into their harmonious cognitive fulfilment; your emotions and volitions pass into it as causes into their effects.

But that percept hangs together with all our other physical percepts. They are of one stuff with it; and if it be our common possession, they must be so likewise. For instance, your hand lays hold of one end of a rope and my hand lays hold of the other end. We pull against each other. Can our two hands be mutual objects in this experience, and the rope not be mutual also? What is true of the rope is true of any other percept. Your objects are over and over again the same as mine. If I ask you *where* some object of yours is, our old Memorial Hall, for example, you point to *my* Memorial Hall with *your* hand which *I* see. If you alter an object in your world, put out a candle, for example, when I am present, *my* candle *ipso facto* goes out. It is only as altering my objects that I guess you to exist. If your objects do not coalesce with my objects, if they be not identically where mine are, they must be proved to be positively somewhere else. But no other location can be assigned for them, so their place must be what it seems to be, the same.[1]

Practically, then, our minds meet in a world of objects which they share in common, which

[1] The notion that our objects are inside of our respective heads is not seriously defensible, so I pass it by.

would still be there, if one or several of the minds were destroyed. I can see no formal objection to this supposition's being literally true. On the principles which I am defending, a 'mind' or 'personal consciousness' is the name for a series of experiences run together by certain definite transitions, and an objective reality is a series of similar experiences knit by different transitions. If one and the same experience can figure twice, once in a mental and once in a physical context (as I have tried, in my article on 'Consciousness,' to show that it can), one does not see why it might not figure thrice, or four times, or any number of times, by running into as many different mental contexts, just as the same point, lying at their intersection, can be continued into many different lines. Abolishing any number of contexts would not destroy the experience itself or its other contexts, any more than abolishing some of the point's linear continuations would destroy the others, or destroy the point itself.

I well know the subtle dialectic which insists

that a term taken in another relation must
needs be an intrinsically different term. The
crux is always the old Greek one, that the same
man can't be tall in relation to one neighbor,
and short in relation to another, for that would
make him tall and short at once. In this essay
I can not stop to refute this dialectic, so I pass
on, leaving my flank for the time exposed.[1]
But if my reader will only allow that the same
'*now*' both ends his past and begins his future;
or that, when he buys an acre of land from his
neighbor, it is the same acre that successively
figures in the two estates; or that when I pay
him a dollar, the same dollar goes into his
pocket that came out of mine; he will also in
consistency have to allow that the same object
may conceivably play a part in, as being related to the rest of, any number of otherwise
entirely different minds. This is enough for
my present point: the common-sense notion of
minds sharing the same object offers no special logical or epistemological difficulties of its
own; it stands or falls with the general possibil-

---

[1] [The argument is resumed below, pp. 101 sq. ED.]

ity of things being in conjunctive relation with other things at all.

In principle, then, let natural realism pass for possible. Your mind and mine *may* terminate in the same percept, not merely against it, as if it were a third external thing, but by inserting themselves into it and coalescing with it, for such is the sort of conjunctive union that appears to be experienced when a perceptual terminus 'fulfils.' Even so, two hawsers may embrace the same pile, and yet neither one of them touch any other part except that pile, of what the other hawser is attached to.

It is therefore not a formal question, but a question of empirical fact solely, whether, when you and I are said to know the 'same' Memorial Hall, our minds do terminate at or in a numerically identical percept. Obviously, as a plain matter of fact, they do *not*. Apart from color-blindness and such possibilities, we see the Hall in different perspectives. You may be on one side of it and I on another. The percept of each of us, as he sees the surface of the Hall, is moreover only his provisional terminus. The

82

next thing beyond my percept is not your mind, but more percepts of my own into which my first percept develops, the interior of the Hall, for instance, or the inner structure of its bricks and mortar. If our minds were in a literal sense *con*terminous, neither could get beyond the percept which they had in common, it would be an ultimate barrier between them — unless indeed they flowed over it and became 'co-conscious' over a still larger part of their content, which (thought-transference apart) is not supposed to be the case. In point of fact the ultimate common barrier can always be pushed, by both minds, farther than any actual percept of either, until at last it resolves itself into the mere notion of imperceptibles like atoms or ether, so that, where we do terminate in percepts, our knowledge is only speciously completed, being, in theoretic strictness, only a virtual knowledge of those remoter objects which conception carries out.

Is natural realism, permissible in logic, refuted then by empirical fact? Do our minds have no object in common after all?

Yes, they certainly have *Space* in common. On pragmatic principles we are obliged to predicate sameness wherever we can predicate no assignable point of difference. If two named things have every quality and function indiscernible, and are at the same time in the same place, they must be written down as numerically one thing under two different names. But there is no test discoverable, so far as I know, by which it can be shown that the place occupied by your percept of Memorial Hall differs from the place occupied by mine. The percepts themselves may be shown to differ; but if each of us be asked to point out where his percept is, we point to an identical spot. All the relations, whether geometrical or causal, of the Hall originate or terminate in that spot wherein our hands meet, and where each of us begins to work if he wishes to make the Hall change before the other's eyes. Just so it is with our bodies. That body of yours which you actuate and feel from within must be in the same spot as the body of yours which I see or touch from without. 'There' for me means where I place my finger. If you do not feel my finger's contact to be 'there' in *my* sense, when I place it on your body, where then do you feel it? Your inner actuations of your body meet my finger *there:* it is *there* that you resist its push, or shrink back, or sweep the finger aside with your hand. Whatever farther knowledge either of us may acquire of the real constitution of the body which we thus feel, you from within and I from without, it is in that same place that the newly conceived or perceived constituents have to be located, and it is *through* that space that your and my mental intercourse with each other has always to be carried on, by the mediation of impressions which I convey thither, and of the reactions thence which those impressions may provoke from you.

In general terms, then, whatever differing contents our minds may eventually fill a place with, the place itself is a numerically identical content of the two minds, a piece of common property in which, through which, and over which they join. The receptacle of certain of our experiences being thus common, the experiences themselves might some day become common also. If that day ever did come, our thoughts would terminate in a complete empirical identity, there would be an end, so far as *those* experiences went, to our discussions about truth. No points of difference appearing, they would have to count as the same.

VII. Conclusion

With this we have the outlines of a philosophy of pure experience before us. At the outset of my essay, I called it a mosaic philosophy. In actual mosaics the pieces are held together by their bedding, for which bedding the Substances, transcendental Egos, or Absolutes of other philosophies may be taken to stand. In radical empiricism there is no bedding; it is as if the pieces clung together by their edges, the transitions experienced between them forming their cement. Of course such a metaphor is misleading, for in actual experience the more substantive and the more transitive parts run into each other continuously, there is in general no separateness needing to be overcome by an external cement; and whatever separateness is actually experienced is not overcome, it stays and counts as separateness to the end. But the metaphor serves to symbolize the fact that Experience itself, taken at large, can grow by its edges. That one moment of it proliferates into the next by transitions which, whether conjunctive or disjunctive, continue the experiential tissue, can not, I contend, be denied. Life is in the transitions as much as in the terms connected; often, indeed, it seems to be there more emphatically, as if our spurts and sallies forward were the real firing-line of the battle, were like the thin line of flame advancing across the dry autumnal field which the farmer proceeds to burn. In this line we live prospectively as well as retrospectively. It is 'of' the past, inasmuch as it comes expressly as the past's continuation; it is 'of' the future in so far as the future, when it comes, will have continued *it*.

These relations of continuous transition experienced are what make our experiences cognitive. In the simplest and completest cases the experiences are cognitive of one another. When one of them terminates a previous series of them with a sense of fulfilment, it, we say, is what those other experiences 'had in view.' The knowledge, in such a case, is verified; the truth is 'salted down.' Mainly, however, we live on speculative investments, or on our prospects only. But living on things *in posse* is as good as living in the actual, so long as our credit remains good. It is evident that for the most part it is good, and that the universe seldom protests our drafts.

In this sense we at every moment can continue to believe in an existing *beyond*. It is only in special cases that our confident rush forward gets rebuked. The beyond must, of course, always in our philosophy be itself of an experiential nature. If not a future experience of our own or a present one of our neighbor, it must be a thing in itself in Dr. Prince's and Professor Strong's sense of the term — that is, it must be an experience *for* itself whose relation to other things we translate into the action of molecules, ether-waves, or whatever else the physical symbols may be.[1] This opens the chapter of the relations of radical empiricism to panpsychism, into which I can not enter now.[2]

The beyond can in any case exist simultaneously — for it can be experienced *to have existed* simultaneously — with the experience that practically postulates it by looking in its direction, or by turning or changing in the direction of which it is the goal. Pending that actuality of union, in the virtuality of which the 'truth,' even now, of the postulation consists, the beyond and its knower are entities split off from each other. The world is in so far forth a pluralism of which the unity is not fully experienced as yet. But, as fast as verifications come, trains of experience, once separate, run into one another; and that is why I said, earlier

---

[1] Our minds and these ejective realities would still have space (or pseudo-space, as I believe Professor Strong calls the medium of interaction between 'things-in-themselves') in common. These would exist *where*, and begin to act *where*, we locate the molecules, etc., and *where* we perceive the sensible phenomena explained thereby. [Cf. Morton Prince: *The Nature of Mind, and Human Automatism*, part I, ch. III, IV; C. A. Strong: *Why the Mind Has a Body*, ch. XII.]

[2] [Cf. below, p. 188; *A Pluralistic Universe*, Lect. IV–VII.]

in my article, that the unity of the world is on the whole undergoing increase. The universe continually grows in quantity by new experiences that graft themselves upon the older mass; but these very new experiences often help the mass to a more consolidated form.

These are the main features of a philosophy of pure experience. It has innumerable other aspects and arouses innumerable questions, but the points I have touched on seem enough to make an entering wedge. In my own mind such a philosophy harmonizes best with a radical pluralism, with novelty and indeterminism, moralism and theism, and with the 'humanism' lately sprung upon us by the Oxford and the Chicago schools.[1] I can not, however, be sure that all these doctrines are its necessary and indispensable allies. It presents so many points of difference, both from the common sense and from the idealism that have made our philosophic language, that it is almost as

---

[1] I have said something of this latter alliance in an article entitled 'Humanism and Truth,' in *Mind*, October, 1904. [Reprinted in *The Meaning of Truth*, pp. 51–101. Cf. also "Humanism and Truth Once More," below, pp. 244–265.]

difficult to state it as it is to think it out clearly, and if it is ever to grow into a respectable system, it will have to be built up by the contributions of many co-operating minds. It seems to me, as I said at the outset of this essay, that many minds are, in point of fact, now turning in a direction that points towards radical empiricism. If they are carried farther by my words, and if then they add their stronger voices to my feebler one, the publication of this essay will have been worth while.

III

THE THING AND ITS RELATIONS[1]

EXPERIENCE in its immediacy seems perfectly fluent. The active sense of living which we all enjoy, before reflection shatters our instinctive world for us, is self-luminous and suggests no paradoxes. Its difficulties are disappointments and uncertainties. They are not intellectual contradictions.

When the reflective intellect gets at work, however, it discovers incomprehensibilities in the flowing process. Distinguishing its elements and parts, it gives them separate names, and what it thus disjoins it can not easily put together. Pyrrhonism accepts the irrationality and revels in its dialectic elaboration. Other philosophies try, some by ignoring, some by resisting, and some by turning the dialectic procedure against itself, negating its first negations, to restore the fluent sense of

[1] [Reprinted from *The Journal of Philosophy, Psychology and Scientific Methods*, vol. II, No. 2, January 19, 1905. Reprinted also as Appendix A in *A Pluralistic Universe*, pp. 347–369. The author's corrections have been adopted in the present text. ED.]

life again, and let redemption take the place of innocence. The perfection with which any philosophy may do this is the measure of its human success and of its importance in philosophic history. In [the last essay], 'A World of Pure Experience,' I tried my own hand sketchily at the problem, resisting certain first steps of dialectics by insisting in a general way that the immediately experienced conjunctive relations are as real as anything else. If my sketch is not to appear too *naïf*, I must come closer to details, and in the present essay I propose to do so.

I

'Pure experience' is the name which I gave to the immediate flux of life which furnishes the material to our later reflection with its conceptual categories. Only new-born babes, or men in semi-coma from sleep, drugs, illnesses, or blows, may be assumed to have an experience pure in the literal sense of a *that* which is not yet any definite *what*, tho' ready to be all sorts of whats; full both of oneness and of manyness, but in respects that don't appear; changing throughout, yet so confusedly that its phases interpenetrate and no points, either of distinction or of identity, can be caught. Pure experience in this state is but another name for feeling or sensation. But the flux of it no sooner comes than it tends to fill itself with emphases, and these salient parts become identified and fixed and abstracted; so that experience now flows as if shot through with adjectives and nouns and prepositions and conjunctions. Its purity is only a relative term, meaning the proportional amount of unverbalized sensation which it still embodies.

Far back as we go, the flux, both as a whole and in its parts, is that of things conjunct and separated. The great continua of time, space, and the self envelope everything, betwixt them, and flow together without interfering. The things that they envelope come as separate in some ways and as continuous in others. Some sensations coalesce with some ideas, and others are irreconcilable. Qualities compenetrate one space, or exclude each other from it. They cling together persistently in groups that move as units, or else they separate. Their changes are abrupt or discontinuous; and their kinds resemble or differ; and, as they do so, they fall into either even or irregular series.

In all this the continuities and the discontinuities are absolutely co-ordinate matters of immediate feeling. The conjunctions are as primordial elements of 'fact' as are the distinctions and disjunctions. In the same act by which I feel that this passing minute is a new pulse of my life, I feel that the old life continues into it, and the feeling of continuance in no wise jars upon the simultaneous feeling of a novelty. They, too, compenetrate harmoniously. Prepositions, copulas, and conjunctions, 'is,' 'is n't,' 'then,' 'before,' 'in,' 'on,' 'beside,' 'between,' 'next,' 'like,' 'unlike,' 'as,' 'but,' flower out of the stream of pure experience, the stream of concretes or the sensational stream, as naturally as nouns and adjectives do, and they melt into it again as fluidly when we apply them to a new portion of the stream.

II

If now we ask why we must thus translate experience from a more concrete or pure into a more intellectualized form, filling it with ever more abounding conceptual distinctions, rationalism and naturalism give different replies.

The rationalistic answer is that the theoretic life is absolute and its interests imperative; that to understand is simply the duty of man; and that who questions this need not be argued with, for by the fact of arguing he gives away his case.

The naturalist answer is that the environment kills as well as sustains us, and that the tendency of raw experience to extinguish the experient himself is lessened just in the degree in which the elements in it that have a practical bearing upon life are analyzed out of the continuum and verbally fixed and coupled together, so that we may know what is in the wind for us and get ready to react in time. Had pure experience, the naturalist says, been always perfectly healthy, there would never

96

have arisen the necessity of isolating or verbalizing any of its terms. We should just have experienced inarticulately and unintellectually enjoyed. This leaning on 'reaction' in the naturalist account implies that, whenever we intellectualize a relatively pure experience, we ought to do so for the sake of redescending to the purer or more concrete level again; and that if an intellect stays aloft among its abstract terms and generalized relations, and does not reinsert itself with its conclusions into some particular point of the immediate stream of life, it fails to finish out its function and leaves its normal race unrun.

Most rationalists nowadays will agree that naturalism gives a true enough account of the way in which our intellect arose at first, but they will deny these latter implications. The case, they will say, resembles that of sexual love. Originating in the animal need of getting another generation born, this passion has developed secondarily such imperious spiritual needs that, if you ask why another generation ought to be born at all, the answer is: 'Chiefly that love may go on.' Just so with our intellect: it originated as a practical means of serving life; but it has developed incidentally the function of understanding absolute truth; and life itself now seems to be given chiefly as a means by which that function may be prosecuted. But truth and the understanding of it lie among the abstracts and universals, so the intellect now carries on its higher business wholly in this region, without any need of redescending into pure experience again.

If the contrasted tendencies which I thus designate as naturalistic and rationalistic are not recognized by the reader, perhaps an example will make them more concrete. Mr. Bradley, for instance, is an ultra-rationalist. He admits that our intellect is primarily practical, but says that, for philosophers, the practical need is simply Truth. Truth, moreover, must be assumed 'consistent.' Immediate experience has to be broken into subjects and qualities, terms and relations, to be understood as truth at all. Yet when so broken it is less consistent then ever. Taken raw, it is all undistinguished. Intellectualized, it is all distinction without oneness. 'Such an arrangement may *work*, but the theoretic problem is not solved.' The question is '*how* the diversity can exist in harmony with the oneness.' To go back to pure experience is unavailing. 'Mere feeling gives no answer to our riddle.' Even if your intuition is a fact, it is not an *understanding*. 'It is a mere experience, and furnishes no consistent view.' The experience offered as facts or truths 'I find that my intellect rejects because they contradict themselves. They offer a complex of diversities conjoined in a way which it feels is not its way and which it can not repeat as its own. . . . For to be satisfied, my intellect must understand, and it can not understand by taking a congeries in the lump.' [1] So Mr. Bradley, in the sole interests of 'understanding' (as he conceives that function), turns his back on finite experience forever. Truth must lie in the opposite direction, the direction of the Absolute; and this kind of

[1] [F. H. Bradley: *Appearance and Reality*, second edition, pp. 152–153, 23, 118, 104, 108–109, 570.]

rationalism and naturalism, or (as I will now call it) pragmatism, walk thenceforward upon opposite paths. For the one, those intellectual products are most true which, turning their face towards the Absolute, come nearest to symbolizing its ways of uniting the many and the one. For the other, those are most true which most successfully dip back into the finite stream of feeling and grow most easily confluent with some particular wave or wavelet. Such confluence not only proves the intellectual operation to have been true (as an addition may 'prove' that a subtraction is already rightly performed), but it constitutes, according to pragmatism, all that we mean by calling it true. Only in so far as they lead us, successfully or unsuccessfully, back into sensible experience again, are our abstracts and universals true or false at all.[1]

III

In Section VI of [the last essay], I adopted

[1] Compare Professor MacLennan's admirable *Auseinandersetzung* with Mr. Bradley, in *The Journal of Philosophy, Psychology and Scientific Methods*, vol. I, [1904], pp. 403 ff., especially pp. 405–4u7.

in a general way the common-sense belief that one and the same world is cognized by our different minds; but I left undiscussed the dialectical arguments which maintain that this is logically absurd. The usual reason given for its being absurd is that it assumes one object (to wit, the world) to stand in two relations at once; to my mind, namely, and again to yours; whereas a term taken in a second relation can not logically be the same term which it was at first.

I have heard this reason urged so often in discussing with absolutists, and it would destroy my radical empiricism so utterly, if it were valid, that I am bound to give it an attentive ear, and seriously to search its strength.

For instance, let the matter in dispute be term M, asserted to be on the one hand related to L, and on the other to $N;$ and let the two cases of relation be symbolized by $L — M$ and $M — N$ respectively. When, now, I assume that the experience may immediately come and be given in the shape $L — M — N$, with no trace of doubling or internal fission in the

M, I am told that this is all a popular delusion; that $L - M - N$ logically means two different experiences, $L - M$ and $M - N$, namely; and that although the Absolute may, and indeed must, from its superior point of view, read its own kind of unity into M's two editions, yet as elements in finite experience the two M's lie irretrievably asunder, and the world between them is broken and unbridged.

In arguing this dialectic thesis, one must avoid slipping from the logical into the physical point of view. It would be easy, in taking a concrete example to fix one's ideas by, to choose one in which the letter M should stand for a collective noun of some sort, which noun, being related to L by one of its parts and to N by another, would inwardly be two things when it stood outwardly in both relations. Thus, one might say: 'David Hume, who weighed so many stone by his body, influences posterity by his doctrine.' The body and the doctrine are two things, between which our finite minds can discover no real sameness, though the same name covers both of them.

And then, one might continue: 'Only an Absolute is capable of uniting such a non-identity.' We must, I say, avoid this sort of example, for the dialectic insight, if true at all, must apply to terms and relations universally. It must be true of abstract units as well as of nouns collective; and if we prove it by concrete examples we must take the simplest, so as to avoid irrelevant material suggestions.

Taken thus in all its generality, the absolutist contention seems to use as its major premise Hume's notion 'that all our distinct perceptions are distinct existences, and that the mind never perceives any real connexion among distinct existences.'[1] Undoubtedly, since we use two phrases in talking first about 'M's relation to L' and then about 'M's relation to N,' we must be having, or must have had, two distinct perceptions; — and the rest would then seem to follow duly. But the starting-point of the reasoning here seems to be the fact of the two *phrases;* and this suggests that

[1] [Hume: *Treatise of Human Nature,* Appendix, Selby-Bigge's edition, p. 636.]

the argument may be merely verbal. Can it be that the whole dialectic consists in attributing to the experience talked-about a constitution similar to that of the language in which we describe it? Must we assert the objective doubleness of the M merely because we have to name it twice over when we name its two relations?

Candidly, I can think of no other reason than this for the dialectic conclusion;[1] for, if we think, not of our words, but of any simple concrete matter which they may be held to signify, the experience itself belies the paradox asserted. We use indeed two separate concepts in analyzing our object, but we know them all the while to be but substitutional, and that the M in $L — M$ and the M in $M — N$ *mean* (*i. e.*, are capable of leading to and terminating in) one self-same piece, M, of sensible experience. This persistent identity of certain units (or emphases, or points, or objects, or members — call them what you will) of the experience-continuum, is just one of those conjunctive

[1] Technically, it seems classable as a 'fallacy of composition.' A duality, predicable of the two wholes, $L — M$ and $M — N$, is forthwith predicated of one of their parts, M.

features of it, on which I am obliged to insist so emphatically.[1] For samenesses are parts of experience's indefeasible structure. When I hear a bell-stroke and, as life flows on, its after image dies away, I still hark back to it as 'that same bell-stroke.' When I see a thing M, with L to the left of it and N to the right of it, I see it *as* one $M;$ and if you tell me I have had to 'take' it twice, I reply that if I 'took' it a thousand times I should still *see* it as a unit.[2] Its unity is aboriginal, just as the multiplicity of my successive takings is aboriginal. It comes unbroken as *that M*, as a singular which I encounter; they come broken, as *those* takings, as my plurality of operations. The unity and the separateness are strictly co-ordinate. I do not easily fathom why my opponents should find the separateness so much more easily understandable that they must needs infect the whole of finite experience with it, and relegate

[1] See above, pp. 42 ff.

[2] I may perhaps refer here to my *Principles of Psychology*, vol. I, pp. 459 ff. It really seems 'weird' to have to argue (as I am forced now to do) for the notion that it is one sheet of paper (with its two surfaces and all that lies between) which is both under my pen and on the table while I write — the 'claim' that it is two sheets seems so brazen. Yet I sometimes suspect the absolutists of sincerity!

the unity (now taken as a bare postulate and no longer as a thing positively perceivable) to the region of the Absolute's mysteries. I do not easily fathom this, I say, for the said opponents are above mere verbal quibbling; yet all that I can catch in their talk is the substitution of what is true of certain words for what is true of what they signify. They stay with the words, — not returning to the stream of life whence all the meaning of them came, and which is always ready to reabsorb them.

IV

For aught this argument proves, then, we may continue to believe that one thing can be known by many knowers. But the denial of one thing in many relations is but one application of a still profounder dialectic difficulty. Man can't be good, said the sophists, for man is *man* and *good* is good; and Hegel [1] and Herbart in their day, more recently A. Spir, [2] and most

[1] [For the author's criticism of Hegel's view of relations, cf. *Will to Believe*, pp. 278-279. ED.]

[2] [Cf. A. Spir: *Denken und Wirklichkeit*, part I, bk. III, ch. IV (containing also account of Herbart). ED.]

recently and elaborately of all, Mr. Bradley, informs us that a term can logically only be a punctiform unit, and that not one of the conjunctive relations between things, which experience seems to yield, is rationally possible.

Of course, if true, this cuts off radical empiricism without even a shilling. Radical empiricism takes conjunctive relations at their face value, holding them to be as real as the terms united by them.[1] The world it represents as a collection, some parts of which are conjunctively and others disjunctively related. Two parts, themselves disjoined, may nevertheless hang together by intermediaries with which they are severally connected, and the whole world eventually may hang together similarly, inasmuch as *some* path of conjunctive transition by which to pass from one of its parts to another may always be discernible. Such determinately various hanging-together may be called *concatenated* union, to distinguish it from the 'through-and-through' type of union,

[1] [See above, pp. 42, 49.]

'each in all and all in each' (union of *total conflux*, as one might call it), which monistic systems hold to obtain when things are taken in their absolute reality. In a concatenated world a partial conflux often is experienced. Our concepts and our sensations are confluent; successive states of the same ego, and feelings of the same body are confluent. Where the experience is not of conflux, it may be of conterminousness (things with but one thing between); or of contiguousness (nothing between); or of likeness; or of nearness; or of simultaneousness; or of in-ness; or of on-ness; or of for-ness; or of simple with-ness; or even of mere and-ness, which last relation would make of however disjointed a world otherwise, at any rate for that occasion a universe 'of discourse.' Now Mr. Bradley tells us that none of these relations, as we actually experience them, can possibly be real.[1] My next duty, accordingly,

[1] Here again the reader must beware of slipping from logical into phenomenal considerations. It may well be that we *attribute* a certain relation falsely, because the circumstances of the case, being complex, have deceived us. At a railway station we may take our own train, and not the one that fills our window, to be moving. We here put motion in the wrong place in the world, but in its original place the

must be to rescue radical empiricism from Mr.
Bradley. Fortunately, as it seems to me, his
general contention, that the very notion of relation is unthinkable clearly, has been successfully met by many critics.[1]

It is a burden to the flesh, and an injustice
both to readers and to the previous writers, to
repeat good arguments already printed. So, in
noticing Mr. Bradley, I will confine myself to
the interests of radical empiricism solely.

V

The first duty of radical empiricism, taking
given conjunctions at their face-value, is to
class some of them as more intimate and some
as more external. When two terms are *similar*, their very natures enter into the relation.

motion is a part of reality. What Mr. Bradley means is nothing like
this, but rather that such things as motion are nowhere real, and
that, even in their aboriginal and empirically incorrigible seats, relations are impossible of comprehension.

[1] Particularly so by Andrew Seth Pringle-Pattison, in his *Man and
the Cosmos;* by L. T. Hobhouse, in chapter XII ("The Validity of
Judgment") of his *Theory of Knowledge;* and by F. C. S. Schiller, in his
Humanism, essay XI. Other fatal reviews (in my opinion) are Hodder's, in the *Psychological Review*, vol. I, [1894], p. 307; Stout's in the
Proceedings of the Aristotelian Society, 1901-2, p. 1; and MacLennan's
in [*The Journal of Philosophy, Psychology and Scientific Methods*,
vol. I, 1904, p. 403].

Being *what* they are, no matter where or when, the likeness never can be denied, if asserted. It continues predicable as long as the terms continue. Other relations, the *where* and the *when*, for example, seem adventitious. The sheet of paper may be 'off' or 'on' the table, for example; and in either case the relation involves only the outside of its terms. Having an outside, both of them, they contribute by it to the relation. It is external: the term's inner nature is irrelevant to it. Any book, any table, may fall into the relation, which is created *pro hac vice*, not by their existence, but by their casual situation. It is just because so many of the conjunctions of experience seem so external that a philosophy of pure experience must tend to pluralism in its ontology. So far as things have space-relations, for example, we are free to imagine them with different origins even. If they could get to *be*, and get into space at all, then they may have done so separately. Once there, however, they are *additives* to one another, and, with no prejudice to their natures, all sorts of space-relations may supervene between them. The question of how things could come to be anyhow, is wholly different from the question what their relations, once the being accomplished, may consist in.

Mr. Bradley now affirms that such external relations as the space-relations which we here talk of must hold of entirely different subjects from those of which the absence of such relations might a moment previously have been plausibly asserted. Not only is the *situation* different when the book is on the table, but the *book itself* is different as a book, from what it was when it was off the table.[1] He admits that "such external relations seem possible and even existing. . . . That you do not alter what you compare or rearrange in space seems to common sense quite obvious, and that on

---

[1] Once more, don't slip from logical into physical situations. Of course, if the table be wet, it will moisten the book, or if it be slight enough and the book heavy enough, the book will break it down. But such collateral phenomena are not the point at issue. The point is whether the successive relations 'on' and 'not-on' can rationally (not physically) hold of the same constant terms, abstractly taken. Professor A. E. Taylor drops from logical into material considerations when he instances color-contrast as a proof that *A*, 'as contra-distinguished from *B*, is not the same thing as mere *A* not in any way affected' (*Elements of Metaphysics*, p. 145). Note the substitution, for 'related' of the word 'affected,' which begs the whole question.

the other side there are as obvious difficulties
does not occur to common sense at all. And I
will begin by pointing out these difficulties....
There is a relation in the result, and this relation, we hear, is to make no difference in its
terms. But, if so, to what does it make a difference? [*Does n't it make a difference to us on-
lookers, at least?*] and what is the meaning and
sense of qualifying the terms by it? [*Surely the
meaning is to tell the truth about their relative
position.*[1]] If, in short, it is external to the terms,
how can it possibly be true *of* them? [*Is it the
'intimacy' suggested by the little word 'of,' here,
which I have underscored, that is the root of Mr.
Bradley's trouble?*] . . . If the terms from their
inner nature do not enter into the relation,
then, so far as they are concerned, they seem
related for no reason at all. . . . Things are spa-
tially related, first in one way, and then become related in another way, and yet in no
way themselves are altered; for the relations,
it is said, are but external. But I reply that, if

---

[1] But "is there any sense," asks Mr. Bradley, peevishly, on p. 579,
"and if so, what sense in truth that is only outside and 'about'
things?" Surely such a question may be left unanswered.

so, I can not *understand* the leaving by the terms of one set of relations and their adoption of another fresh set. The process and its result to the terms, if they contribute nothing to it [*Surely they contribute to it all there is 'of' it!*] seem irrational throughout. [*If 'irrational' here means simply 'non-rational,' or non-deducible from the essence of either term singly, it is no reproach; if it means 'contradicting' such essence, Mr. Bradley should show wherein and how.*] But, if they contribute anything, they must surely be affected internally. [*Why so, if they contribute only their surface? In such relations as 'on,' 'a foot away,' 'between,' 'next,' etc., only surfaces are in question.*] . . . If the terms contribute anything whatever, then the terms are affected [*inwardly altered?*] by the arrangement. . . . That for working purposes we treat, and do well to treat, some relations as external merely I do not deny, and that of course is not the question at issue here. That question is . . . whether in the end and in principle a mere external relation [*i. e., a relation which can change without forcing its terms to change their nature simultaneously*] is possible and forced on us by the facts." [1]

Mr. Bradley next reverts to the antinomies of space, which, according to him, prove it to be unreal, although it appears as so prolific a medium of external relations; and he then concludes that "Irrationality and externality can not be the last truth about things. Somewhere there must be a reason why this and that appear together. And this reason and reality must reside in the whole from which terms and relations are abstractions, a whole in which their internal connection must lie, and out of which from the background appear those fresh results which never could have come from the premises." And he adds that "Where the whole is different, the terms that qualify and contribute to it must so far be different. . . . They are altered so far only [*How far? farther than externally, yet not through and through?*] but still they are altered. . . . I must insist that in each case the terms are qualified by their whole [*Qualified how? — Do their external*

---

[1] *Appearance and Reality*, second edition, pp. 575–576.

*relations, situations, dates, etc., changed as these
are in the new whole, fail to qualify them 'far'
enough?*], and that in the second case there is a
whole which differs both logically and psychologically from the first whole; and I urge that
in contributing to the change the terms so far
are altered."

Not merely the relations, then, but the terms
are altered: *und zwar* 'so far.' But just *how*
far is the whole problem; and 'through-and-
through' would seem (in spite of Mr. Bradley's
somewhat undecided utterances [1]) to be the

---

[1] I say 'undecided,' because, apart from the 'so far,' which sounds
terribly half-hearted, there are passages in these very pages in which
Mr. Bradley admits the pluralistic thesis. Read, for example, what he
says, on p. 578, of a billiard ball keeping its 'character' unchanged,
though, in its change of place, its 'existence' gets altered; or what he
says, on p. 579, of the possibility that an abstract quality A, B, or C,
in a thing, 'may throughout remain unchanged' although the thing be
altered; or his admission that in red-hairedness, both as analyzed out
of a man and when given with the rest of him, there may be 'no
change' p. 580). Why does he immediately add that for the pluralist
to plead the non-mutation of such abstractions would be an *ignoratio
elenchi?* It is impossible to admit it to be such. The entire *elenchus*
and inquest is just as to whether parts which you can abstract from
existing wholes can also contribute to other wholes without changing
their inner nature. If they can thus mould various wholes into new
gestaltqualitäten, then it follows that the same elements are logically
able to exist in different wholes [whether physically able would depend
on additional hypotheses]; that partial changes are thinkable, and
through-and-through change not a dialectic necessity; that monism
is only an hypothesis; and that an additively constituted universe

full Bradleyan answer. The 'whole' which he here treats as primary and determinative of each part's manner of 'contributing,' simply *must*, when it alters, alter in its entirety. There *must* be total conflux of its parts, each into and through each other. The 'must' appears here as a *Machtspruch*, as an *ipse dixit* of Mr. Bradley's absolutistically tempered 'understanding,' for he candidly confesses that how the parts *do* differ as they contribute to different wholes, is unknown to him.[1]

Although I have every wish to comprehend the authority by which Mr. Bradley's understanding speaks, his words leave me wholly unconverted. 'External relations' stand with their withers all unwrung, and remain, for aught he proves to the contrary, not only practically workable, but also perfectly intelligible factors of reality.

is a rationally respectable hypothesis also. All the theses of radical empiricism, in short, follow.

[1] *Op. cit.*, pp. 577–579.

VI

Mr. Bradley's understanding shows the most extraordinary power of perceiving separations and the most extraordinary impotence in comprehending conjunctions. One would naturally say 'neither or both,' but not so Mr. Bradley. When a common man analyzes certain *whats* from out the stream of experience, he understands their distinctness *as thus isolated*. But this does not prevent him from equally well understanding their combination with each other *as originally experienced in the concrete*, or their confluence with new sensible experiences in which they recur as 'the same.' Returning into the stream of sensible presentation, nouns and adjectives, and *thats* and abstract *whats*, grow confluent again, and the word 'is' names all these experiences of conjunction. Mr. Bradley understands the isolation of the abstracts, but to understand the combination is to him impossible.[1] "To under-

[1] So far as I catch his state of mind, it is somewhat like this: 'Book,' 'table,' 'on' — how does the existence of these three abstract elements result in *this* book being livingly on *this* table. Why is n't the table on

stand a complex AB," he says, "I must begin with A or B. And beginning, say with A, if I then merely find B, I have either lost A, or I have got beside A, [*the word 'beside' seems here vital, as meaning a conjunction 'external' and therefore unintelligible*] something else, and in neither case have I understood.[1] For my intellect can not simply unite a diversity, nor has it in itself any form or way of togetherness, and you gain nothing if, beside A and B, you offer me their conjunction in fact. For to my intellect that is no more than another external element. And 'facts,' once for all, are for my intellect not true unless they satisfy it. . . . The intellect has in its nature no principle of mere togetherness."[2]

the book? Or why does n't the 'on' connect itself with another book, or something that is not a table? Must n't something *in* each of the three elements already determine the two others to *it*, so that they do not settle elsewhere or float vaguely? Must n't the *whole fact be prefigured in each part*, and exist *de jure* before it can exist *de facto*? But, if so, in what can the jural existence consist, if not in a spiritual miniature of the whole fact's constitution actuating every partial factor as its purpose? But is this anything but the old metaphysical fallacy of looking behind a fact *in esse* for the ground of the fact, and finding it in the shape of the very same fact *in posse*? Somewhere we must leave off with a *constitution* behind which there is nothing.

[1] Apply this to the case of 'book-on-table'! W. J.

[2] *Op. cit.*, pp. 570, 572.

Of course Mr. Bradley has a right to define 'intellect' as the power by which we perceive separations but not unions — provided he give due notice to the reader. But why then claim that such a maimed and amputated power must reign supreme in philosophy, and accuse on its behoof the whole empirical world of irrationality? It is true that he elsewhere attributes to the intellect a *proprius motus* of transition, but says that when he looks for *these* transitions in the detail of living experience, he 'is unable to verify such a solution.' [1]

Yet he never explains what the intellectual transitions would be like in case we had them. He only defines them negatively — they are not spatial, temporal, predicative, or causal; or qualitatively or otherwise serial; or in any way relational as we naïvely trace relations, for relations *separate* terms, and need themselves to be hooked on *ad infinitum*. The nearest approach he makes to describing a truly intellectual transition is where he speaks of

[1] *Op. cit.*, pp. 568, 569.

119

A and *B* as being 'united, each from its own nature, in a whole which is the nature of both alike.' [1] But this (which, *pace* Mr. Bradley, seems exquisitely analogous to 'taking' a congeries in a 'lump,' if not to 'swamping') suggests nothing but that *conflux* which pure experience so abundantly offers, as when 'space,' 'white' and 'sweet' are confluent in a 'lump of sugar,' or kinesthetic, dermal, and optical sensations confluent in 'my hand.' [2] All that I can verify in the transitions which Mr. Bradley's intellect desiderates as its *proprius motus* is a reminiscence of these and other sensible conjunctions (especially space-conjunctions), but a reminiscence so vague that its originals are not recognized. Bradley in short repeats the fable of the dog, the bone, and its image in the water. With a world of particulars, given in loveliest union, in conjunction definitely various, and variously de-

[1] *Op. cit.*, p. 570.

[2] How meaningless is the contention that in such wholes (or in 'book-on-table,' 'watch-in-pocket,' etc.) the relation is an additional entity *between* the terms, needing itself to be related again to each! Both Bradley (*op. cit.*, pp. 32–33) and Royce (*The World and the Individual*, vol. I, p. 128) lovingly repeat this piece of profundity.

finite, the 'how' of which you 'understand' as soon as you see the fact of them,[1] for there is no 'how' except the constitution of the fact as given; with all this given him, I say, in pure experience, he asks for some ineffable union in the abstract instead, which, if he gained it, would only be a duplicate of what he has already in his full possession. Surely he abuses the privilege which society grants to all us philosophers, of being puzzle-headed.

Polemic writing like this is odious; but with absolutism in possession in so many quarters, omission to defend my radical empiricism against its best known champion would count as either superficiality or inability. I have to conclude that its dialectic has not invalidated in the least degree the usual conjunctions by which the world, as experienced, hangs so variously together. In particular it leaves an empirical theory of knowledge[2] intact, and lets us continue to believe with common sense that

[1] The 'why' and the 'whence' are entirely other questions, not under discussion, as I understand Mr. Bradley. Not how experience gets itself born, but how it can be what it is after it is born, is the puzzle.

[2] Above, p. 52.

one object *may* be known, if we have any ground for thinking that it *is* known, to many knowers.

In [the next essay] I shall return to this last supposition, which seems to me to offer other difficulties much harder for a philosophy of pure experience to deal with than any of absolutism's dialectic objections.

IV

HOW TWO MINDS CAN KNOW ONE THING[1]

I~N~ [the essay] entitled 'Does Consciousness Exist?' I have tried to show that when we call an experience 'conscious,' that does not mean that it is suffused throughout with a peculiar modality of being ('psychic' being) as stained glass may be suffused with light, but rather that it stands in certain determinate relations to other portions of experience extraneous to itself. These form one peculiar 'context' for it; while, taken in another context of experiences, we class it as a fact in the physical world. This 'pen,' for example, is, in the first instance, a bald *that*, a datum, fact, phenomenon, content, or whatever other neutral or ambiguous name you may prefer to apply. I called it in that article a 'pure experience.' To get classed either as a physical pen or as some one's percept of a pen, it must assume a *func-*

---

[1] [Reprinted from *The Journal of Philosophy, Psychology and Scientific Methods*, vol. II, No. 7, March 30, 1905.]

tion, and that can only happen in a more complicated world. So far as in that world it is a stable feature, holds ink, marks paper and obeys the guidance of a hand, it is a physical pen. That is what we mean by being 'physical,' in a pen. So far as it is instable, on the contrary, coming and going with the movements of my eyes, altering with what I call my fancy, continuous with subsequent experiences of its 'having been' (in the past tense), it is the percept of a pen in my mind. Those peculiarities are what we mean by being 'conscious,' in a pen.

In Section VI of another [essay][1] I tried to show that the same *that,* the same numerically identical pen of pure experience, can enter simultaneously into many conscious contexts, or, in other words, be an object for many different minds. I admitted that I had not space to treat of certain possible objections in that article; but in [the last essay] I took some of the objections up. At the end of that [essay] I said that still more formidable-sounding

[1] "A World of Pure Experience," above, pp. 39-91.

objections remained; so, to leave my pure-experience theory in as strong a state as possible, I propose to consider those objections now.

I

The objections I previously tried to dispose of were purely logical or dialectical. No one identical term, whether physical or psychical, it had been said, could be the subject of two relations at once. This thesis I sought to prove unfounded. The objections that now confront us arise from the nature supposed to inhere in psychic facts specifically. Whatever may be the case with physical objects, a fact of consciousness, it is alleged (and indeed very plausibly), can not, without self-contradiction, be treated as a portion of two different minds, and for the following reasons.

In the physical world we make with impunity the assumption that one and the same material object can figure in an indefinitely large number of different processes at once. When, for instance, a sheet of rubber is pulled at its four corners, a unit of rubber in the middle of the sheet is affected by all four of the pulls. It *transmits* them each, as if it pulled in four different ways at once itself. So, an air-particle or an ether-particle 'compounds' the different directions of movement imprinted on it without obliterating their several individualities. It delivers them distinct, on the contrary, at as many several 'receivers' (ear, eye or what not) as may be 'tuned' to that effect. The apparent paradox of a distinctness like this surviving in the midst of compounding is a thing which, I fancy, the analyses made by physicists have by this time sufficiently cleared up.

But if, on the strength of these analogies, one should ask: "Why, if two or more lines can run through one and the same geometrical point, or if two or more distinct processes of activity can run through one and the same physical thing so that it simultaneously plays a rôle in each and every process, might not two or more streams of personal consciousness include one and the same unit of experience so that it would simultaneously be a part of the experience of all the different minds?" one would be checked by thinking of a certain peculiarity by which phenomena of consciousness differ from physical things.

While physical things, namely, are supposed to be permanent and to have their 'states,' a fact of consciousness exists but once and *is* a state. Its *esse* is *sentiri;* it is only so far as it is felt; and it is unambiguously and unequivocally exactly *what* is felt. The hypothesis under consideration would, however, oblige it to be felt equivocally, felt now as part of my mind and again at the same time *not* as a part of my mind, but of yours (for my mind is *not* yours), and this would seem impossible without doubling it into two distinct things, or, in other words, without reverting to the ordinary dualistic philosophy of insulated minds each knowing its object representatively as a third thing, — and that would be to give up the pureexperience scheme altogether.

Can we see, then, any way in which a unit of pure experience might enter into and figure in two diverse streams of consciousness without turning itself into the two units which, on our hypothesis, it must not be?

II

There is a way; and the first step towards it is to see more precisely how the unit enters into either one of the streams of consciousness alone. Just what, from being 'pure,' does its becoming 'conscious' *once* mean?

It means, first, that new experiences have supervened; and, second, that they have borne a certain assignable relation to the unit supposed. Continue, if you please, to speak of the pure unit as 'the pen.' So far as the pen's successors do but repeat the pen or, being different from it, are 'energetically' [1] related to it, it and they will form a group of stably existing physical things. So far, however, as its successors differ from it in another well-determined way, the pen will figure in their context, not as a physical, but as a mental fact. It will become a passing 'percept,' *my* percept of that pen. What now is that decisive well-determined way?

In the chapter on 'The Self,' in my *Principles*

[1] [For an explanation of this expression, see above, p. 32.]

of Psychology, I explained the continuous identity of each personal consciousness as a name for the practical fact that new experiences [1] come which look back on the old ones, find them 'warm,' and greet and appropriate them as 'mine.' These operations mean, when analyzed empirically, several tolerably definite things, viz.:

1. That the new experience has past time for its 'content,' and in that time a pen that 'was';

2. That 'warmth' was also about the pen, in the sense of a group of feelings ('interest' aroused, 'attention' turned, 'eyes' employed, etc.) that were closely connected with it and that now recur and evermore recur with unbroken vividness, though from the pen of now, which may be only an image, all such vividness may have gone;

3. That these feelings are the nucleus of 'me';

4. That whatever once was associated with them was, at least for that one moment, 'mine' — my implement if associated with

---

[1] I call them 'passing thoughts' in the book — the passage in point goes from pages 330 to 342 of vol. I.

hand-feelings, my 'percept' only, if only eye-feelings and attention-feelings were involved.

The pen, realized in this retrospective way as my percept, thus figures as a fact of 'conscious' life. But it does so only so far as 'appropriation' has occurred; and appropriation is *part of the content of a later experience* wholly additional to the originally 'pure' pen. *That* pen, virtually both objective and subjective, is at its own moment actually and intrinsically neither. It has to be looked back upon and *used*, in order to be classed in either distinctive way. But its use, so called, is in the hands of the other experience, while *it* stands, throughout the operation, passive and unchanged.

If this pass muster as an intelligible account of how an experience originally pure can enter into one consciousness, the next question is as to how it might conceivably enter into two.

III

Obviously no new kind of condition would have to be supplied. All that we should have to postulate would be a second subsequent experience, collateral and contemporary with the first subsequent one, in which a similar act of appropriation should occur. The two acts would interfere neither with one another nor with the originally pure pen. It would sleep undisturbed in its own past, no matter how many such successors went through their several appropriative acts. Each would know it as 'my' percept, each would class it as a 'conscious' fact.

Nor need their so classing it interfere in the least with their classing it at the same time as a physical pen. Since the classing in both cases depends upon the taking of it in one group or another of associates, if the superseding experience were of wide enough 'span' it could think the pen in both groups simultaneously, and yet distinguish the two groups. It would then see the whole situation conformably to what we call 'the representative theory of cognition,' and that is what we all spontaneously do. As a man philosophizing 'popularly,' I believe that what I see myself writing with is double — I think it in its relations to physical nature, and also in its relations to my personal life; I see that it is in my mind, but that it also is a physical pen.

The paradox of the same experience figuring in two consciousnesses seems thus no paradox at all. To be 'conscious' means not simply to be, but to be reported, known, to have awareness of one's being added to that being; and this is just what happens when the appropriative experience supervenes. The pen-experience in its original immediacy is not aware of itself, it simply *is*, and the second experience is required for what we call awareness of it to occur.[1] The difficulty of understanding what happens here is, therefore, not a logical difficulty: there is no contradiction involved. It is an ontological difficulty rather. Experiences come on an enormous scale, and if we take

---

[1] Shadworth Hodgson has laid great stress on the fact that the minimum of consciousness demands two subfeelings, of which the second retrospects the first. (Cf. the section 'Analysis of Minima' in his *Philosophy of Reflection*, vol. I, p. 248; also the chapter entitled 'The Moment of Experience' in his *Metaphysic of Experience*, vol. I, p. 34.) 'We live forward, but we understand backward' is a phrase of Kierkegaard's which Höffding quotes. [H. Höffding: "A Philosophical Confession," *Journal of Philosophy, Psychology and Scientific Methods*, vol. II, 1905, p. 86.]

them all together, they come in a chaos of incommensurable relations that we can not straighten out. We have to abstract different groups of them, and handle these separately if we are to talk of them at all. But how the experiences ever *get themselves made*, or *why* their characters and relations are just such as appear, we can not begin to understand. Granting, however, that, by hook or crook, they *can* get themselves made, and can appear in the successions that I have so schematically described, then we have to confess that even although (as I began by quoting from the adversary) 'a feeling only is as it is felt,' there is still nothing absurd in the notion of its being felt in two different ways at once, as yours, namely, and as mine. It is, indeed, 'mine' only as it is felt as mine, and 'yours' only as it is felt as yours. But it is felt as neither *by itself*, but only when 'owned' by our two several remembering experiences, just as one undivided estate is owned by several heirs.

IV

One word, now, before I close, about the corollaries of the views set forth. Since the acquisition of conscious quality on the part of an experience depends upon a context coming to it, it follows that the sum total of all experiences, having no context, can not strictly be called conscious at all. It is a *that*, an Absolute, a 'pure' experience on an enormous scale, undifferentiated and undifferentiable into thought and thing. This the post-Kantian idealists have always practically acknowledged by calling their doctrine an *Identitäts-philosophie*. The question of the *Beseelung* of the All of things ought not, then, even to be asked. No more ought the question of its *truth* to be asked, for truth is a relation inside of the sum total, obtaining between thoughts and something else, and thoughts, as we have seen, can only be contextual things. In these respects the pure experiences of our philosophy are, in themselves considered, so many little absolutes, the philosophy of pure experience being only a more comminuted *Identitätsphilosophie.*[1]

Meanwhile, a pure experience can be postulated with any amount whatever of span or field. If it exert the retrospective and appropriative function on any other piece of experience, the latter thereby enters into its own conscious stream. And in this operation time intervals make no essential difference. After sleeping, my retrospection is as perfect as it is between two successive waking moments of my time. Accordingly if, millions of years later, a similarly retrospective experience should anyhow come to birth, my present thought would form a genuine portion of its long-span conscious life. 'Form a portion,' I say, but not in the sense that the two things could be entitatively or substantively one — they cannot, for they are numerically discrete facts — but only in the sense that the *functions* of my present thought, its knowledge, its purpose, its content and 'consciousness,' in short, being inherited, would be continued practically

---

[1] [Cf. below, pp. 197, 202.]

unchanged. Speculations like Fechner's, of an Earth-soul, of wider spans of consciousness enveloping narrower ones throughout the cosmos, are, therefore, philosophically quite in order, provided they distinguish the functional from the entitative point of view, and do not treat the minor consciousness under discussion as a kind of standing material of which the wider ones *consist.*[1]

[1] [Cf. *A Pluralistic Universe*, Lect. IV, 'Concerning Fechner,' and Lect. V, 'The Compounding of Consciousness.']

V

THE PLACE OF AFFECTIONAL FACTS IN A WORLD OF PURE EXPERIENCE[1]

COMMON sense and popular philosophy are as
dualistic as it is possible to be. Thoughts, we
all naturally think, are made of one kind of
substance, and things of another. Consciousness, flowing inside of us in the forms of conception or judgment, or concentrating itself in
the shape of passion or emotion, can be directly
felt as the spiritual activity which it is, and
known in contrast with the space-filling objective 'content' which it envelopes and accompanies. In opposition to this dualistic
philosophy, I tried, in [the first essay] to show
that thoughts and things are absolutely homogeneous as to their material, and that their
opposition is only one of relation and of function. There is no thought-stuff different from
thing-stuff, I said; but the same identical piece

---

[1] [Reprinted from *The Journal of Philosophy, Psychology and
Scientific Methods*, vol. II, No. 11, May 25, 1905.]

of 'pure experience' (which was the name I gave to the *materia prima* of everything) can stand alternately for a 'fact of consciousness' or for a physical reality, according as it is taken in one context or in another. For the right understanding of what follows, I shall have to presuppose that the reader will have read that [essay].[1]

The commonest objection which the doctrine there laid down runs up against is drawn from the existence of our 'affections.' In our pleasures and pains, our loves and fears and angers, in the beauty, comicality, importance or preciousness of certain objects and situations, we have, I am told by many critics, a great realm of experience intuitively recognized as spiritual, made, and felt to be made, of consciousness exclusively, and different in nature from the space-filling kind of being which is enjoyed by physical objects. In Section VII. of [the first essay], I treated of this class of experiences very inadequately,

[1] It will be still better if he shall have also read the [essay] entitled 'A World of Pure Experience,' which follows [the first] and develops its ideas still farther.

because I had to be so brief. I now return to the subject, because I believe that, so far from invalidating my general thesis, these phenomena, when properly analyzed, afford it powerful support.

The central point of the pure-experience theory is that 'outer' and 'inner' are names for two groups into which we sort experiences according to the way in which they act upon their neighbors. Any one 'content,' such as *hard*, let us say, can be assigned to either group. In the outer group it is 'strong,' it acts 'energetically' and aggressively. Here whatever is hard interferes with the space its neighbors occupy. It dents them; is impenetrable by them; and we call the hardness then a physical hardness. In the mind, on the contrary, the hard thing is nowhere in particular, it dents nothing, it suffuses through its mental neighbors, as it were, and interpenetrates them. Taken in this group we call both it and them 'ideas' or 'sensations'; and the basis of the two groups respectively is the different type of interrelation, the mutual impenetrability, on the one hand, and the lack of physical interference and interaction, on the other.

That what in itself is one and the same entity should be able to function thus differently in different contexts is a natural consequence of the extremely complex reticulations in which our experiences come. To her offspring a tigress is tender, but cruel to every other living thing — both cruel and tender, therefore, at once. A mass in movement resists every force that operates contrariwise to its own direction, but to forces that pursue the same direction, or come in at right angles, it is absolutely inert. It is thus both energetic and inert; and the same is true (if you vary the associates properly) of every other piece of experience. It is only towards certain specific groups of associates that the physical energies, as we call them, of a content are put forth. In another group it may be quite inert.

It is possible to imagine a universe of experiences in which the only alternative between neighbors would be either physical interaction or complete inertness. In such a world the mental or the physical *status* of any piece of experience would be unequivocal. When active, it would figure in the physical, and when inactive, in the mental group.

But the universe we live in is more chaotic than this, and there is room in it for the hybrid or ambiguous group of our affectional experiences, of our emotions and appreciative perceptions. In the paragraphs that follow I shall try to show:

(1) That the popular notion that these experiences are intuitively given as purely inner facts is hasty and erroneous; and

(2) That their ambiguity illustrates beautifully my central thesis that subjectivity and objectivity are affairs not of what an experience is aboriginally made of, but of its classification. Classifications depend on our temporary purposes. For certain purposes it is convenient to take things in one set of relations, for other purposes in another set. In the two cases their contexts are apt to be different. In the case of our affectional experiences we have no permanent and steadfast purpose that

obliges us to be consistent, so we find it easy to let them float ambiguously, sometimes classing them with our feelings, sometimes with more physical realities, according to caprice or to the convenience of the moment. Thus would these experiences, so far from being an obstacle to the pure experience philosophy, serve as an excellent corroboration of its truth.

First of all, then, it is a mistake to say, with the objectors whom I began by citing, that anger, love and fear are affections purely of the mind. That, to a great extent at any rate, they are simultaneously affections of the body is proved by the whole literature of the James-Lange theory of emotion.[1] All our pains, moreover, are local, and we are always free to speak of them in objective as well as in subjective terms. We can say that we are aware of a painful place, filling a certain bigness in our organism, or we can say that we are inwardly in a 'state' of pain. All our adjectives of

[1] [Cf. *The Principles of Psychology*, vol. II, ch. XXV; and "The Physical Basis of Emotion," *The Psychological Review*, vol. I, 1894, p. 516.]

worth are similarly ambiguous — I instanced
some of the ambiguities [in the first essay].[1]
Is the preciousness of a diamond a quality of
the gem? or is it a feeling in our mind? Practically we treat it as both or as either, according to the temporary direction of our thought.
'Beauty,' says Professor Santayana, 'is pleasure objectified'; and in Sections 10 and 11 of
his work, *The Sense of Beauty*, he treats in a
masterly way of this equivocal realm. The
various pleasures we receive from an object
may count as 'feelings' when we take them
singly, but when they combine in a total richness, we call the result the 'beauty' of the
object, and treat it as an outer attribute which
our mind perceives. We discover beauty just as
we discover the physical properties of things.
Training is needed to make us expert in either
line. Single sensations also may be ambiguous.
Shall we say an 'agreeable degree of heat,' or
an 'agreeable feeling' occasioned by the degree
of heat? Either will do; and language would
lose most of its esthetic and rhetorical value

---

[1] [See above, pp. **34, 35**.]

were we forbidden to project words primarily connoting our affections upon the objects by which the affections are aroused. The man is really hateful; the action really mean; the situation really tragic — all in themselves and quite apart from our opinion. We even go so far as to talk of a weary road, a giddy height, a jocund morning or a sullen sky; and the term 'indefinite' while usually applied only to our apprehensions, functions as a fundamental physical qualification of things in Spencer's 'law of evolution,' and doubtless passes with most readers for all right.

Psychologists, studying our perceptions of movement, have unearthed experiences in which movement is felt in general but not ascribed correctly to the body that really moves. Thus in optical vertigo, caused by unconscious movements of our eyes, both we and the external universe appear to be in a whirl. When clouds float by the moon, it is as if both clouds and moon and we ourselves shared in the motion. In the extraordinary case of amnesia of the Rev. Mr. Hanna, published by Sidis and Goodhart in their important work on *Multiple Personality*, we read that when the patient first recovered consciousness and "noticed an attendant walk across the room, he identified the movement with that of his own. He did not yet discriminate between his own movements and those outside himself." [1] Such experiences point to a primitive stage of perception in which discriminations afterwards needful have not yet been made. A piece of experience of a determinate sort is there, but there at first as a 'pure' fact. Motion originally simply *is;* only later is it confined to this thing or to that. Something like this is true of every experience, however complex, at the moment of its actual presence. Let the reader arrest himself in the act of reading this article now. *Now* this is a pure experience, a phenomenon, or datum, a mere *that* or content of fact. '*Reading*' *simply is, is there;* and whether there for some one's consciousness, or there for physical nature, is a question not yet put. At the moment, it is there for

[1] Page 102.

neither; later we shall probably judge it to have been there for both.

With the affectional experiences which we are considering, the relatively 'pure' condition lasts. In practical life no urgent need has yet arisen for deciding whether to treat them as rigorously mental or as rigorously physical facts. So they remain equivocal; and, as the world goes, their equivocality is one of their great conveniences.

The shifting place of 'secondary qualities' in the history of philosophy [1] is another excellent proof of the fact that 'inner' and 'outer' are not coefficients with which experiences come to us aboriginally stamped, but are rather results of a later classification performed by us for particular needs. The common-sense stage of thought is a perfectly definite practical halting-place, the place where we ourselves can proceed to act unhesitatingly. On this stage of thought things act on each other as well as on us by means of their secondary quali-

[1] [Cf. Janet and Séailles: *History of the Problems of Philosophy,* trans. by Monahan, part I, ch. III.]

ties. Sound, as such, goes through the air and can be intercepted. The heat of the fire passes over, as such, into the water which it sets a-boiling. It is the very light of the arc-lamp which displaces the darkness of the midnight street, etc. By engendering and trans-locating just these qualities, actively efficacious as they seem to be, we ourselves succeed in altering nature so as to suit us; and until more purely intellectual, as distinguished from practical, needs had arisen, no one ever thought of calling these qualities subjective. When, however, Galileo, Descartes, and others found it best for philosophic purposes to class sound, heat, and light along with pain and pleasure as purely mental phenomena, they could do so with impunity.[1]

Even the primary qualities are undergoing the same fate. Hardness and softness are effects on us of atomic interactions, and the atoms themselves are neither hard nor soft, nor solid nor liquid. Size and shape are deemed

---

[1] [Cf. Descartes: *Meditation* II; *Principles of Philosophy*, part I, XLVIII.]

subjective by Kantians; time itself is subjective according to many philosophers;[1] and even the activity and causal efficacy which lingered in physics long after secondary qualities were banished are now treated as illusory projections outwards of phenomena of our own consciousness. There are no activities or effects in nature, for the most intellectual contemporary school of physical speculation. Nature exhibits only *changes*, which habitually coincide with one another so that their habits are describable in simple 'laws.'[2]

There is no original spirituality or materiality of being, intuitively discerned, then; but only a translocation of experiences from one world to another; a grouping of them with one set or another of associates for definitely practical or intellectual ends.

I will say nothing here of the persistent ambiguity of *relations*. They are undeniable parts of pure experience; yet, while common sense and what I call radical empiricism stand

[1] [Cf. A. E. Taylor: *Elements of Metaphysics*, bk. III, ch. IV.]
[2] [Cf. K. Pearson: *Grammar of Science*, ch. III.]

for their being objective, both rationalism and the usual empiricism claim that they are exclusively the 'work of the mind' — the finite mind or the absolute mind, as the case may be.

Turn now to those affective phenomena which more directly concern us.

We soon learn to separate the ways in which things appeal to our interests and emotions from the ways in which they act upon one another. It does not *work* to assume that physical objects are going to act outwardly by their sympathetic or antipathetic qualities. The beauty of a thing or its value is no force that can be plotted in a polygon of compositions, nor does its 'use' or 'significance' affect in the minutest degree its vicissitudes or destiny at the hands of physical nature. Chemical 'affinities' are a purely verbal metaphor; and, as I just said, even such things as forces, tensions, and activities can at a pinch be regarded as anthropomorphic projections. So far, then, as the physical world means the collection of contents that determine in each other certain regular changes, the whole collection of our appreciative attributes has to be treated as falling outside of it. If we mean by physical nature whatever lies beyond the surface of our bodies, these attributes are inert throughout the whole extent of physical nature.

Why then do men leave them as ambiguous as they do, and not class them decisively as purely spiritual?

The reason would seem to be that, although they are inert as regards the rest of physical nature, they are not inert as regards that part of physical nature which our own skin covers. It is those very appreciative attributes of things, their dangerousness, beauty, rarity, utility, etc., that primarily appeal to our attention. In our commerce with nature these attributes are what give *emphasis* to objects; and for an object to be emphatic, whatever spiritual fact it may mean, means also that it produces immediate bodily effects upon us, alterations of tone and tension, of heart-beat and breathing, of vascular and visceral action. The 'interesting' aspects of things are thus not wholly inert physically, though they be active only in these small corners of physical nature which our bodies occupy. That, however, is enough to save them from being classed as absolutely non-objective.

The attempt, if any one should make it, to sort experiences into two absolutely discrete groups, with nothing but inertness in one of them and nothing but activities in the other, would thus receive one check. It would receive another as soon as we examined the more distinctively mental group; for though in that group it be true that things do not act on one another by their physical properties, do not dent each other or set fire to each other, they yet act on each other in the most energetic way by those very characters which are so inert extracorporeally. It is by the interest and importance that experiences have for us, by the emotions they excite, and the purposes they subserve, by their affective values, in short, that their consecution in our several conscious streams, as 'thoughts' of ours, is mainly ruled. Desire introduces them; interest holds them; fitness fixes their order and connection. I need only refer for this aspect of our mental life, to Wundt's article 'Ueber psychische Causalität,' which begins Volume X. of his *Philosophische Studien*.[1]

It thus appears that the ambiguous or amphibious *status* which we find our epithets of value occupying is the most natural thing in the world. It would, however, be an unnatural status if the popular opinion which I cited at the outset were correct. If 'physical' and 'mental' meant two different kinds of intrinsic nature, immediately, intuitively, and infallibly discernible, and each fixed forever in whatever bit of experience it qualified, one does not see how there could ever have arisen any room for doubt or ambiguity. But if, on the contrary, these words are words of sorting, ambiguity is natural. For then, as soon as the relations of a thing are sufficiently various it can be sorted variously.

[1] It is enough for my present purpose if the appreciative characters but *seem* to act thus. Believers in an activity *an sich*, other than our mental experiences of activity, will find some farther reflections on the subject in my address on 'The Experience of Activity.' [The next essay. Cf. especially, p. 169. ED.]

Take a mass of carrion, for example, and the 'disgustingness' which for us is part of the experience. The sun caresses it, and the zephyr wooes it as if it were a bed of roses. So the disgustingness fails to *operate* within the realm of suns and breezes, — it does not function as a physical quality. But the carrion 'turns our stomach' by what seems a direct operation — it *does* function physically, therefore, in that limited part of physics. We can treat it as physical or as non-physical according as we take it in the narrower or in the wider context, and conversely, of course, we must treat it as non-mental or as mental.

Our body itself is the palmary instance of the ambiguous. Sometimes I treat my body purely as a part of outer nature. Sometimes, again, I think of it as 'mine,' I sort it with the 'me,' and then certain local changes and determinations in it pass for spiritual happenings. Its breathing is my 'thinking,' its sensorial adjustments are my 'attention,' its kinesthetic alterations are my 'efforts,' its visceral perturbations are my 'emotions.'

153

The obstinate controversies that have arisen over such statements as these (which sound so paradoxical, and which can yet be made so seriously) prove how hard it is to decide by bare introspection what it is in experiences that shall make them either spiritual or material. It surely can be nothing intrinsic in the individual experience. It is their way of behaving towards each other, their system of relations, their function; and all these things vary with the context in which we find it opportune to consider them.

I think I may conclude, then (and I hope that my readers are now ready to conclude with me), that the pretended spirituality of our emotions and of our attributes of value, so far from proving an objection to the philosophy of pure experience, does, when rightly discussed and accounted for, serve as one of its best corroborations.

VI

THE EXPERIENCE OF ACTIVITY[1]

Brethren of the Psychological Association:

In casting about me for a subject for your President this year to talk about it has seemed to me that our experiences of activity would form a good one; not only because the topic is so naturally interesting, and because it has lately led to a good deal of rather inconclusive discussion, but because I myself am growing more and more interested in a certain systematic way of handling questions, and want to get others interested also, and this question strikes me as one in which, although I am painfully aware of my inability to communicate new discoveries or to reach definitive conclusions, I yet can show, in a rather definite manner, how the method works.

[1] President's Address before the American Psychological Association, Philadelphia Meeting, December, 1904. [Reprinted from *The Psychological Review*, vol. xii, No. 1, Jan., 1905. Also reprinted, with some omissions, as Appendix B, *A Pluralistic Universe*, pp. 370–394. Pp. 166–167 have also been reprinted in *Some Problems of Philosophy*, p. 212. The present essay is referred to in *ibid.*, p. 219, note. The author's corrections have been adopted for the present text. Ed.]

The way of handling things I speak of, is, as you already will have suspected, that known sometimes as the pragmatic method, sometimes as humanism, sometimes as Deweyism, and in France, by some of the disciples of Bergson, as the Philosophie nouvelle. Professor Woodbridge's *Journal of Philosophy* [1] seems unintentionally to have become a sort of meeting place for those who follow these tendencies in America. There is only a dim identity among them; and the most that can be said at present is that some sort of gestation seems to be in the atmosphere, and that almost any day a man with a genius for finding the right word for things may hit upon some unifying and conciliating formula that will make so much vaguely similar aspiration crystallize into more definite form.

I myself have given the name of 'radical empiricism' to that version of the tendency in question which I prefer; and I propose, if you will now let me, to illustrate what I mean by radical empiricism, by applying it to activity

---

[1] [*The Journal of Philosophy, Psychology and Scientific Methods.*]

as an example, hoping at the same time incidentally to leave the general problem of activity in a slightly — I fear very slightly — more manageable shape than before.

Mr. Bradley calls the question of activity a scandal to philosophy, and if one turns to the current literature of the subject — his own writings included — one easily gathers what he means. The opponents cannot even understand one another. Mr. Bradley says to Mr. Ward: "I do not care what your oracle is, and your preposterous psychology may here be gospel if you please; . . . but if the revelation does contain a meaning, I will commit myself to this: either the oracle is so confused that its signification is not discoverable, or, upon the other hand, if it can be pinned down to any definite statement, then that statement will be false." [1] Mr. Ward in turn says of Mr. Bradley: "I cannot even imagine the state of mind to which his description applies. . . . [It] reads like an unintentional travesty

[1] *Appearance and Reality*, second edition, pp. 116–117. — Obviously written *at* Ward, though Ward's name is not mentioned.

of Herbartian psychology by one who has tried to improve upon it without being at the pains to master it."[1] Münsterberg excludes a view opposed to his own by saying that with any one who holds it a *Verständigung* with him is "*grundsätzlich ausgeschlossen*"; and Royce, in a review of Stout,[2] hauls him over the coals at great length for defending 'efficacy' in a way which I, for one, never gathered from reading him, and which I have heard Stout himself say was quite foreign to the intention of his text.

In these discussions distinct questions are habitually jumbled and different points of view are talked of *durcheinander*.

(1) There is a psychological question: "Have we perceptions of activity? and if so, what are they like, and when and where do we have them?"

(2) There is a metaphysical question: "Is there a *fact* of activity? and if so, what idea must we frame of it? What is it like? and what

---

[1] [*Mind*, vol. XII, 1887, pp. 573–574.]
[2] *Mind*, N. S., vol. VI, [1897], p. 379.

does it do, if it does anything?" And finally there is a logical question:

(3) "Whence do we *know* activity? By our own feelings of it solely? or by some other source of information?" Throughout page after page of the literature one knows not which of these questions is before one; and mere description of the surface-show of experience is proferred as if it implicitly answered every one of them. No one of the disputants, moreover, tries to show what pragmatic consequences his own view would carry, or what assignable particular differences in any one's experience it would make if his adversary's were triumphant.

It seems to me that if radical empiricism be good for anything, it ought, with its pragmatic method and its principle of pure experience, to be able to avoid such tangles, or at least to simplify them somewhat. The pragmatic method starts from the postulate that there is no difference of truth that does n't make a difference of fact somewhere; and it seeks to determine the meaning of all differences of opinion by making the discussion hinge as soon as possible upon some practical or particular issue. The principle of pure experience is also a methodical postulate. Nothing shall be admitted as fact, it says, except what can be experienced at some definite time by some experient; and for every feature of fact ever so experienced, a definite place must be found somewhere in the final system of reality. In other words: Everything real must be experienceable somewhere, and every kind of thing experienced must somewhere be real.

Armed with these rules of method let us see what face the problems of activity present to us.

By the principle of pure experience, either the word 'activity' must have no meaning at all, or else the original type and model of what it means must lie in some concrete kind of experience that can be definitely pointed out. Whatever ulterior judgments we may eventually come to make regarding activity, *that sort* of thing will be what the judgments are about. The first step to take, then, is to ask where in the stream of experience we seem to find what we speak of as activity. What we are to think of the activity thus found will be a later question.

Now it is obvious that we are tempted to affirm activity wherever we find anything *going on*. Taken in the broadest sense, any apprehension of something *doing*, is an experience of activity. Were our world describable only by the words 'nothing happening,' 'nothing changing,' 'nothing doing,' we should unquestionably call it an 'inactive' world. Bare activity then, as we may call it, means the bare fact of event or change. 'Change taking place' is a unique content of experience, one of those 'conjunctive' objects which radical empiricism seeks so earnestly to rehabilitate and preserve. The sense of activity is thus in the broadest and vaguest way synonymous with the sense of 'life.' We should feel our own subjective life at least, even in noticing and proclaiming an otherwise inactive world. Our own reaction on its monotony would be the one thing experienced there in the form of something coming to pass.

This seems to be what certain writers have in mind when they insist that for an experient to be at all is to be active. It seems to justify, or at any rate to explain, Mr. Ward's expression that we *are* only as we are active,[1] for we *are* only as experients; and it rules out Mr. Bradley's contention that "there is no original experience of anything like activity." [2] What we ought to say about activities thus elementary, whose they are, what they effect, or whether indeed they effect anything at all — these are later questions, to be answered only when the field of experience is enlarged.

Bare activity would thus be predicable, though there were no definite direction, no actor, and no aim. Mere restless zigzag movement, or a wild *Ideenflucht*, or *Rhapsodie der Wahrnehmungen*, as Kant would say,[3] would

---

[1] *Naturalism and Agnosticism*, vol. II, p. 245. One thinks naturally of the peripatetic *actus primus* and *actus secundus* here. ["Actus autem est *duplex: primus* et *secundus*. Actus quidem primus est forma, et integritas sei. Actus autem secundus est operatio." Thomas Aquinas : *Summa Theologica*, edition of Leo XIII, (1894), vol. I, p. 391. Cf. also Blanc: *Dictionnaire de Philosophie*, under 'acte.' ED.]

[2] [*Appearance and Reality*, second edition, p. 116.]

[3] [*Kritik der reinen Vernunft, Werke*, (1905), vol. IV, p. 110 (trans. by Max Müller, second edition, p. 128).]

constitute an active as distinguished from an inactive world.

But in this actual world of ours, as it is given, a part at least of the activity comes with definite direction; it comes with desire and sense of goal; it comes complicated with resistances which it overcomes or succumbs to, and with the efforts which the feeling of resistance so often provokes; and it is in complex experiences like these that the notions of distinct agents, and of passivity as opposed to activity arise. Here also the notion of causal efficacy comes to birth. Perhaps the most elaborate work ever done in descriptive psychology has been the analysis by various recent writers of the more complex activity-situations.[1] In their descriptions, exquisitely

---

[1] I refer to such descriptive work as Ladd's (*Psychology, Descriptive and Explanatory*, part I, chap. V, part II, chap. XI, part III, chaps. XXV and XXVI); as Sully's (*The Human Mind*, part V); as Stout's (*Analytic Psychology*, book I, chap. VI, and book II, chaps. I, II, and III); as Bradley's (in his long series of analytic articles on Psychology in *Mind*); as Titchener's (*Outline of Psychology*, part I, chap. VI); as Shand's (*Mind*, N. S., III, 449; IV, 450; VI, 289); as Ward's (*Mind*, XII, 67; 564); as Loveday's (*Mind*, N. S., X, 455); as Lipps's (Vom Fühlen, Wollen und Denken, 1902, chaps. II, IV, VI); and as Bergson's (*Revue Philosophique*, LIII, 1) — to mention only a few writings which I immediately recall.

subtle some of them,[1] the activity appears as the *gestaltqualität* or the *fundirte inhalt* (or as whatever else you may please to call the conjunctive form) which the content falls into when we experience it in the ways which the describers set forth. Those factors in those relations are what we mean by activity-situations; and to the possible enumeration and accumulation of their circumstances and ingredients there would seem to be no natural bound. Every hour of human life could contribute to the picture gallery; and this is the only fault that one can find with such descriptive industry — where is it going to stop? Ought we to listen forever to verbal pictures of what we have already in concrete form in our own breasts? [2] They never take us off the superficial plane. We knew the facts already — less spread out and separated, to be sure — but

[1] Their existence forms a curious commentary on Prof. Münsterberg's dogma that will-attitudes are not describable. He himself has contributed in a superior way to their description, both in his *Willenshandlung*, and in his *Grundzüge [der Psychologie]*, part II, chap. IX, § 7.

[2] I ought myself to cry *peccavi*, having been a voluminous sinner in my own chapter on the will. [*Principles of Psychology*, vol. II, chap. XXVI.]

we knew them still. We always felt our own activity, for example, as 'the expansion of an idea with which our Self is identified, against an obstacle'; [1] and the following out of such a definition through a multitude of cases elaborates the obvious so as to be little more than an exercise in synonymic speech.

All the descriptions have to trace familiar outlines, and to use familiar terms. The activity is, for example, attributed either to a physical or to a mental agent, and is either aimless or directed. If directed it shows tendency. The tendency may or may not be resisted. If not, we call the activity immanent, as when a body moves in empty space by its momentum, or our thoughts wander at their own sweet will. If resistance is met, *its* agent complicates the situation. If now, in spite of resistance, the original tendency continues, effort makes its appearance, and along with effort, strain or squeeze. Will, in the narrower sense of the word, then comes upon the scene, when-

---

[1] [Cf. F. H. Bradley, *Appearance and Reality*, second edition, pp. 96–97.]

ever, along with the tendency, the strain and squeeze are sustained. But the resistance may be great enough to check the tendency, or even to reverse its path. In that case, we (if 'we' were the original agents or subjects of the tendency) are overpowered. The phenomenon turns into one of tension simply, or of necessity succumbed-to, according as the opposing power is only equal, or is superior to ourselves.

Whosoever describes an experience in such terms as these describes an experience *of* activity. If the word have any meaning, it must denote what there is found. *There* is complete activity in its original and first intention. What it is 'known-as' is what there appears. The experiencer of such a situation possesses all that the idea contains. He feels the tendency, the obstacle, the will, the strain, the triumph, or the passive giving up, just as he feels the time, the space, the swiftness or intensity, the movement, the weight and color, the pain and pleasure, the complexity, or whatever remaining characters the situation may involve. He goes through all that ever can be imagined where

166

activity is supposed. If we suppose activities to go on outside of our experience, it is in forms like these that we must suppose them, or else give them some other name; for the word 'activity' has no imaginable content whatever save these experiences of process, obstruction, striving, strain, or release, ultimate *qualia* as they are of the life given us to be known.

Were this the end of the matter, one might think that whenever we had successfully lived through an activity-situation we should have to be permitted, without provoking contradiction, to say that we had been really active, that we had met real resistance and had really prevailed. Lotze somewhere says that to be an entity all that is necessary is to *gelten* as an entity, to operate, or be felt, experienced, recognized, or in any way realized, as such.[1] In our activity-experiences the activity assuredly fulfils Lotze's demand. It makes itself *gelten*. It is witnessed at its work. No matter what activities there may really be in this extraordinary universe of ours, it is impossible

---

[1] [Cf. above, p. 59, note.]

for us to conceive of any one of them being either lived through or authentically known otherwise than in this dramatic shape of something sustaining a felt purpose against felt obstacles and overcoming or being overcome. What 'sustaining' means here is clear to anyone who has lived through the experience, but to no one else; just as 'loud,' 'red,' 'sweet,' mean something only to beings with ears, eyes, and tongues. The *percipi* in these originals of experience is the *esse*; the curtain is the picture. If there is anything hiding in the background, it ought not to be called activity, but should get itself another name.

This seems so obviously true that one might well experience astonishment at finding so many of the ablest writers on the subject flatly denying that the activity we live through in these situations is real. Merely to feel active is not to be active, in their sight. The agents that appear in the experience are not real agents, the resistances do not really resist, the effects that appear are not really effects at all.[1]

---

[1] *Verborum gratiâ:* "The feeling of activity is not able, *quâ* feeling,

THE EXPERIENCE OF ACTIVITY

It is evident from this that mere descriptive
analysis of any one of our activity-experiences
is not the whole story, that there is something

to tell us anything about activity" (Loveday: *Mind*, N. S., vol. **x**,
[1901], p. 463); "A sensation or feeling or sense *of* activity . . . is not,
looked at in another way, an experience *of* activity at all. It is a mere
sensation shut up within which you could by no reflection get the
idea of activity. . . . Whether this experience is or is not later on a
character essential to our perception and our idea of activity, it, as it
comes first, is not in itself an experience of activity at all. It, as it
comes first, is only so for extraneous reasons and only so for an outside
observer" (Bradley, *Appearance and Reality*, second edition, p. 605);
"In dem Tätigkeitsgefühle liegt an sich nicht der geringste Beweis
für das Vorhandensein einer psychischen Tätigkeit" (Münsterberg:
Grundzüge der Psychologie). I could multiply similar quotations and
would have introduced some of them into my text to make it more
concrete, save that the mingling of different points of view in most of
these author's discussions (not in Münsterberg's) make it impossible to
disentangle exactly what they mean. I am sure in any case, to be
accused of misrepresenting them totally, even in this note, by omission
of the context, so the less I name names and the more I stick to abstract characterization of a merely possible style of opinion, the safer
it will be. And apropos of misunderstandings, I may add to this note
a complaint on my own account. Professor Stout, in the excellent
chapter on 'Mental Activity,' in vol. I of his *Analytic Psychology*,
takes me to task for identifying spiritual activity with certain muscular feelings and gives quotations to bear him out. They are from
certain paragraphs on 'the Self,' in which my attempt was to show
what the central nucleus of the activities that we call 'ours' is.
[*Principles of Psychology*, vol. I, pp. 299–305.] I found it in certain
intracephalic movements which we habitually oppose, as 'subjective,' to the activities of the transcorporeal world. I sought to show
that there is no direct evidence that we feel the activity of an
inner spiritual agent as such (I should now say the activity of
'consciousness' as such, see [the first essay], 'Does Consciousness
Exist?'). There are, in fact, three distinguishable 'activities' in
the field of discussion: the elementary activity involved in the mere
that of experience, in the fact that *something* is going on, and the farther specification of this *something* into two *whats*, an activity felt **as**

still to tell *about* them that has led such able
writers to conceive of a *Simon-pure* activity,
of an activity *an sich*, that does, and does n't

'ours,' and an activity ascribed to objects. Stout, as I apprehend him,
identifies 'our' activity with that of the total experience-process, and
when I circumscribe it as a part thereof, accuses me of treating it as a
sort of external appendage to itself (Stout: *op. cit.*, vol. I, pp. 162–163),
as if I 'separated the activity from the process which is active.' But
all the processes in question are active, and their activity is inseparable
from their being. My book raised only the question of *which* activity
deserved the name of 'ours.' So far as we are 'persons,' and contrasted
and opposed to an 'environment,' movements in our body figure as
our activities; and I am unable to find any other activities that are
ours in this strictly personal sense. There is a wider sense in which
the whole 'choir of heaven and furniture of the earth,' and their
activities, are ours, for they are our 'objects.' But 'we' are here only
another name for the total process of experience, another name for all
that is, in fact; and I was dealing with the personal and individualized
self exclusively in the passages with which Professor Stout finds fault.

The individualized self, which I believe to be the only thing properly called self, is a part of the content of the world experienced. The
world experienced (otherwise called the 'field of consciousness') comes
at all times with our body as its centre, centre of vision, centre of action, centre of interest. Where the body is is 'here'; when the body
acts is 'now'; what the body touches is 'this'; all other things are
'there' and 'then' and 'that.' These words of emphasized position
imply a systematization of things with reference to a focus of action
and interest which lies in the body; and the systematization is now so
instinctive (was it ever not so?) that no developed or active experience
exists for us at all except in that ordered form. So far as 'thoughts'
and 'feelings' can be active, their activity terminates in the activity
of the body, and only through first arousing its activities can they
begin to change those of the rest of the world. [Cf. also *A Pluralistic
Universe*, p. 344, note 8. Ed.] The body is the storm centre, the origin
of co-ordinates, the constant place of stress in all that experience-
train. Everything circles round it, and is felt from its point of view.
The word 'I,' then, is primarily a noun of position, just like 'this' and
'here.' Activities attached to 'this' position have prerogative emphasis, and, if activities have feelings, must be felt in a peculiar way. The

merely appear to us to do, and compared with whose real doing all this phenomenal activity is but a specious sham.

The metaphysical question opens here; and I think that the state of mind of one possessed by it is often something like this: "It is all very well," we may imagine him saying, "to talk about certain experience-series taking on the form of feelings of activity, just as they might take on musical or geometric forms. Suppose that they do so; suppose we feel a will to stand a strain. Does our feeling do more than *record* the fact that the strain is sustained? The *real* activity, meanwhile, is the *doing* of the fact; and what is the doing made of before the record is made. What in the will *enables* it to act thus? And these trains of experience themselves, in which activities appear, what makes them *go* at all? Does the activity in one bit of experience bring the next bit into being? As an em-

word. 'my' designates the kind of emphasis. I see no inconsistency whatever in defending, on the one hand, 'my' activities as unique and opposed to those of outer nature, and, on the other hand, in affirming, after introspection, that they consist in movements in the head. The 'my' of them is the emphasis, the feeling of perspective-interest in which they are dyed.

piricist you cannot say so, for you have just declared activity to be only a kind of synthetic object, or conjunctive relation experienced between bits of experience already made. But what made them at all? What propels experience *überhaupt* into being? *There* is the activity that *operates;* the activity *felt* is only its superficial sign."

To the metaphysical question, popped upon us in this way, I must pay serious attention ere I end my remarks; but, before doing so, let me show that without leaving the immediate reticulations of experience, or asking what makes activity itself act, we still find the distinction between less real and more real activities forced upon us, and are driven to much soul-searching on the purely phenomenal plane.

We must not forget, namely, in talking of the ultimate character of our activity-experiences, that each of them is but a portion of a wider world, one link in the vast chain of processes of experience out of which history is made. Each partial process, to him who lives through it, defines itself by its origin and its goal; but to an observer with a wider mind-span who should live outside of it, that goal would appear but as a provisional halting-place, and the subjectively felt activity would be seen to continue into objective activities that led far beyond. We thus acquire a habit, in discussing activity-experiences, of defining them by their relation to something more. If an experience be one of narrow span, it will be mistaken as to what activity it is and whose. You think that *you* are acting while you are only obeying someone's push. You think you are doing *this*, but you are doing something of which you do not dream. For instance, you think you are but drinking this glass; but you are really creating the liver-cirrhosis that will end your days. You think you are just driving this bargain, but, as Stevenson says somewhere, you are laying down a link in the policy of mankind.

Generally speaking, the onlooker, with his wider field of vision, regards the *ultimate outcome* of an activity as what it is more really doing; and *the most previous agent* ascertain-

able, being the first source of action, he regards
as the most real agent in the field. The others
but transmit that agent's impulse; on him
we put responsibility; we name him when one
asks us 'Who's to blame?'

But the most previous agents ascertainable,
instead of being of longer span, are often of
much shorter span than the activity in view.
Brain-cells are our best example. My brain-
cells are believed to excite each other from
next to next (by contiguous transmission of
katabolic alteration, let us say) and to have
been doing so long before this present stretch
of lecturing-activity on my part began. If any
one cell-group stops its activity, the lecturing
will cease or show disorder of form. *Cessante
causa, cessat et effectus* — does not this look as
if the short-span brain activities were the more
real activities, and the lecturing activities
on my part only their effects? Moreover, as
Hume so clearly pointed out,[1] in my mental
activity-situation the words physically to be

---

[1] [*Enquiry Concerning Human Understanding*, sect. VII, part I,
Selby-Bigge's edition, pp. 65 ff.]

uttered are represented as the activity's immediate goal. These words, however, cannot be uttered without intermediate physical processes in the bulb and vagi nerves, which processes nevertheless fail to figure in the mental activity-series at all. That series, therefore, since it leaves out vitally real steps of action, cannot represent the real activities. It is something purely subjective; the *facts* of activity are elsewhere. They are something far more interstitial, so to speak, than what my feelings record.

The *real* facts of activity that have in point of fact been systematically pleaded for by philosophers have, so far as my information goes, been of three principal types.

The first type takes a consciousness of wider time-span than ours to be the vehicle of the more real activity. Its will is the agent, and its purpose is the action done.

The second type assumes that 'ideas' struggling with one another are the agents, and that the prevalence of one set of them is the action.

The third type believes that nerve-cells are the agents, and that resultant motor discharges are the acts achieved.

Now if we must de-realize our immediately felt activity-situations for the benefit of either of these types of substitute, we ought to know what the substitution practically involves. *What practical difference ought it to make if*, instead of saying naïvely that 'I' am active now in delivering this address, I say that *a wider thinker is active*, or that *certain ideas are active*, or that *certain nerve-cells are active*, in producing the result?

This would be the pragmatic meaning of the three hypotheses. Let us take them in succession in seeking a reply.

If we assume a wider thinker, it is evident that his purposes envelope mine. I am really lecturing *for* him; and although I cannot surely know to what end, yet if I take him religiously, I can trust it to be a good end, and willingly connive. I can be happy in thinking that my activity transmits his impulse, and that his ends prolong my own. So long as I take him religiously, in short, he does not de-realize my activities. He tends rather to corroborate the reality of them, so long as I believe both them and him to be good.

When now we turn to ideas, the case is different, inasmuch as ideas are supposed by the association psychology to influence each other only from next to next. The 'span' of an idea or pair of ideas, is assumed to be much smaller instead of being larger than that of my total conscious field. The same results may get worked out in both cases, for this address is being given anyhow. But the ideas supposed to 'really' work it out had no prevision of the whole of it; and if I was lecturing for an absolute thinker in the former case, so, by similar reasoning, are my ideas now lecturing for me, that is, accomplishing unwittingly a result which I approve and adopt. But, when this passing lecture is over, there is nothing in the bare notion that ideas have been its agents that would seem to guarantee that my present purposes in lecturing will be prolonged. *I* may have ulterior developments in view; but there is no certainty that my ideas as such will wish to, or be able to, work them out.

The like is true if nerve-cells be the agents. The activity of a nerve-cell must be conceived of as a tendency of exceedingly short reach, an 'impulse' barely spanning the way to the next cell — for surely that amount of actual 'process' must be 'experienced' by the cells if what happens between them is to deserve the name of activity at all. But here again the gross resultant, as *I* perceive it, is indifferent to the agents, and neither wished or willed or foreseen. Their being agents now congruous with my will gives me no guarantee that like results will recur again from their activity. In point of fact, all sorts of other results do occur. My mistakes, impotencies, perversions, mental obstructions, and frustrations generally, are also results of the activity of cells. Although these are letting me lecture now, on other occasions they make me do things that I would willingly not do.

The question *Whose is the real activity?* is thus tantamount to the question *What will be the actual results?* Its interest is dramatic; how will things work out? If the agents are of one sort, one way; if of another sort, they may work out very differently. The pragmatic meaning of the various alternatives, in short, is great. It makes no merely verbal difference which opinion we take up.

You see it is the old dispute come back! Materialism and teleology; elementary short-span actions summing themselves 'blindly,' or far foreseen ideals coming with effort into act.

Naïvely we believe, and humanly and dramatically we like to believe, that activities both of wider and of narrower span are at work in life together, that both are real, and that the long-span tendencies yoke the others in their service, encouraging them in the right direction, and damping them when they tend in other ways. But how to represent clearly the *modus operandi* of such steering of small tendencies by large ones is a problem which metaphysical thinkers will have to ruminate upon for many years to come. Even if such control should eventually grow clearly picturable, the question how far it is successfully exerted in this actual world can be answered only by investigating the details of fact. No philosophic knowledge of the general nature and constitution of tendencies, or of the relation of larger to smaller ones, can help us to predict which of all the various competing tendencies that interest us in this universe are likeliest to prevail. We know as an empirical fact that far-seeing tendencies often carry out their purpose, but we know also that they are often defeated by the failure of some comtemptibly small process on which success depends. A little thrombus in a statesman's meningeal artery will throw an empire out of gear. I can therefore not even hint at any solution of the pragmatic issue. I have only wished to show you that that issue is what gives the real interest to all inquiries into what kinds of activity may be real. Are the forces that really act in the world more foreseeing or more blind? As between 'our' activities as 'we' experience them, and those of our ideas, or of our brain-cells, the issue is well-defined.

THE EXPERIENCE OF ACTIVITY

I said a while back [1] that I should return to the 'metaphysical' question before ending; so, with a few words about that, I will now close my remarks.

In whatever form we hear this question propounded, I think that it always arises from two things, a belief that *causality* must be exerted in activity, and a wonder as to how causality is made. If we take an activity-situation at its face-value, it seems as if we caught *in flagrante delicto* the very power that makes facts come and be. I now am eagerly striving, for example, to get this truth which I seem half to perceive, into words which shall make it show more clearly. If the words come, it will seem as if the striving itself had drawn or pulled them into actuality out from the state of merely possible being in which they were. How is this feat performed? How does the pulling *pull?* How do I get my hold on words not yet existent, and when they come by what means have I *made* them come? Really it is the problem of creation; for in the end the question is: How do

[1] Page 172.

I make them *be?* Real activities are those that really make things be, without which the things are not, and with which they are there. Activity, so far as we merely feel it, on the other hand, is only an impression of ours, it may be maintained; and an impression is, for all this way of thinking, only a shadow of another fact.

Arrived at this point, I can do little more than indicate the principles on which, as it seems to me, a radically empirical philosophy is obliged to rely in handling such a dispute.

If there *be* real creative activities in being, radical empiricism must say, somewhere they must be immediately lived. Somewhere the *that* of efficacious causing and the *what* of it must be experienced in one, just as the what and the that of 'cold' are experienced in one whenever a man has the sensation of cold here and now. It boots not to say that our sensations are fallible. They are indeed; but to see the thermometer contradict us when we say 'it is cold' does not abolish cold as a specific nature from the universe. Cold is in the arctic

circle if not here. Even so, to feel that our
train is moving when the train beside our window moves, to see the moon through a telescope come twice as near, or to see two pictures as one solid when we look through a
stereoscope at them, leaves motion, nearness, and solidity still in being — if not here,
yet each in its proper seat elsewhere. And
wherever the seat of real causality *is*, as ultimately known 'for true' (in nerve-processes,
if you will, that cause our feelings of activity as well as the movements which these
seem to prompt), a philosophy of pure experience can consider the real causation as no other
nature of thing than that which even in our
most erroneous experiences appears to be at
work. Exactly what appears there is what we
mean by working, though we may later come
to learn that working was not exactly *there*.
Sustaining, persevering, striving, paying with
effort as we go, hanging on, and finally achiev-
ing our intention — this *is* action, this *is* effectuation in the only shape in which, by a pure
experience-philosophy, the whereabouts of it

anywhere can be discussed. Here is creation in its first intention, here is causality at work.[1] To treat this offhand as the bare illusory surface of a world whose real causality is an unimaginable ontological principle hidden in the cubic deeps, is, for the more empirical way of thinking, only animism in another shape. You explain your given fact by your 'principle,' but the principle itself, when you look clearly at it, turns out to be nothing but a previous little spiritual copy of the fact. Away from that one and only kind of fact your mind, considering causality, can never get.[2]

[1] Let me not be told that this contradicts [the first essay], 'Does Consciousness Exist?' (see especially page 32), in which it was said that while 'thoughts' and 'things' have the same natures, the natures work 'energetically' on each other in the things (fire burns, water wets, etc.) but not in the thoughts. Mental activity-trains are composed of thoughts, yet their members do work on each other, they check, sustain, and introduce. They do so when the activity is merely associational as well as when effort is there. But, and this is my reply, they do so by other parts of their nature than those that energize physically. One thought in every developed activity-series is a desire or thought of purpose, and all the other thoughts acquire a feeling tone from their relation of harmony or oppugnancy to this. The interplay of these secondary tones (among which 'interest,' 'difficulty,' and 'effort' figure) runs the drama in the mental series. In what we term the physical drama these qualities play absolutely no part. The subject needs careful working out; but I can see no inconsistency.

[2] I have found myself more than once accused in print of being the assertor of a metaphysical principle of activity. Since literary misunderstandings retard the settlement of problems, I should like to say

THE EXPERIENCE OF ACTIVITY

I conclude, then, that real effectual causation as an ultimate nature, as a 'category,' if you like, of reality, is *just what we feel it to be*, just that kind of conjunction which our own activity-series reveal. We have the whole butt and being of it in our hands; and the healthy thing

that such an interpretation of the pages I have published on Effort and on Will is absolutely foreign to what I meant to express. [*Principles of Psychology*, vol. II, ch. XXVI.] I owe all my doctrines on this subject to Renouvier; and Renouvier, as I understand him, is (or at any rate then was) an out and out phenomenist, a denier of 'forces' in the most strenuous sense. [Cf. Ch. Renouvier: *Esquisse d'une Classification Systématique des Doctrines Philosophiques* (1885), vol. II, pp. 390–392; *Essais de Critique Générale* (1859), vol. II, §§ ix, xiii. For an acknowledgment of the author's general indebtedness to Renouvier, cf. *Some Problems of Philosophy*, p. 165, note. ED.] Single clauses in my writing, or sentences read out of their connection, may possibly have been compatible with a transphenomenal principle of energy; but I defy anyone to show a single sentence which, taken with its context, should be naturally held to advocate that view. The misinterpretation probably arose at first from my defending (after Renouvier) the indeterminism of our efforts. 'Free will' was supposed by my critics to involve a supernatural agent. As a matter of plain history the only 'free will' I have ever thought of defending is the character of novelty in fresh activity-situations. If an activity-process is the form of a whole 'field of consciousness,' and if each field of consciousness is not only in its totality unique (as is now commonly admitted) but has its elements unique (since in that situation they are all dyed in the total) then novelty is perpetually entering the world and what happens there is not pure *repetition*, as the dogma of the literal uniformity of nature requires. Activity-situations come, in short, each with an original touch. A 'principle' of free will if there were one, would doubtless manifest itself in such phenomena, but I never saw, nor do I now see, what the principle could do except rehearse the phenomenon beforehand, or why it ever should be invoked.

for philosophy is to leave off grubbing underground for what effects effectuation, or what makes action act, and to try to solve the concrete questions of where effectuation in this world is located, of which things are the true causal agents there, and of what the more remote effects consist.

From this point of view the greater sublimity traditionally attributed to the metaphysical inquiry, the grubbing inquiry, entirely disappears. If we could know what causation really and transcendentally is in itself, the only *use* of the knowledge would be to help us to recognize an actual cause when we had one, and so to track the future course of operations more intelligently out. The mere abstract inquiry into causation's hidden nature is not more sublime than any other inquiry equally abstract. Causation inhabits no more sublime level than anything else. It lives, apparently, in the dirt of the world as well as in the absolute, or in man's unconquerable mind. The worth and interest of the world consists not in its elements, be these elements things, or be they the conjunctions of things; it exists rather in the dramatic outcome in the whole process, and in the meaning of the succession stages which the elements work out.

My colleague and master, Josiah Royce, in a page of his review of Stout's *Analytic Psychology* [1] has some fine words on this point with which I cordially agree. I cannot agree with his separating the notion of efficacy from that of activity altogether (this I understand to be one contention of his) for activities are efficacious whenever they are real activities at all. But the inner nature both of efficacy and of activity are superficial problems, I understand Royce to say; and the only point for us in solving them would be their possible use in helping us to solve the far deeper problem of the course and meaning of the world of life. Life, says our colleague, is full of significance, of meaning, of success and of defeat, of hoping and of striving, of longing, of desire, and of inner value. It is a total presence that embodies worth. To live our own lives better in

[1] *Mind*, N. S., vol. VI, 1897; cf. pp. 392-393.

this presence is the true reason why we wish to know the elements of things; so even we psychologists must end on this pragmatic note.

The urgent problems of activity are thus more concrete. They are all problems of the true relation of longer-span to shorter-span activities. When, for example, a number of 'ideas' (to use the name traditional in psychology) grow confluent in a larger field of consciousness, do the smaller activities still co-exist with the wider activities then experienced by the conscious subject? And, if so, do the wide activities accompany the narrow ones inertly, or do they exert control? Or do they perhaps utterly supplant and replace them and short-circuit their effects? Again, when a mental activity-process and a brain-cell series of activities both terminate in the same muscular movement, does the mental process steer the neural processes or not? Or, on the other hand, does it independently short-circuit their effects? Such are the questions that we must begin with. But so far am I from suggesting any definitive answer to such questions, that I hardly yet can put them clearly. They lead, however, into that region of panpsychic and ontologic speculation of which Professors Bergson and Strong have lately enlarged the literature in so able and interesting a way.[1] The results of these authors seem in many respects dissimilar, and I understand them as yet but imperfectly; but I cannot help suspecting that the direction of their work is very promising, and that they have the hunter's instinct for the fruitful trails.

[1] [Cf. *A Pluralistic Universe*, Lect. VI (on Bergson) ; H. Bergson: *Creative Evolution*, trans. by A. Mitchell; C. A. Strong: *Why the Mind has a Body*, ch. XII. ED.]

VII

THE ESSENCE OF HUMANISM[1]

Humanism is a ferment that has 'come to stay.' [2] It is not a single hypothesis or theorem, and it dwells on no new facts. It is rather a slow shifting in the philosophic perspective, making things appear as from a new centre of interest or point of sight. Some writers are strongly conscious of the shifting, others half unconscious, even though their own vision may have undergone much change. The result is no small confusion in debate, the half-conscious humanists often taking part against the radical ones, as if they wished to count upon the other side. [3]

[1] [Reprinted from *The Journal of Philosophy, Psychology and Scientific Methods*, vol. II, No. 5, March 2, 1905. Also reprinted, with slight changes in *The Meaning of Truth*, pp. 121–135. The author's corrections have been adopted for the present text. ED.]

[2] [Written *apropos* of the appearance of three articles in *Mind*, N. S., vol. XIV, No. 53, January, 1905: " 'Absolute' and 'Relative' Truth," H. H. Joachim; "Professor James on 'Humanism and Truth,'" H. W. B. Joseph; "Applied Axioms," A. Sidgwick. Of these articles the second and third "continue the humanistic (or pragmatistic) controversy," the first "deeply connects with it." ED.]

[3] Professor Baldwin, for example. His address 'On Selective Thinking' (*Psychological Review*, [vol. V], 1898, reprinted in his volume, *Development and Evolution*) seems to me an unusually well-written

190

THE ESSENCE OF HUMANISM

If humanism really be the name for such a shifting of perspective, it is obvious that the whole scene of the philosophic stage will change in some degree if humanism prevails. The emphasis of things, their foreground and background distribution, their sizes and values, will not keep just the same.[1] If such pervasive consequences be involved in humanism, it is clear that no pains which philosophers may take, first in defining it, and then in furthering, checking, or steering its progress, will be thrown away.

It suffers badly at present from incomplete definition. Its most systematic advocates, Schiller and Dewey, have published fragment-

pragmatic manifesto. Nevertheless in 'The Limits of Pragmatism' (*ibid.*, [vol. xi], 1904), he (much less clearly) joins in the attack.

[1] The ethical changes, it seems to me, are beautifully made evident in Professor Dewey's series of articles, which will never get the attention they deserve till they are printed in a book. I mean: 'The Significance of Emotions,' *Psychological Review*, vol. ii, [1895], p. 13; 'The Reflex Arc Concept in Psychology,' *ibid.*, vol. iii, [1896], p. 357; 'Psychology and Social Practice,' *ibid.*, vol. vii, [1900], p. 105; 'Interpretation of Savage Mind,' *ibid.*, vol. ix, [1902], p. 217; 'Green's Theory of the Moral Motive,' *Philosophical Review*, vol. i, [1892], p. 593; 'Self-realization as the Moral Ideal,' *ibid.*, vol. ii, [1893], p. 652; 'The Psychology of Effort,' *ibid.*, vol. vi, [1897], p. 43; 'The Evolutionary Method as Applied to Morality,' *ibid.*, vol. xi, [1902], pp. 107, 353; 'Evolution and Ethics,' *Monist*, vol. viii, [1898], p. 321; to mention only a few.

ary programs only; and its bearing on many vital philosophic problems has not been traced except by adversaries who, scenting heresies in advance, have showered blows on doctrines — subjectivism and scepticism, for example — that no good humanist finds it necessary to entertain. By their still greater reticences, the anti-humanists have, in turn, perplexed the humanists. Much of the controversy has involved the word 'truth.' It is always good in debate to know your adversary's point of view authentically. But the critics of humanism never define exactly what the word 'truth' signifies when they use it themselves. The humanists have to guess at their view; and the result has doubtless been much beating of the air. Add to all this, great individual differences in both camps, and it becomes clear that nothing is so urgently needed, at the stage which things have reached at present, as a sharper definition by each side of its central point of view.

Whoever will contribute any touch of sharpness will help us to make sure of what's what and who is who. Anyone can contribute such a definition, and, without it, no one knows exactly where he stands. If I offer my own provisional definition of humanism [1] now and here, others may improve it, some adversary may be led to define his own creed more sharply by the contrast, and a certain quickening of the crystallization of general opinion may result.

I

The essential service of humanism, as I conceive the situation, is to have seen that *though one part of our experience may lean upon another part to make it what it is in any one of several aspects in which it may be considered, experience as a whole is self-containing and leans on nothing.*

Since this formula also expresses the main contention of transcendental idealism, it needs abundant explication to make it unambigu-

[1] [The author employs the term 'humanism' either as a synonym for 'radical empiricism' (cf. *e.g.*, above, p. 156); or as that general philosophy of life of which 'radical empiricism' is the theoretical ground (cf. below, p. 194). For other discussions of 'humanism,' cf. below, essay XI, and *The Meaning of Truth*, essay III. ED.]

ous. It seems, at first sight, to confine itself to denying theism and pantheism. But, in fact, it need not deny either; everything would depend on the exegesis; and if the formula ever became canonical, it would certainly develop both right-wing and left-wing interpreters. I myself read humanism theistically and pluralistically. If there be a God, he is no absolute all-experiencer, but simply the experiencer of widest actual conscious span. Read thus, humanism is for me a religion susceptible of reasoned defence, though I am well aware how many minds there are to whom it can appeal religiously only when it has been monistically translated. Ethically the pluralistic form of it takes for me a stronger hold on reality than any other philosophy I know of — it being essentially a *social* philosophy, a philosophy of '*co*,' in which conjunctions do the work. But my primary reason for advocating it is its matchless intellectual economy. It gets rid, not only of the standing 'problems' that monism engenders ('problem of evil,' 'problem of freedom,' and the like), but of other metaphysical mysteries and paradoxes as well.

It gets rid, for example, of the whole agnostic controversy, by refusing to entertain the hypothesis of trans-empirical reality at all. It gets rid of any need for an absolute of the Bradleyan type (avowedly sterile for intellectual purposes) by insisting that the conjunctive relations found within experience are faultlessly real. It gets rid of the need of an absolute of the Roycean type (similarly sterile) by its pragmatic treatment of the problem of knowledge [a treatment of which I have already given a version in two very inadequate articles].[1] As the views of knowledge, reality and truth imputed to humanism have been those so far most fiercely attacked, it is in regard to these ideas that a sharpening of focus seems most urgently required. I proceed therefore to bring the views which *I* impute to humanism in these respects into focus as briefly as I can.

[1] [Omitted from reprint in *Meaning of Truth*. The articles referred to are 'Does Consciousness Exist?' and 'A World of Pure Experience,' reprinted above.]

II

If the central humanistic thesis, printed above in italics, be accepted, it will follow that, if there be any such thing at all as knowing, the knower and the object known must both be portions of experience. One part of experience must, therefore, either

(1) Know another part of experience — in other words, parts must, as Professor Woodbridge says,[1] represent *one another* instead of representing realities outside of 'consciousness' — this case is that of conceptual knowledge; or else

(2) They must simply exist as so many ultimate *thats* or facts of being, in the first instance; and then, as a secondary complication, and without doubling up its entitative singleness, any one and the same *that* must figure alternately as a thing known and as a knowledge of the thing, by reason of two divergent kinds of context into which, in the general course of experience, it gets woven.[2]

---

[1] In *Science*, November 4, 1904, p. 599.

[2] This statement is probably excessively obscure to any one who

This second case is that of sense-perception. There is a stage of thought that goes beyond common sense, and of it I shall say more presently; but the common-sense stage is a perfectly definite halting-place of thought, primarily for purposes of action; and, so long as we remain on the common-sense stage of thought, object and subject *fuse* in the fact of 'presentation' or sense-perception — the pen and hand which I now *see* writing, for example, *are* the physical realities which those words designate. In this case there is no self-transcendency implied in the knowing. Humanism, here, is only a more comminuted *Identitätsphilosophie*.[1]

In case (1), on the contrary, the representative experience does transcend itself in knowing the other experience that is its object. No one can talk of the knowledge of the one by the other without seeing them as numerically distinct entities, of which the one lies beyond the other and away from it, along some direction

has not read my two articles, 'Does Consciousness Exist?' and 'A World of Pure Experience.'

[1] [Cf. above, p. 134; and below, p. 202.]

and with some interval, that can be definitely named. But, if the talker be a humanist, he must also see this distance-interval concretely and pragmatically, and confess it to consist of other intervening experiences — of possible ones, at all events, if not of actual. To call my present idea of my dog, for example, cognitive of the real dog means that, as the actual tissue of experience is constituted, the idea is capable of leading into a chain of other experiences on my part that go from next to next and terminate at last in vivid sense-perceptions of a jumping, barking, hairy body. Those *are* the real dog, the dog's full presence, for my common sense. If the supposed talker is a profound philosopher, although they may not *be* the real dog for him, they *mean* the real dog, are practical substitutes for the real dog, as the representation was a practical substitute for them, that real dog being a lot of atoms, say, or of mind-stuff, that lie *where* the sense-perceptions lie in his experience as well as in my own.

III

The philosopher here stands for the stage of thought that goes beyond the stage of common sense; and the difference is simply that he 'interpolates' and 'extrapolates,' where common sense does not. For common sense, two men see the same identical real dog. Philosophy, noting actual differences in their perceptions, points out the duality of these latter, and interpolates something between them as a more real terminus — first, organs, viscera, etc.; next, cells; then, ultimate atoms; lastly, mind-stuff perhaps. The original sense-termini of the two men, instead of coalescing with each other and with the real dog-object, as at first supposed, are thus held by philosophers to be separated by invisible realities with which, at most, they are conterminous.

Abolish, now, one of the percipients, and the interpolation changes into 'extrapolation.' The sense-terminus of the remaining percipient is regarded by the philosopher as not quite reaching reality. He has only carried the procession of experiences, the philosopher thinks, to a definite, because practical, halting-place somewhere on the way towards an absolute truth that lies beyond.

The humanist sees all the time, however, that there is no absolute transcendency even about the more absolute realities thus conjectured or believed in. The viscera and cells are only possible percepts following upon that of the outer body. The atoms again, though we may never attain to human means of perceiving them, are still defined perceptually. The mind-stuff itself is conceived as a kind of experience; and it is possible to frame the hypothesis (such hypotheses can by no logic be excluded from philosophy) of two knowers of a piece of mind-stuff and the mind-stuff itself becoming 'confluent' at the moment at which our imperfect knowing might pass into knowing of a completed type. Even so do you and I habitually represent our two perceptions and the real dog as confluent, though only provisionally, and for the common-sense stage of thought. If my pen be inwardly made of mind-stuff, there is no confluence *now* between that mind-stuff and my visual perception of the pen. But conceivably there might come to be such confluence; for, in the case of my hand, the visual sensations and the inward feelings of the hand, its mind-stuff, so to speak, are even now as confluent as any two things can be.

There is, thus, no breach in humanistic epistemology. Whether knowledge be taken as ideally perfected, or only as true enough to pass muster for practice, it is hung on one continuous scheme. Reality, howsoever remote, is always defined as a terminus within the general possibilities of experience; and what knows it is defined as an experience *that 'represents' it, in the sense of being substitutable for it in our thinking* because it leads to the same associates, *or in the sense of 'pointing to it'* through a chain of other experiences that either intervene or may intervene.

Absolute reality here bears the same relation to sensation as sensation bears to conception or imagination. Both are provisional or final termini, sensation being only the terminus at which the practical man habitually stops, while the philosopher projects a 'beyond' in the shape of more absolute reality. These termini, for the practical and the philosophical stages of thought respectively, are self-supporting. They are not 'true' of anything else, they simply *are*, are *real*. They 'lean on nothing,' as my italicized formula said. Rather does the whole fabric of experience lean on them, just as the whole fabric of the solar system, including many relative positions, leans, for its absolute position in space, on any one of its constituent stars. Here, again, one gets a new *Identitätsphilosophie* in pluralistic form.[1]

IV

If I have succeeded in making this at all clear (though I fear that brevity and abstractness between them may have made me fail), the reader will see that the 'truth' of our mental operations must always be an intra-experiential affair. A conception is reckoned true by common sense when it can be made to lead to a

[1] [Cf. above, pp. 134, 197.]

sensation. The sensation, which for common sense is not so much 'true' as 'real,' is held to be *provisionally* true by the philosopher just in so far as it *covers* (abuts at, or occupies the place of) a still more absolutely real experience, in the possibility of which to some remoter experient the philosopher finds reason to believe.

Meanwhile what actually *does* count for true to any individual trower, whether he be philosopher or common man, is always a result of his *apperceptions*. If a novel experience, conceptual or sensible, contradict too emphatically our pre-existent system of beliefs, in ninety-nine cases out of a hundred it is treated as false. Only when the older and the newer experiences are congruous enough to mutually apperceive and modify each other, does what we treat as an advance in truth result. [Having written of this point in an article in reply to Mr. Joseph's criticism of my humanism, I will say no more about truth here, but refer the reader to that review.[1]] In no case, however, need truth

[1] [Omitted from reprint in *Meaning of Truth*. The review re-

consist in a relation between our experiences and something archetypal or trans-experiential. Should we ever reach absolutely terminal experiences, experiences in which we all agreed, which were superseded by no revised continuations, these would not be *true*, they would be *real*, they would simply *be*, and be indeed the angles, corners, and linchpins of all reality, on which the truth of everything else would be stayed. Only such *other* things as led to these by satisfactory conjunctions would be 'true.' Satisfactory connection of some sort with such termini is all that the word 'truth' means. On the common-sense stage of thought sense-presentations serve as such termini. Our ideas and concepts and scientific theories pass for true only so far as they harmoniously lead back to the world of sense.

I hope that many humanists will endorse this attempt of mine to trace the more essential features of that way of viewing things. I feel almost certain that Messrs. Dewey and

ferred to is reprinted below, pp. 244–265, under the title "Humanism and Truth Once More." ED.]

Schiller will do so. If the attackers will also take some slight account of it, it may be that discussion will be a little less wide of the mark than it has hitherto been.

VIII

LA NOTION DE CONSCIENCE[1]

Je voudrais vous communiquer quelques doutes qui me sont venus au sujet de la notion de Conscience qui règne dans tous nos traités de psychologie.

On définit habituellement la Psychologie comme la Science des faits de Conscience, ou des *phénomènes*, ou encore des *états* de la Conscience. Qu'on admette qu'elle se rattache à des *moi* personnels, ou bien qu'on la croie impersonnelle à la façon du "moi transcendental" de Kant, de la *Bewusstheit* ou du *Bewusstsein überhaupt* de nos contemporains en Allemagne, cette conscience est toujours regardée comme possédant une essence propre, absolument distincte de l'essence des choses matérielles, qu'elle a le don mystérieux de représenter et de

[1] [A communication made (in French) at the Fifth International Congress of Psychology, in Rome, April 30, 1905. It is reprinted from the *Archives de Psychologie*, vol. v, No. 17, June, 1905.] Cette communication est le résumé, forcément très condensé, de vues que l'auteur a exposées, au cours de ces derniers mois, en une série d'articles publiés dans le *Journal of Philosophy, Psychology and Scientific Methods*, 1904 et 1905. [The series of articles referred to is reprinted above. Ed.]

connaître. Les faits matériels, pris dans leur matérialité, ne sont pas *éprouvés*, ne sont pas objets d'*expérience*, ne se *rapportent* pas. Pour qu'ils prennent la forme du système dans lequel nous nous sentons vivre, il faut qu'ils *apparaissent*, et ce fait d'apparaître, surajouté à leur existence brute, s'appelle la conscience que nous en avons, ou peut-être, selon l'hypothèse panpsychiste, qu'ils ont d'eux-mêmes.

Voilà ce dualisme invétéré qu'il semble impossible de chasser de notre vue du monde. Ce monde peut bien exister en soi, mais nous n'en savons rien, car pour nous il est exclusivement un objet d'expérience; et la condition indispensable à cet effet, c'est qu'il soit rapporté à des témoins, qu'il soit connu par un sujet ou par des sujets spirituels. Objet et sujet, voilà les deux jambes sans lesquelles il semble que la philosophie ne saurait faire un pas en avant.

Toutes les écoles sont d'accord là-dessus, scolastique, cartésianisme, kantisme, néo-kantisme, tous admettent le dualisme fondamental. Le positivisme ou agnosticisme de nos

jours, qui se pique de relever des sciences
naturelles, se donne volontiers, il est vrai, le
nom de monisme. Mais ce n'est qu'un monisme verbal. Il pose une réalité inconnue,
mais nous dit que cette réalité se présente toujours sous deux "aspects," un côté conscience
et un côté matière, et ces deux côtés demeurent aussi irréductibles que les attributs fon-
damentaux, étendue et pensée, du Dieu de
Spinoza. Au fond, le monisme contemporain
est du spinozisme pur.

Or, comment se représente-t-on cette conscience dont nous sommes tous si portés à
admettre l'existence? Impossible de la définir,
nous dit-on, mais nous en avons tous une intuition immédiate: tout d'abord la conscience a
conscience d'elle-même. Demandez à la première personne que vous rencontrerez, homme
ou femme, psychologue ou ignorant, et elle
vous répondra qu'elle *se sent* penser, jouir,
souffrir, vouloir, tout comme elle se sent re-
spirer. Elle perçoit directement sa vie spirituelle comme une espèce de courant intérieur,
actif, léger, fluide, délicat, diaphane pour ainsi

dire, et absolument opposé à quoi que ce soit de matériel. Bref, la vie subjective ne paraît pas seulement être une condition logiquement indispensable pour qu'il y ait un monde objectif qui *apparaisse*, c'est encore un élément de l'expérience même que nous éprouvons directement, au même titre que nous éprouvons notre propre corps.

Idées et Choses, comment donc ne pas reconnaître leur dualisme? Sentiments et Objets, comment douter de leur hétérogénéité absolue?

La psychologie soi-disant scientifique admet cette hétérogénéité comme l'ancienne psychologie spiritualiste l'admettait. Comment ne pas l'admettre? Chaque science découpe arbitrairement dans la trame des faits un champ où elle se parque, et dont elle décrit et étudie le contenu. La psychologie prend justement pour son domaine le champ des faits de conscience. Elle les postule sans les critiquer, elle les oppose aux faits matériels; et sans critiquer non plus la notion de ces derniers, elle les rattache à la conscience par le lien mystérieux de la *connaissance*, de l'*aperception* qui, pour elle, est

un troisième genre de fait fondamental et
ultime. En suivant cette voie, la psychologie
contemporaine a fêté de grands triomphes.
Elle a pu faire une esquisse de l'évolution de
la vie consciente, en concevant cette dernière
comme s'adaptant de plus en plus complètement au milieu physique environnant. Elle
a pu établir un parallélisme dans le dualisme,
celui des faits psychiques et des événements
cérébraux. Elle a expliqué les illusions, les
hallucinations, et jusqu'à un certain point, les
maladies mentales. Ce sont de beaux progrès;
mais il reste encore bien des problèmes. La
philosophie générale surtout, qui a pour devoir
de scruter tous les postulats, trouve des paradoxes et des empêchements là où la science
passe outre; et il n'y a que les amateurs de
science populaire qui ne sont jamais perplexes.
Plus on va au fond des choses, plus on trouve
d'énigmes; et j'avoue pour ma part que depuis
que je m'occupe sérieusement de psychologie,
ce vieux dualisme de matière et de pensée,
cette hétérogénéité posée comme absolue des
deux essences, m'a toujours présenté des diffi-

cultés. C'est de quelques-unes de ces difficul-
tés que je voudrais maintenant vous entretenir.

D'abord il y en a une, laquelle, j'en suis
convaincu, vous aura frappés tous. Prenons la
perception extérieure, la sensation directe que
nous donnent par exemple les murs de cette
salle. Peut-on dire ici que le psychique et le
physique sont absolument hétérogènes? Au
contraire, ils sont si peu hétérogènes que si
nous nous plaçons au point de vue du sens
commun; si nous faisons abstraction de toutes
les inventions explicatives, des molécules et des
ondulations éthérées, par exemple, qui au fond
sont des entités métaphysiques; si, en un mot,
nous prenons la réalité naïvement et telle
qu'elle nous est donnée tout d'abord, cette
réalité sensible d'où dépendent nos intérêts
vitaux, et sur laquelle se portent toutes nos
actions; eh bien, cette réalité sensible et la
sensation que nous en avons sont, au moment
où la sensation se produit, absolument iden-
tiques l'une à l'autre. La réalité est l'aperception même. Les mots "murs de cette salle" ne
signifient que cette blancheur fraîche et sonore

qui nous entoure, coupée par ces fenêtres,
bornée par ces lignes et ces angles. Le physique
ici n'a pas d'autre contenu que le psychique.
Le sujet et l'objet se confondent.

C'est Berkeley qui le premier a mis cette
vérité en honneur. *Esse est percipi.* Nos sensations ne sont pas de petits duplicats in-
térieurs des choses, elles sont les choses mêmes
en tant que les choses nous sont présentes. Et
quoi que l'on veuille penser de la vie absente,
cachée, et pour ainsi dire privée, des choses, et
quelles que soient les constructions hypothé-
tiques qu'on en fasse, il reste vrai que la vie
publique des choses, cette actualité présente
par laquelle elles nous confrontent, d'où déri-
vent toutes nos constructions théoriques, et
à laquelle elles doivent toutes revenir et se
rattacher sous peine de flotter dans l'air et
dans l'irréel; cette actualité, dis-je, est homogène, et non pas seulement homogène, mais
numériquement une, avec une certaine partie
de notre vie intérieure.

Voilà pour la perception extérieure. Quand
on s'adresse à l'imagination, à la mémoire ou

aux facultés de représentation abstraite, bien
que les faits soient ici beaucoup plus compli-
qués, je crois que la même homogénéité essentielle se dégage. Pour simplifier le problème,
excluons d'abord toute réalité sensible. Prenons la pensée pure, telle qu'elle s'effectue dans
le rêve ou la rêverie, ou dans la mémoire du
passé. Ici encore, l'étoffe de l'expérience ne
fait-elle pas double emploi, le physique et le
psychique ne se confondent-ils pas? Si je rêve
d'une montagne d'or, elle n'existe sans doute
pas en dehors du rêve, mais *dans* le rêve elle est
de nature ou d'essence parfaitement physique,
c'est *comme* physique qu'elle m'apparaît. Si en
ce moment je me permets de me souvenir de
ma maison en Amérique, et des détails de mon
embarquement récent pour l'Italie, le phénomène pur, le fait qui se produit, qu'est-il? C'est,
dit-on, ma pensée, avec son contenu. Mais encore ce contenu, qu'est-il? Il porte la forme
d'une partie du monde réel, partie distante, il
est vrai, de six mille kilomètres d'espace et de
six semaines de temps, mais reliée à la salle où
nous sommes par une foule de choses, objets

et événements, homogènes d'une part avec la salle et d'autre part avec l'objet de mes souvenirs.

Ce contenu ne se donne pas comme étant d'abord un tout petit fait intérieur que je projetterais ensuite au loin, il se présente d'emblée comme le fait éloigné même. Et l'acte de penser ce contenu, la conscience que j'en ai, que sont-ils? Sont-ce au fond autre chose que des manières rétrospectives de nommer le contenu lui-même, lorsqu'on l'aura séparé de tous ces intermédiaires physiques, et relié à un nouveau groupe d'associés qui le font rentrer dans ma vie mentale, les émotions par exemple qu'il a éveillées en moi, l'attention que j'y porte, mes idées de tout à l'heure qui l'ont suscité comme souvenir? Ce n'est qu'en se rapportant à ces derniers associés que le phénomène arrive à être classé comme *pensée;* tant qu'il ne se rapporte qu'aux premiers il demeure phénomène *objectif*.

Il est vrai que nous opposons habituellement nos images intérieures aux objets, et que nous les considérons comme de petites copies, comme des calques ou doubles, affaiblis, de ces derniers. C'est qu'un objet présent a une vivacité et une netteté supérieures à celles de l'image. Il lui fait ainsi contraste; et pour me servir de l'excellent mot de Taine, il lui sert de *réducteur.* Quand les deux sont présents ensemble, l'objet prend le premier plan et l'image "recule," devient une chose "absente." Mais cet objet présent, qu'est-il en lui-même? De quelle étoffe est-il fait? De la même étoffe que l'image. Il est fait de *sensations;* il est chose perçue. Son *esse* est *percipi,* et lui et l'image sont génériquement homogènes.

Si je pense en ce moment à mon chapeau que j'ai laissé tout à l'heure au vestiaire, où est le dualisme, le discontinu, entre le chapeau pensé et le chapeau réel? C'est d'un vrai *chapeau absent* que mon esprit s'occupe. J'en tiens compte pratiquement comme d'une réalité. S'il était présent sur cette table, le chapeau déterminerait un mouvement de ma main: je l'enlèverais. De même ce chapeau conçu, ce chapeau en idée, déterminera tantôt la direction de mes pas. J'irai le prendre.

L'idée que j'en ai se continuera jusqu'à la présence sensible du chapeau, et s'y fondra harmonieusement.

Je conclus donc que, — bien qu'il y ait un dualisme pratique — puisque les images se distinguent des objets, en tiennent lieu, et nous y mènent, il n'y a pas lieu de leur attribuer une différence de nature essentielle. Pensée et actualité sont faites d'une seule et même étoffe, qui est l'étoffe de l'expérience en général.

La psychologie de la perception extérieure nous mène à la même conclusion. Quand j'aperçois l'objet devant moi comme une table de telle forme, à telle distance, on m'explique que ce fait est dû à deux facteurs, à une matière de sensation qui me pénètre par la voie des yeux et qui donne l'élément d'extériorité réelle, et à des idées qui se réveillent, vont à la rencontre de cette réalité, la classent et l'interprètent. Mais qui peut faire la part, dans la table concrètement aperçue, de ce qui est sensation et de ce qui est idée? L'externe et l'interne, l'étendu et l'inétendu, se fusionnent et font un mariage indissoluble. Cela rappelle ces panoramas circulaires, où des objets réels, rochers, herbe, chariots brisés, etc., qui occupent l'avant-plan, sont si ingénieusement reliés à la toile qui fait le fond, et qui représente une bataille ou un vaste paysage, que l'on ne sait plus distinguer ce qui est objet de ce qui est peinture. Les coutures et les joints sont imperceptibles.

Cela pourrait-il advenir si l'objet et l'idée étaient absolument dissemblables de nature?

Je suis convaincu que des considérations pareilles à celles que je viens d'exprimer auront déjà suscité, chez vous aussi, des doutes au sujet du dualisme prétendu.

Et d'autres raisons de douter surgissent encore. Il y a toute une sphère d'adjectifs et d'attributs qui ne sont ni objectifs, ni subjectifs d'une manière exclusive, mais que nous employons tantôt d'une manière et tantôt d'une autre, comme si nous nous complaisions dans leur ambiguïté. Je parle des qualités que nous *apprécions*, pour ainsi dire, dans les

217

choses, leur côté esthétique, moral, leur valeur
pour nous. La beauté, par exemple, où réside-
t-elle? Est-elle dans la statue, dans la sonate,
ou dans notre esprit? Mon collègue à Harvard, George Santayana, a écrit un livre d'esthétique,[1] où il appelle la beauté "le plaisir
objectifié"; et en vérité, c'est bien ici qu'on
pourrait parler de projection au dehors. On
dit indifféremment une chaleur agréable, ou
une sensation agréable de chaleur. La rareté,
le précieux du diamant nous en paraissent des
qualités essentielles. Nous parlons d'un orage
affreux, d'un homme haïssable, d'une action
indigne, et nous croyons parler objectivement,
bien que ces termes n'expriment que des
rapports à notre sensibilité émotive propre.
Nous disons même un chemin pénible, un ciel
triste, un coucher de soleil superbe. Toute
cette manière animiste de regarder les choses
qui paraît avoir été la façon primitive de penser des hommes, peut très bien s'expliquer (et
M. Santayana, dans un autre livre tout récent,[2]

---

[1] *The Sense of Beauty*, pp. 44 ff.
[2] *The Life of Reason* [vol. I, "Reason in Common Sense," p. 142].

l'a bien expliquée ainsi) par l'habitude d'attribuer à l'objet *tout* ce que nous ressentons en sa présence. Le partage du subjectif et de l'objectif est le fait d'une réflexion très avancée, que nous aimons encore ajourner dans beaucoup d'endroits. Quand les besoins pratiques ne nous en tirent pas forcément, il semble que nous aimons à nous bercer dans le vague.

Les qualités secondes elles-mêmes, chaleur, son, lumière, n'ont encore aujourd'hui qu'une attribution vague. Pour le sens commun, pour la vie pratique, elles sont absolument objectives, physiques. Pour le physicien, elles sont subjectives. Pour lui, il n'y a que la forme, la masse, le mouvement, qui aient une réalité extérieure. Pour le philosophe idéaliste, au contraire, forme et mouvement sont tout aussi subjectifs que lumière et chaleur, et il n'y a que la chose-en-soi inconnue, le "noumène," qui jouisse d'une réalité extramentale complète.

Nos sensations intimes conservent encore de cette ambiguïté. Il y a des illusions de mouvement qui prouvent que nos premières sensations de mouvement étaient généralisées. C'est le monde entier, avec nous, qui se mouvait. Maintenant nous distinguons notre propre mouvement de celui des objets qui nous entourent, et parmi les objets nous en distinguons qui demeurent en repos. Mais il est des états de vertige où nous retombons encore aujourd'hui dans l'indifférenciation première.

Vous connaissez tous sans doute cette théorie qui a voulu faire des émotions des sommes de sensations viscérales et musculaires. Elle a donné lieu à bien des controverses, et aucune opinion n'a encore conquis l'unanimité des suffrages. Vous connaissez aussi les controverses sur la nature de l'activité mentale. Les uns soutiennent qu'elle est une force purement spirituelle que nous sommes en état d'apercevoir immédiatement comme telle. Les autres prétendent que ce que nous nommons activité mentale (effort, attention, par exemple) n'est que le reflet senti de certains effets dont notre organisme est le siège, tensions musculaires au crâne et au gosier, arrêt ou passage de la respiration, afflux de sang, etc.

De quelque manière que se résolvent ces controverses, leur existence prouve bien clairement une chose, c'est qu'il est très difficile, ou même absolument impossible de savoir, par la seule inspection intime de certains phénomènes, s'ils sont de nature physique, occupant de l'étendue, etc., ou s'ils sont de nature purement psychique et intérieure. Il nous faut toujours trouver des raisons pour appuyer notre avis; il nous faut chercher la classification la plus probable du phénomène; et en fin de compte il pourrait bien se trouver que toutes nos classifications usuelles eussent eu leurs motifs plutôt dans les besoins de la pratique que dans quelque faculté que nous aurions d'apercevoir deux essences ultimes et diverses qui composeraient ensemble la trame des choses. Le corps de chacun de nous offre un contraste pratique presque violent à tout le reste du milieu ambiant. Tout ce qui arrive au dedans de ce corps nous est plus intime et important que ce qui arrive ailleurs. Il s'identifie avec notre moi, il se classe avec lui. Ame, vie, souffle, qui saurait bien les distinguer exactement? Même nos images et nos souvenirs, qui n'agissent sur le monde physique que par le moyen de notre corps, semblent appartenir à ce dernier. Nous les traitons comme internes, nous les classons avec nos sentiments affectifs. Il faut bien avouer, en somme, que la question du dualisme de la pensée et de la matière est bien loin d'être finalement résolue.

Et voilà terminée la première partie de mon discours. J'ai voulu vous pénétrer, Mesdames et Messieurs, de mes doutes et de la réalité, aussi bien que de l'importance, du problème.

Quant à moi, après de longues années d'hésitation, j'ai fini par prendre mon parti carrément. Je crois que la conscience, telle qu'on se la représente communément, soit comme entité, soit comme activité pure, mais en tout cas comme fluide, inétendue, diaphane, vide de tout contenu propre, mais se connaissant directement elle-même, spirituelle enfin, je crois, dis-je, que cette conscience est une pure chimère, et que la somme de réalités concrètes que le mot conscience devrait couvrir, mérite une toute autre description, description, du reste, qu'une philosophie attentive aux faits et

sachant faire un peu d'analyse, serait désormais en état de fournir ou plutôt de commencer
à fournir. Et ces mots m'amènent à la seconde
partie de mon discours. Elle sera beaucoup
plus courte que la première, parce que si je la
développais sur la même échelle, elle serait
beaucoup trop longue. Il faut, par conséquent,
que je me restreigne aux seules indications
indispensables.

Admettons que la conscience, la *Bewusstheit*,
conçue comme essence, entité, activité, moitié
irréductible de chaque expérience, soit sup-
primée, que le dualisme fondamental et pour
ainsi dire ontologique soit aboli et que ce que
nous supposions exister soit seulement ce qu'on
a appelé jusqu'ici le *contenu*, le *Inhalt*, de la
conscience; comment la philosophie va-t-elle se
tirer d'affaire avec l'espèce de monisme vague
qui en résultera? Je vais tâcher de vous insinuer
quelques suggestions positives là-dessus, bien
que je craigne que, faute du développement
nécessaire, mes idées ne répandront pas une
clarté très grande. Pourvu que j'indique un

commencement de sentier, ce sera peut-être assez.

Au fond, pourquoi nous accrochons-nous d'une manière si tenace à cette idée d'une conscience surajoutée à l'existence du contenu des choses? Pourquoi la réclamons-nous si fortement, que celui qui la nierait nous semblerait plutôt un mauvais plaisant qu'un penseur? N'est-ce pas pour sauver ce fait indéniable que le contenu de l'expérience n'a pas seulement une existence propre et comme immanente et intrinsèque, mais que chaque partie de ce contenu déteint pour ainsi dire sur ses voisines, rend compte d'elle-même à d'autres, sort en quelque sorte de soi pour être sue et qu'ainsi tout le champ de l'expérience se trouve être transparent de part en part, ou constitué comme un espace qui serait rempli de miroirs?

Cette bilatéralité des parties de l'expérience, — à savoir d'une part, qu'elles *sont* avec des qualités propres; d'autre part, qu'elles sont rapportées à d'autres parties et *sues* — l'opinion régnante la constate et l'explique par un dualisme fondamental de constitution apparte-

nant à chaque morceau d'expérience en propre.
Dans cette feuille de papier il n'y a pas seulement, dit-on, le contenu, blancheur, minceur,
etc., mais il y a ce second fait de la conscience
de cette blancheur et de cette minceur. Cette
fonction d'être "rapporté," de faire partie de la
trame entière d'une expérience plus compré-
hensive, on l'érige en fait ontologique, et on
loge ce fait dans l'intérieur même du papier, en
l'accouplant à sa blancheur et à sa minceur.
Ce n'est pas un rapport extrinsèque qu'on
suppose, c'est une moitié du phénomène même.

Je crois qu'en somme on se représente la
réalité comme constituée de la façon dont sont
faites les "couleurs" qui nous servent à la
peinture. Il y a d'abord des matières coloran-
tes qui répondent au contenu, et il y a un vé-
hicule, huile ou colle, qui les tient en suspen-
sion et qui répond à la conscience. C'est un
dualisme complet, où, en employant certains
procédés, on peut séparer chaque élément de
l'autre par voie de soustraction. C'est ainsi
qu'on nous assure qu'en faisant un grand effort
d'abstraction introspective, nous pouvons sai-

sir notre conscience sur le vif, comme une activité spirituelle pure, en négligeant à peu près complètement les matières qu'à un moment donné elle éclaire.

Maintenant je vous demande si on ne pourrait pas tout aussi bien renverser absolument cette manière de voir. Supposons, en effet, que la réalité première soit de nature neutre, et appelons-la par quelque nom encore ambigu, comme *phénomène*, *donné*, *Vorfindung*. Moimême j'en parle volontiers au pluriel, et je lui donne le nom d'*expériences pures*. Ce sera un monisme, si vous voulez, mais un monisme tout à fait rudimentaire et absolument opposé au soi-disant monisme bilatéral du positivisme scientifique ou spinoziste.

Ces expériences pures existent et se succèdent, entrent dans des rapports infiniment variés les unes avec les autres, rapports qui sont eux-mêmes des parties essentielles de la trame des expériences. Il y a "Conscience" de ces rapports au même titre qu'il y a "Conscience" de leurs termes. Il en résulte que des *groupes* d'expériences se font remarquer et

distinguer, et qu'une seule et même expérience,
vu la grande variété de ses rapports, peut
jouer un rôle dans plusieurs groupes à la fois.
C'est ainsi que dans un certain contexte de
voisins, elle serait classée comme un phénomène physique, tandis que dans un autre
entourage elle figurerait comme un fait de
conscience, à peu près comme une même par-
ticule d'encre peut appartenir simultanément
à deux lignes, l'une verticale, l'autre horizon-
tale, pourvu qu'elle soit située à leur intersection.

Prenons, pour fixer nos idées, l'expérience
que nous avons à ce moment du local où nous
sommes, de ces murailles, de cette table, de ces
chaises, de cet espace. Dans cette expérience
pleine, concrète et indivise, telle qu'elle est là,
donnée, le monde physique objectif et le monde
intérieur et personnel de chacun de nous se
rencontrent et se fusionnent comme des lignes
se fusionnent à leur intersection. Comme chose
physique, cette salle a des rapports avec tout
le reste du bâtiment, bâtiment que nous autres
nous ne connaissons et ne connaîtrons pas.

Elle doit son existence à toute une histoire de financiers, d'architectes, d'ouvriers. Elle pèse sur le sol; elle durera indéfiniment dans le temps; si le feu y éclatait, les chaises et la table qu'elle contient seraient vite réduites en cendres.

Comme expérience personnelle, au contraire, comme chose "rapportée," connue, consciente, cette salle a de tout autres tenants et aboutissants. Ses antécédents ne sont pas des ouvriers, ce sont nos pensées respectives de tout à l'heure. Bientôt elle ne figurera que comme un fait fugitif dans nos biographies, associé à d'agréables souvenirs. Comme expérience psychique, elle n'a aucun poids, son ameublement n'est pas combustible. Elle n'exerce de force physique que sur nos seuls cerveaux, et beaucoup d'entre nous nient encore cette influence; tandis que la salle physique est en rapport d'influence physique avec tout le reste du monde.

Et pourtant c'est de la même salle absolument qu'il s'agit dans les deux cas. Tant que nous ne faisons pas de physique spéculative, tant que nous nous plaçons dans le sens commun, c'est la salle vue et sentie qui est bien la salle physique. De quoi parlons-nous donc si ce n'est de *cela*, de cette même partie de la nature matérielle que tous nos esprits, à ce même moment, embrassent, qui entre telle quelle dans l'expérience actuelle et intime de chacun de nous, et que notre souvenir regardera toujours comme une partie intégrante de notre histoire. C'est absolument une même étoffe qui figure simultanément, selon le contexte que l'on considère, comme fait matériel et physique, ou comme fait de conscience intime.

Je crois donc qu'on ne saurait traiter conscience et matière comme étant d'essence disparate. On n'obtient ni l'une ni l'autre par soustraction, en négligeant chaque fois l'autre moitié d'une expérience de composition double. Les expériences sont au contraire primitivement de nature plutôt simple. Elles *deviennent* conscientes dans leur entier, elles *deviennent* physiques dans leur entier; et c'est *par voie d'addition* que ce résultat se réalise. Pour autant que des expériences se prolongent dans le temps, entrent dans des rapports d'influence physique, se brisant, se chauffant, s'éclairant, etc., mutuellement, nous en faisons un groupe à part que nous appelons le monde physique. Pour autant, au contraire, qu'elles sont fugitives, inertes physiquement, que leur succession ne suit pas d'ordre déterminé, mais semble plutôt obéir à des caprices émotifs, nous en faisons un autre groupe que nous appelons le monde psychique. C'est en entrant à présent dans un grand nombre de ces groupes psychiques que cette salle devient maintenant chose consciente, chose rapportée, chose sue. En faisant désormais partie de nos biographies respectives, elle ne sera pas suivie de cette sotte et monotone répétition d'elle-même dans le temps qui caractérise son existence physique. Elle sera suivie, au contraire, par d'autres expériences qui seront discontinues avec elle, ou qui auront ce genre tout particulier de continuité que nous appelons souvenir. Demain, elle aura eu sa place dans chacun de nos passés; mais les présents divers auxquels tous ces passés seront liés demain seront bien différents du présent dont cette salle jouira demain comme entité physique.

Les deux genres de groupes sont formés d'expériences, mais les rapports des expériences entre elles diffèrent d'un groupe à l'autre. C'est donc par addition d'autres phénomènes qu'un phénomène donné devient conscient ou connu, ce n'est pas par un dédoublement d'essence intérieure. La connaissance des choses leur *survient*, elle ne leur est pas immanente. Ce n'est le fait ni d'un moi transcendental, ni d'une *Bewusstheit* ou acte de conscience qui les animerait chacune. *Elles se connaissent l'une l'autre*, ou plutôt il y en a qui connaissent les autres; et le rapport que nous nommons connaissance n'est lui-même, dans beaucoup de cas, qu'une suite d'expériences intermédiaires parfaitement susceptibles d'être décrites en termes concrets. Il n'est nullement le mystère transcendant où se sont complus tant de philosophes.

Mais ceci nous mènerait beaucoup trop loin. Je ne puis entrer ici dans tous les replis de la théorie de la connaissance, ou de ce que, vous autres Italiens, vous appelez la gnoséologie. Je dois me contenter de ces remarques écourtées, ou simples suggestions, qui sont, je le crains, encore bien obscures faute des développements nécessaires.

Permettez donc que je me résume — trop sommairement, et en style dogmatique — dans les six thèses suivantes :

1° *La Conscience, telle qu'on l'entend ordinairement, n'existe pas, pas plus que la Matière, à laquelle Berkeley a donné le coup de grâce;*

2° *Ce qui existe et forme la part de vérité que le mot de "Conscience" recouvre, c'est la susceptibilité que possèdent les parties de l'expérience d'être rapportées ou connues;*

3° *Cette susceptibilité s'explique par le fait que certaines expériences peuvent mener les unes aux autres par des expériences intermédiaires nettement caractérisées, de telle sorte que les unes se trouvent jouer le rôle de choses connues, les autres celui de sujets connaissants;*

4° *On peut parfaitement définir ces deux rôles*

sans sortir de la trame de l'expérience même, et sans invoquer rien de transcendant ;

5° Les attributions sujet et objet, représenté et représentatif, chose et pensée, signifient donc une distinction pratique qui est de la dernière importance, mais qui est d'ordre FONCTIONNEL *seulement, et nullement ontologique comme le dualisme classique se la représente ;*

6° En fin de compte, les choses et les pensées ne sont point foncièrement hétérogènes, mais elles sont faites d'une même étoffe, étoffe qu'on ne peut définir comme telle, mais seulement éprouver, et que l'on peut nommer, si on veut, l'étoffe de l'expérience en général.

Volume II

A PLURALISTIC UNIVERSE

HIBBERT LECTURES ON THE
CURRENT SITUATION IN
PHILOSOPHY DELIVERED AT
MANCHESTER COLLEGE, OXFORD
IN 1909

I

THE TYPES OF PHILOSOPHIC THINKING

LECTURE I

THE TYPES OF PHILOSOPHIC THINKING

As these lectures are meant to be public, and so few, I have assumed all very special problems to be excluded, and some topic of general interest required. Fortunately, our age seems to be growing philosophical again — still in the ashes live the wonted fires. Oxford, long the seed-bed, for the english world, of the idealism inspired by Kant and Hegel, has recently become the nursery of a very different way of thinking. Even non-philosophers have begun to take an interest in a controversy over what is known as pluralism or humanism. It looks a little as if the ancient english empiricism, so long put out of fashion here by nobler sounding germanic formulas, might be re-pluming itself and getting ready for a stronger flight than ever. It looks as if foundations were being sounded and examined afresh.

Individuality outruns all classification, yet we insist on classifying every one we meet under some general head. As these heads usually suggest prejudicial associations to some hearer or other, the life of philosophy largely consists of resentments at the classing, and complaints of being misunderstood. But there are signs of clearing up, and, on the whole, less acrimony in discussion, for which both Oxford and Harvard are partly to be thanked. As I look back into the sixties, Mill, Bain, and Hamilton were the only official philosophers in Britain. Spencer, Martineau, and Hodgson were just beginning. In France, the pupils of Cousin were delving into history only, and Renouvier alone had an original system. In Germany, the hegelian impetus had spent itself, and, apart from historical scholarship, nothing but the materialistic controversy remained, with such men as Büchner and Ulrici as its champions. Lotze and Fechner were the sole original thinkers, and Fechner was not a professional philosopher at all.

The general impression made was of crude issues and oppositions, of small subtlety and of a widely spread ignorance. Amateurishness was rampant. Samuel Bailey's 'letters on the philosophy of the human mind,' published in 1855, are one of the ablest expressions of english associationism, and a book of real power. Yet hear how he writes of Kant: 'No one, after reading the extracts, etc., can be surprised to hear of a declaration by men of eminent abilities, that, after years of study, they had not succeeded in gathering one clear idea from the speculations of Kant. I should have been almost surprised if they had. In or about 1818, Lord Grenville, when visiting the Lakes of England, observed to Professor Wilson that, after five years' study of Kant's philosophy, he had not gathered from it one clear idea. Wilberforce, about the same time, made the same confession to another friend of my own. "I am endeavoring," exclaims Sir James Mackintosh, in the irritation, evidently, of baffled efforts, "to understand this accursed german philosophy." ' [1]

What Oxford thinker would dare to print such *naïf* and provincial-sounding citations of authority to-day?

The torch of learning passes from land to land as the spirit bloweth the flame. The deepening of philosophic consciousness came to us english folk from Germany, as it will probably pass back ere long. Ferrier, J. H. Stirling, and, most of all, T. H. Green are to be thanked. If asked to tell in broad strokes what the main doctrinal change has been, I should call it a change from the crudity of the older english thinking, its ultra-simplicity of mind, both when it was religious and when it was anti-religious, toward a rationalism derived in the first instance from Germany, but relieved from german technicality and shrillness, and content to suggest, and to remain vague, and to be, in the english fashion, devout.

By the time T. H. Green began at Oxford, the generation seemed to feel as if it had fed on the chopped straw of psychology and of associationism long enough, and as if a little vastness, even though it went with vagueness, as of some moist wind from far away, reminding us of our pre-natal sublimity, would be welcome.

Green's great point of attack was the dis-

connectedness of the reigning english sensationalism. *Relating* was the great intellectual
activity for him, and the key to this relating
was believed by him to lodge itself at last in
what most of you know as Kant's unity of
apperception, transformed into a living spirit
of the world.

Hence a monism of a devout kind. In some
way we must be fallen angels, one with intelligence as such; and a great disdain for empiricism of the sensationalist sort has always characterized this school of thought, which, on the
whole, has reigned supreme at Oxford and in
the scottish universities until the present day.

But now there are signs of its giving way to
a wave of revised empiricism. I confess that l
should be glad to see this latest wave prevail;
so — the sooner I am frank about it the better
— I hope to have my voice counted in its favor
as one of the results of this lecture-course.

What do the terms empiricism and rationalism mean? Reduced to their most preg-
nant difference, *empiricism means the habit of
explaining wholes by parts, and rationalism*

means the habit of explaining parts by wholes.
Rationalism thus preserves affinities with monism, since wholeness goes with union, while
empiricism inclines to pluralistic views. No
philosophy can ever be anything but a summary sketch, a picture of the world in abridg-
ment, a foreshortened bird's-eye view of the
perspective of events. And the first thing to
notice is this, that the only material we have
at our disposal for making a picture of the
whole world is supplied by the various portions
of that world of which we have already had
experience. We can invent no new forms of
conception, applicable to the whole exclusively,
and not suggested originally by the parts. All
philosophers, accordingly, have conceived of
the whole world after the analogy of some
particular feature of it which has particularly
captivated their attention. Thus, the theists
take their cue from manufacture, the pantheists from growth. For one man, the world is
like a thought or a grammatical sentence in
which a thought is expressed. For such a philosopher, the whole must logically be prior to

8

the parts; for letters would never have been invented without syllables to spell, or syllables without words to utter.

Another man, struck by the disconnectedness and mutual accidentality of so many of the world's details, takes the universe as a whole to have been such a disconnectedness originally, and supposes order to have been superinduced upon it in the second instance, possibly by attrition and the gradual wearing away by internal friction of portions that originally interfered.

Another will conceive the order as only a statistical appearance, and the universe will be for him like a vast grab-bag with black and white balls in it, of which we guess the quantities only probably, by the frequency with which we experience their egress.

For another, again, there is no really inherent order, but it is we who project order into the world by selecting objects and tracing relations so as to gratify our intellectual interests. We *carve out* order by leaving the disorderly parts out; and the world is conceived thus after the analogy of a forest or a block of marble from which parks or statues may be produced by eliminating irrelevant trees or chips of stone.

Some thinkers follow suggestions from human life, and treat the universe as if it were essentially a place in which ideals are realized. Others are more struck by its lower features, and for them, brute necessities express its character better.

All follow one analogy or another; and all the analogies are with some one or other of the universe's subdivisions. Every one is nevertheless prone to claim that his conclusions are the only logical ones, that they are necessities of universal reason, they being all the while, at bottom, accidents more or less of personal vision which had far better be avowed as such; for one man's vision may be much more valuable than another's, and our visions are usually not only our most interesting but our most respectable contributions to the world in which we play our part. What was reason given to men for, said some eighteenth century writer, except to enable them to find reasons for what they want to think and do? — and I think the history of philosophy largely bears him out. 'The aim of knowledge,' says Hegel,[2] 'is to divest the objective world of its strangeness, and to make us more at home in it.' Different men find their minds more at home in very different fragments of the world.

Let me make a few comments, here, on the curious antipathies which these partialities arouse. They are sovereignly unjust, for all the parties are human beings with the same essential interests, and no one of them is the wholly perverse demon which another often imagines him to be. Both are loyal to the world that bears them; neither wishes to spoil it; neither wishes to regard it as an insane incoherence; both want to keep it as a universe of some kind; and their differences are all secondary to this deep agreement. They may be only propensities to emphasize differently. Or one man may care for finality and security more than the other. Or their tastes in language may be different. One may like a universe that lends itself to lofty and exalted characterization. To another this may seem sentimental or rhetorical. One may wish for the right to use a clerical vocabulary, another a technical or professorial one. A certain old farmer of my acquaintance in America was called a rascal by one of his neighbors. He immediately smote the man, saying, 'I won't stand none of your diminutive epithets.' Empiricist minds, putting the parts before the whole, appear to rationalists, who start from the whole, and consequently enjoy magniloquent privileges, to use epithets offensively diminutive. But all such differences are minor matters which ought to be subordinated in view of the fact that, whether we be empiricists or rationalists, we are, ourselves, parts of the universe and share the same one deep concern in its destinies. We crave alike to feel more truly at home with it, and to contribute our mite to its amelioration. It would be pitiful if small æsthetic discords were to keep honest men asunder.

I shall myself have use for the diminutive epithets of empiricism. But if you look behind the words at the spirit, I am sure you will not find it matricidal. I am as good a son as any rationalist among you to our common mother.

What troubles me more than this misapprehension is the genuine abstruseness of many of the matters I shall be obliged to talk about, and the difficulty of making them intelligible at one hearing. But there are two pieces, 'zwei stücke,' as Kant would have said, in every philosophy — the final outlook, belief, or attitude to which it brings us, and the reasonings by which that attitude is reached and mediated. A philosophy, as James Ferrier used to tell us, must indeed be true, but that is the least of its requirements. One may be true without being a philosopher, true by guesswork or by revelation. What distinguishes a philosopher's truth is that it is *reasoned*. Argument, not supposition, must have put it in his possession. Common men find themselves inheriting their beliefs, they know not how. They jump into them with both feet, and stand there. Philosophers must do more; they must first get reason's license for them; and to the professional philosophic mind the operation of procuring the license is usually a thing of much more pith and moment than any particular beliefs to which the license may give the rights of access. Suppose, for example, that a philosopher believes in what is called free-will. That a common man alongside of him should also share that belief, possessing it by a sort of inborn intuition, does not endear the man to the philosopher at all — he may even be ashamed to be associated with such a man. What interests the philosopher is the particular premises on which the free-will he believes in is established, the sense in which it is taken, the objections it eludes, the difficulties it takes account of, in short the whole form and temper and manner and technical apparatus that goes with the belief in question. A philosopher across the way who should use the same technical apparatus, making the same distinctions, etc., but drawing opposite conclusions and denying free-will entirely, would fascinate the first philosopher far more than would the *naïf* co-believer. Their common technical interests would unite them more than their opposite conclusions separate them.

14

I. THE TYPES OF THINKING

Each would feel an essential consanguinity in the other, would think of him, write *at* him, care for his good opinion. The simple-minded believer in free-will would be disregarded by either. Neither as ally nor as opponent would his vote be counted.

In a measure this is doubtless as it should be, but like all professionalism it can go to abusive extremes. The end is after all more than the way, in most things human, and forms and methods may easily frustrate their own purpose. The abuse of technicality is seen in the infrequency with which, in philosophical literature, metaphysical questions are discussed directly and on their own merits. Almost always they are handled as if through a heavy woolen curtain, the veil of previous philosophers' opinions. Alternatives are wrapped in proper names, as if it were indecent for a truth to go naked. The late Professor John Grote of Cambridge has some good remarks about this. 'Thought,' he says, 'is not a professional matter, not something for so-called philosophers only or for professed thinkers. The best phi-

losopher is the man who can think most *simply*.
. . . I wish that people would consider that
thought — and philosophy is no more than
good and methodical thought — is a matter *intimate* to them, a portion of their real selves . . .
that they would *value* what they think, and be
interested in it. . . . In my own opinion,' he
goes on, ' there is something depressing in this
weight of learning, with nothing that can come
into one's mind but one is told, Oh, that is the
opinion of such and such a person long ago.
. . . I can conceive of nothing more noxious
for students than to get into the habit of saying
to themselves about their ordinary philosophic
thought, Oh, somebody must have thought it
all before.' [8] Yet this is the habit most en-
couraged at our seats of learning. You must
tie your opinion to Aristotle's or Spinoza's;
you must define it by its distance from Kant's;
you must refute your rival's view by identifying
it with Protagoras's. Thus does all spontaneity of thought, all freshness of conception, get
destroyed. Everything you touch is shopworn.
The over-technicality and consequent dreari-

ness of the younger disciples at our american universities is appalling. It comes from too much following of german models and manners. Let me fervently express the hope that in this country you will hark back to the more humane english tradition. American students have to regain direct relations with our subject by painful individual effort in later life. Some of us have done so. Some of the younger ones, I fear, never will, so strong are the professional shop-habits already.

In a subject like philosophy it is really fatal to lose connexion with the open air of human nature, and to think in terms of shop-tradition only. In Germany the forms are so professionalized that anybody who has gained a teaching chair and written a book, however distorted and eccentric, has the legal right to figure forever in the history of the subject like a fly in amber. All later comers have the duty of quoting him and measuring their opinions with his opinion. Such are the rules of the professorial game — they think and write from each other and for each other and at each other exclusively. With this exclusion of the open air all true perspective gets lost, extremes and oddities count as much as sanities, and command the same attention; and if by chance any one writes popularly and about results only, with his mind directly focussed on the subject, it is reckoned *oberflächliches zeug* and *ganz unwissenschaftlich*. Professor Paulsen has recently written some feeling lines about this over-professionalism, from the reign of which in Germany his own writings, which sin by being 'literary,' have suffered loss of credit. Philosophy, he says, has long assumed in Germany the character of being an esoteric and occult science. There is a genuine fear of popularity. Simplicity of statement is deemed synonymous with hollowness and shallowness. He recalls an old professor saying to him once: 'Yes, we philosophers, whenever we wish, can go so far that in a couple of sentences we can put ourselves where nobody can follow us.' The professor said this with conscious pride, but he ought to have been ashamed of it. Great as technique is, results are greater. To teach

18

philosophy so that the pupils' interest in technique exceeds that in results is surely a vicious aberration. It is bad form, not good form, in a discipline of such universal human interest. Moreover, technique for technique, does n't David Hume's technique set, after all, the kind of pattern most difficult to follow? Is n't it the most admirable? The english mind, thank heaven, and the french mind, are still kept, by their aversion to crude technique and barbarism, closer to truth's natural probabilities. Their literatures show fewer obvious falsities and monstrosities than that of Germany. Think of the german literature of æsthetics, with the preposterousness of such an unæsthetic personage as Immanuel Kant enthroned in its centre! Think of german books on *religions-philosophie*, with the heart's battles translated into conceptual jargon and made dialectic. The most persistent setter of questions, feeler of objections, insister on satisfactions, is the religious life. Yet all its troubles can be treated with absurdly little technicality. The wonder is that, with their way of working philosophy,

19

individual Germans should preserve any spontaneity of mind at all. That they still manifest freshness and originality in so eminent a degree, proves the indestructible richness of the german cerebral endowment.

Let me repeat once more that a man's vision is the great fact about him. Who cares for Carlyle's reasons, or Schopenhauer's, or Spencer's ? A philosophy is the expression of a man's intimate character, and all definitions of the universe are but the deliberately adopted reactions of human characters upon it. In the recent book from which I quoted the words of Professor Paulsen, a book of successive chapters by various living german philosophers,[3] we pass from one idiosyncratic personal atmosphere into another almost as if we were turning over a photograph album.

If we take the whole history of philosophy, the systems reduce themselves to a few main types which, under all the technical verbiage in which the ingenious intellect of man envelops them, are just so many visions, modes of feeling the whole push, and seeing the whole drift of life, forced on one by one's total character and experience, and on the whole *preferred* — there is no other truthful word — as one's best working attitude. Cynical characters take one general attitude, sympathetic characters another. But no general attitude is possible towards the world as a whole, until the intellect has developed considerable generalizing power and learned to take pleasure in synthetic formulas. The thought of very primitive men has hardly any tincture of philosophy. Nature can have little unity for savages. It is a Walpurgis-nacht procession, a checkered play of light and shadow, a medley of impish and elfish friendly and inimical powers. 'Close to nature' though they live, they are anything but Wordsworthians. If a bit of cosmic emotion ever thrills them, it is likely to be at midnight, when the camp smoke rises straight to the wicked full moon in the zenith, and the forest is all whispering with witchery and danger. The eeriness of the world, the mischief and the manyness, the littleness of the forces, the magical surprises, the unaccountability of every agent,

these surely are the characters most impressive
at that stage of culture, these communicate the
thrills of curiosity and the earliest intellectual
stirrings. Tempests and conflagrations, pesti-
lences and earthquakes, reveal supramundane
powers, and instigate religious terror rather
than philosophy. Nature, more demonic than
divine, is above all things *multifarious*. So
many creatures that feed or threaten, that help
or crush, so many beings to hate or love, to
understand or start at — which is on top and
which subordinate? Who can tell? They are
co-ordinate, rather, and to adapt ourselves to
them singly, to 'square' the dangerous powers
and keep the others friendly, regardless of consistency or unity, is the chief problem. The
symbol of nature at this stage, as Paulsen well
says, is the sphinx, under whose nourishing
breasts the tearing claws are visible.

But in due course of time the intellect awoke,
with its passion for generalizing, simplifying,
and subordinating, and then began those diver-
gences of conception which all later experience
seems rather to have deepened than to have

effaced, because objective nature has contributed to both sides impartially, and has let the thinkers emphasize different parts of her, and pile up opposite imaginary supplements.

Perhaps the most interesting opposition is that which results from the clash between what I lately called the sympathetic and the cynical temper. Materialistic and spiritualistic philosophies are the rival types that result: the former defining the world so as to leave man's soul upon it as a sort of outside passenger or alien, while the latter insists that the intimate and human must surround and underlie the brutal. This latter is the spiritual way of thinking.

Now there are two very distinct types or stages in spiritualistic philosophy, and my next purpose in this lecture is to make their contrast evident. Both types attain the sought-for intimacy of view, but the one attains it somewhat less successfully than the other.

The generic term spiritualism, which I began by using merely as the opposite of materialism, thus subdivides into two species, the more intimate one of which is monistic and the less intimate dualistic. The dualistic species is the *theism* that reached its elaboration in the scholastic philosophy, while the monistic species is the *pantheism* spoken of sometimes simply as idealism, and sometimes as 'post-kantian' or 'absolute' idealism. Dualistic theism is professed as firmly as ever at all catholic seats of learning, whereas it has of late years tended to disappear at our british and american universities, and to be replaced by a monistic pantheism more or less open or disguised. I have an impression that ever since T. H. Green's time absolute idealism has been decidedly in the ascendent at Oxford. It is in the ascendent at my own university of Harvard.

Absolute idealism attains, I said, to the more intimate point of view; but the statement needs some explanation. So far as theism represents the world as God's world, and God as what Matthew Arnold called a magnified non-natural man, it would seem as if the inner quality of the world remained human, and as if our relations with it might be intimate enough — for what is best in ourselves appears then also outside of ourselves, and we and the universe are of the same spiritual species. So far, so good, then; and one might consequently ask, What more of intimacy do you require? To which the answer is that to be like a thing is not as intimate a relation as to be substantially fused into it, to form one continuous soul and body with it; and that pantheistic idealism, making us entitatively one with God, attains this higher reach of intimacy.

The theistic conception, picturing God and his creation as entities distinct from each other, still leaves the human subject outside of the deepest reality in the universe. God is from eternity complete, it says, and sufficient unto himself; he throws off the world by a free act and as an extraneous substance, and he throws off man as a third substance, extraneous to both the world and himself. Between them, God says 'one,' the world says 'two,' and man says 'three,' — that is the orthodox theistic view. And orthodox theism has been so jealous of God's glory that it has taken pains to exaggerate everything in the notion of him that could make for isolation and separateness. Page upon page in scholastic books go to prove that God is in no sense implicated by his creative act, or involved in his creation. That his relation to the creatures he has made should make any difference to him, carry any consequence, or qualify his being, is repudiated as a pantheistic slur upon his self-sufficingness. I said a moment ago that theism treats us and God as of the same species, but from the orthodox point of view that was a slip of language. God and his creatures are *toto genere* distinct in the scholastic theology, they have absolutely *nothing* in common; nay, it degrades God to attribute to him any generic nature whatever; he can be classed with nothing. There is a sense, then, in which philosophic theism makes us outsiders and keeps us foreigners in relation to God, in which, at any rate, his connexion with us appears as unilateral and not reciprocal. His action can affect us, but he can never be affected by our reaction. Our relation, in short, is not a strictly social relation. Of course in common men's religion the relation is believed to be social, but that is only one of the many differences between religion and theology.

This essential dualism of the theistic view has all sorts of collateral consequences. Man being an outsider and a mere subject to God, not his intimate partner, a character of externality invades the field. God is not heart of our heart and reason of our reason, but our magistrate, rather; and mechanically to obey his commands, however strange they may be, remains our only moral duty. Conceptions of criminal law have in fact played a great part in defining our relations with him. Our relations with speculative truth show the same externality. One of our duties is to know truth, and rationalist thinkers have always assumed it to be our sovereign duty. But in scholastic theism we find truth already instituted and established without our help, complete apart from our knowing; and the most we can do is to acknowledge it passively and adhere to it, altho such adhesion as ours can make no jot of difference to what is adhered to. The situation here again is radically dualistic. It is not as if the world came to know itself, or God came to know himself, partly through us, as pantheistic idealists have maintained, but truth exists *per se* and absolutely, by God's grace and decree, no matter who of us knows it or is ignorant, and it would continue to exist unaltered, even though we finite knowers were all annihilated.

It has to be confessed that this dualism and lack of intimacy has always operated as a drag and handicap on christian thought. Orthodox theology has had to wage a steady fight within the schools against the various forms of pantheistic heresy which the mystical experiences of religious persons, on the one hand, and the formal or æsthetic superiorities of monism to dualism, on the other, kept producing. God as intimate soul and reason of the universe has always seemed to some people a more worthy conception than God as external creator. So conceived, he appeared to unify the world more perfectly, he made it less finite and mechanical, and in comparison with such a God an external creator seemed more like the product of a childish fancy. I have been told by Hindoos that the great obstacle to the spread of Christianity in their country is the puerility of our dogma of creation. It has not sweep and infinity enough to meet the requirements of even the illiterate natives of India.

Assuredly most members of this audience are ready to side with Hinduism in this matter. Those of us who are sexagenarians have witnessed in our own persons one of those gradual mutations of intellectual climate, due to innumerable influences, that make the thought of a past generation seem as foreign to its successor as if it were the expression of a different race of men. The theological machinery that spoke so livingly to our ancestors, with its finite age of the world, its creation out of nothing, its juridical morality and eschatology, its relish for rewards and punishments, its treatment of God as an external contriver, an 'intelligent and moral governor,' sounds as odd to most of us as if it were some outlandish savage religion.

The vaster vistas which scientific evolutionism has opened, and the rising tide of social democratic ideals, have changed the type of our imagination, and the older monarchical theism is obsolete or obsolescent. The place of the divine in the world must be more organic and intimate. An external creator and his institutions may still be verbally confessed at Church in formulas that linger by their mere inertia, but the life is out of them, we avoid dwelling on them, the sincere heart of us is elsewhere.

I shall leave cynical materialism entirely out of our discussion as not calling for treatment before this present audience, and I shall ignore old-fashioned dualistic theism for the same reason. Our contemporary mind having once for all grasped the possibility of a more intimate *weltanschauung*, the only opinions quite worthy of arresting our attention will fall within the general scope of what may roughly be called the pantheistic field of vision, the vision of God as the indwelling divine rather than the external creator, and of human life as part and parcel of that deep reality.

30

I. THE TYPES OF THINKING

As we have found that spiritualism in general breaks into a more intimate and a less intimate species, so the more intimate species itself breaks into two subspecies, of which the one is more monistic, the other more pluralistic in form. I say in form, for our vocabulary gets unmanageable if we don't distinguish between form and substance here. The inner life of things must be substantially akin anyhow to the tenderer parts of man's nature in any spiritualistic philosophy. The word 'intimacy' probably covers the essential difference. Materialism holds the foreign in things to be more primary and lasting, it sends us to a lonely corner with our intimacy. The brutal aspects overlap and outwear; refinement has the feebler and more ephemeral hold on reality.

From a pragmatic point of view the difference between living against a background of foreignness and one of intimacy means the difference between a general habit of wariness and one of trust. One might call it a social difference, for after all, the common *socius* of us all is the great universe whose children we are.

If materialistic, we must be suspicious of this socius, cautious, tense, on guard. If spiritualistic, we may give way, embrace, and keep no ultimate fear.

The contrast is rough enough, and can be cut across by all sorts of other divisions, drawn from other points of view than that of foreignness and intimacy. We have so many different businesses with nature that no one of them yields us an all-embracing clasp. The philosophic attempt to define nature so that no one's business is left out, so that no one lies outside the door saying 'Where do *I* come in?' is sure in advance to fail. The most a philosophy can hope for is not to lock out any interest forever. No matter what doors it closes, it must leave other doors open for the interests which it neglects. I have begun by shutting ourselves up to intimacy and foreignness because that makes so generally interesting a contrast, and because it will conveniently introduce a farther contrast to which I wish this hour to lead.

The majority of men are sympathetic. Comparatively few are cynics because they like cynicism, and most of our existing materialists are such because they think the evidence of facts impels them, or because they find the idealists they are in contact with too private and tender-minded; so, rather than join their company, they fly to the opposite extreme. I therefore propose to you to disregard materialists altogether for the present, and to consider the sympathetic party alone.

It is normal, I say, to be sympathetic in the sense in which I use the term. Not to demand intimate relations with the universe, and not to wish them satisfactory, should be accounted signs of something wrong. Accordingly when minds of this type reach the philosophic level, and seek some unification of their vision, they find themselves compelled to correct that aboriginal appearance of things by which savages are not troubled. That sphinx-like presence, with its breasts and claws, that first bald multifariousness, is too discrepant an object for philosophic contemplation. The intimacy and the foreignness cannot be written down as simply coexisting. An order must be made; and in that order the higher side of things must dominate. The philosophy of the absolute agrees with the pluralistic philosophy which I am going to contrast with it in these lectures, in that both identify human substance with the divine substance. But whereas absolutism thinks that the said substance becomes fully divine only in the form of totality, and is not its real self in any form but the *all*-form, the pluralistic view which I prefer to adopt is willing to believe that there may ultimately never be an all-form at all, that the substance of reality may never get totally collected, that some of it may remain outside of the largest combination of it ever made, and that a distributive form of reality, the *each*-form, is logically as acceptable and empirically as probable as the all-form commonly acquiesced in as so obviously the self-evident thing. The contrast between these two forms of a reality which we will agree to suppose substantially spiritual is practically the topic of this course of lectures. You see now what I mean by pantheism's two subspecies. If we give to the monistic subspecies the name of philosophy of the absolute, we may give that of radical empiricism to its pluralistic rival, and it may be well to distinguish them occasionally later by these names.

As a convenient way of entering into the study of their differences, I may refer to a recent article by Professor Jacks of Manchester College. Professor Jacks, in some brilliant pages in the 'Hibbert Journal' for last October, studies the relation between the universe and the philosopher who describes and defines it for us. You may assume two cases, he says. Either what the philosopher tells us is extraneous to the universe he is accounting for, an indifferent parasitic outgrowth, so to speak; or the fact of his philosophizing is itself one of the things taken account of in the philosophy, and self-included in the description. In the former case the philosopher means by the universe everything *except* what his own presence brings; in the latter case his philosophy is itself an intimate part of the universe, and may be a

part momentous enough to give a different turn
to what the other parts signify. It may be a
supreme reaction of the universe upon itself
by which it rises to self-comprehension. It
may handle itself differently in consequence
of this event.

Now both empiricism and absolutism bring
the philosopher inside and make man intimate,
but the one being pluralistic and the other
monistic, they do so in differing ways that
need much explanation. Let me then contrast
the one with the other way of representing the
status of the human thinker.

For monism the world is no collection, but
one great all-inclusive fact outside of which is
nothing — nothing is its only alternative. When
the monism is idealistic, this all-enveloping fact
is represented as an absolute mind that makes
the partial facts by thinking them, just as we
make objects in a dream by dreaming them, or
personages in a story by imagining them. To
be, on this scheme, is, on the part of a finite
thing, to be an object for the absolute; and on
the part of the absolute it is to be the thinker of

36

that assemblage of objects. If we use the word 'content' here, we see that the absolute and the world have an identical content. The absolute is nothing but the knowledge of those objects; the objects are nothing but what the absolute knows. The world and the all-thinker thus compenetrate and soak each other up without residuum. They are but two names for the same identical material, considered now from the subjective, and now from the objective point of view — gedanke and gedachtes, as we would say if we were Germans. We philosophers naturally form part of the material, on the monistic scheme. The absolute makes us by thinking us, and if we ourselves are enlightened enough to be believers in the absolute, one may then say that our philosophizing is one of the ways in which the absolute is conscious of itself. This is the full pantheistic scheme, the *identitätsphilosophie*, the immanence of God in his creation, a conception sublime from its tremendous unity. And yet that unity is incomplete, as closer examination will show.

The absolute and the world are one fact, I

said, when materially considered. Our philosophy, for example, is not numerically distinct from the absolute's own knowledge of itself, not a duplicate and copy of it, it is part of that very knowledge, is numerically identical with as much of it as our thought covers. The absolute just *is* our philosophy, along with everything else that is known, in an act of knowing which (to use the words of my gifted absolutist colleague Royce) forms in its wholeness one luminously transparent conscious moment.

But one as we are in this material sense with the absolute substance, that being only the whole of us, and we only the parts of it, yet in a formal sense something like a pluralism breaks out. When we speak of the absolute we *take* the one universal known material collectively or integrally; when we speak of its objects, of our finite selves, etc., we *take* that same identical material distributively and separately. But what is the use of a thing's *being* only once if it can be *taken* twice over, and if being taken in different ways makes different things true of it? As the absolute takes me, for example, I appear *with* everything else in its field of perfect knowledge. As I take myself, I appear *without* most other things in my field of relative ignorance. And practical differences result from its knowledge and my ignorance. Ignorance breeds mistake, curiosity, misfortune, pain, for me; I suffer those consequences. The absolute knows of those things, of course, for it knows me and my suffering, but it does n't itself suffer. It can't be ignorant, for simultaneous with its knowledge of each question goes its knowledge of each answer. It can't be patient, for it has to wait for nothing, having everything at once in its possession. It can't be surprised; it can't be guilty. No attribute connected with succession can be applied to it, for it is all at once and wholly what it is, 'with the unity of a single instant,' and succession is not of it but in it, for we are continually told that it is ' timeless.'

Things true of the world in its finite aspects, then, are not true of it in its infinite capacity. *Quâ* finite and plural its accounts of itself to itself are different from what its account to itself *quâ* infinite and one must be.

With this radical discrepancy between the absolute and the relative points of view, it seems to me that almost as great a bar to intimacy between the divine and the human breaks out in pantheism as that which we found in monarchical theism, and hoped that pantheism might not show. We humans are incurably rooted in the temporal point of view. The eternal's ways are utterly unlike our ways. 'Let us imitate the All,' said the original prospectus of that admirable Chicago quarterly called the 'Monist.' As if we could, either in thought or conduct! We are invincibly parts, let us talk as we will, and must always apprehend the absolute as if it were a foreign being. If what I mean by this is not wholly clear to you at this point, it ought to grow clearer as my lectures proceed.

II

MONISTIC IDEALISM

LECTURE II

MONISTIC IDEALISM

LET me recall to you the programme which I indicated to you at our last meeting. After agreeing not to consider materialism in any shape, but to place ourselves straightway upon a more spiritualistic platform, I pointed out three kinds of spiritual philosophy between which we are asked to choose. The first way was that of the older dualistic theism, with ourselves represented as a secondary order of substances created by God. We found that this allowed of a degree of intimacy with the creative principle inferior to that implied in the pantheistic belief that we are substantially one with it, and that the divine is therefore the most intimate of all our possessions, heart of our heart, in fact. But we saw that this pantheistic belief could be held in two forms, a monistic form which I called philosophy of the absolute, and a pluralistic form which I called radical empiricism, the former conceiving that the divine exists authentically only when the world is experienced all at once in its absolute totality, whereas radical empiricism allows that the absolute sum-total of things may never be actually experienced or realized in that shape at all, and that a disseminated, distributed, or incompletely unified appearance is the only form that reality may yet have achieved.

I may contrast the monistic and pluralistic forms in question as the 'all-form' and the 'each-form.' At the end of the last hour I animadverted on the fact that the all-form is so radically different from the each-form, which is our human form of experiencing the world, that the philosophy of the absolute, so far as insight and understanding go, leaves us almost as much outside of the divine being as dualistic theism does. I believe that radical empiricism, on the contrary, holding to the each-form, and making of God only one of the eaches, affords the higher degree of intimacy. The general thesis of these lectures I said would be a defence of the pluralistic against the monistic view. Think of the universe as existing

solely in the each-form, and you will have on
the whole a more reasonable and satisfactory
idea of it than if you insist on the all-form being
necessary. The rest of my lectures will do little
more than make this thesis more concrete, and
I hope more persuasive.

It is curious how little countenance radical
pluralism has ever had from philosophers.
Whether materialistically or spiritualistically
minded, philosophers have always aimed at
cleaning up the litter with which the world
apparently is filled. They have substituted
economical and orderly conceptions for the
first sensible tangle; and whether these were
morally elevated or only intellectually neat,
they were at any rate always æsthetically pure
and definite, and aimed at ascribing to the
world something clean and intellectual in the
way of inner structure. As compared with all
these rationalizing pictures, the pluralistic empiricism which I profess offers but a sorry
appearance. It is a turbid, muddled, gothic
sort of an affair, without a sweeping outline
and with little pictorial nobility. Those of you

who are accustomed to the classical constructions of reality may be excused if your first reaction upon it be absolute contempt—a shrug
of the shoulders as if such ideas were unworthy of explicit refutation. But one must have
lived some time with a system to appreciate
its merits. Perhaps a little more familiarity
may mitigate your first surprise at such a programme as I offer.

First, one word more than what I said last
time about the relative foreignness of the divine
principle in the philosophy of the absolute.
Those of you who have read the last two chapters of Mr. Bradley's wonderful book, 'Appearance and reality,' will remember what
an elaborately foreign aspect *his* absolute is
finally made to assume. It is neither intelligence nor will, neither a self nor a collection of
selves, neither truthful, good, nor beautiful, as
we understand these terms. It is, in short, a
metaphysical monster, all that we are permitted to say of it being that whatever it is, it is at
any rate *worth* more (worth more to itself, that
is) than if any eulogistic adjectives of ours

applied to it. It is us, and all other appearances, but none of us *as such*, for in it we are all 'transmuted,' and its own as-suchness is of another denomination altogether.

Spinoza was the first great absolutist, and the impossibility of being intimate with *his* God is universally recognized. *Quatenus infinitus est* he is other than what he is *quatenus humanam mentem constituit*. Spinoza's philosophy has been rightly said to be worked by the word *quatenus*. Conjunctions, prepositions, and adverbs play indeed the vital part in all philosophies; and in contemporary idealism the words 'as' and 'quâ' bear the burden of reconciling metaphysical unity with phenomenal diversity. Quâ absolute the world is one and perfect, quâ relative it is many and faulty, yet it is identically the self-same world — instead of talking of it as many facts, we call it one fact in many aspects.

As absolute, then, or *sub specie eternitatis*, or *quatenus infinitus est*, the world repels our sympathy because it has no history. *As such,* the absolute neither acts nor suffers, nor loves

nor hates; it has no needs, desires, or aspira-
tions, no failures or successes, friends or enemies, victories or defeats. All such things per-
tain to the world quâ relative, in which our
finite experiences lie, and whose vicissitudes
alone have power to arouse our interest. What
boots it to tell me that the absolute way is the
true way, and to exhort me, as Emerson says,
to lift mine eye up to its style, and manners of
the sky, if the feat is impossible by definition?
I am finite once for all, and all the categories of
my sympathy are knit up with the finite world
as such, and with things that have a history.
'Aus dieser erde quellen meine freuden, und
ihre sonne scheinet meinen leiden.' I have
neither eyes nor ears nor heart nor mind for
anything of an opposite description, and the
stagnant felicity of the absolute's own perfection moves me as little as I move it. If we
were *readers* only of the cosmic novel, things
would be different: we should then share the
author's point of view and recognize villains
to be as essential as heroes in the plot. But
we are not the readers but the very personages

of the world-drama. In your own eyes each of you here is its hero, and the villains are your respective friends or enemies. The tale which the absolute reader finds so perfect, we spoil for one another through our several vital identifications with the destinies of the particular personages involved.

The doctrine on which the absolutists lay most stress is the absolute's 'timeless' character. For pluralists, on the other hand, time remains as real as anything, and nothing in the universe is great or static or eternal enough not to have some history. But the world that each of us feels most intimately at home with is that of beings with histories that play into our history, whom we can help in their vicissitudes even as they help us in ours. This satisfaction the absolute denies us; we can neither help nor hinder it, for it stands outside of history. It surely is a merit in a philosophy to make the very life we lead seem real and earnest. Pluralism, in exorcising the absolute, exorcises the great de-realizer of the only life we are at home in, and thus redeems the nature of reality from essential foreignness. Every end, reason, motive, object of desire or aversion, ground of sorrow or joy that we feel is in the world of finite multifariousness, for only in that world does anything really happen, only there do events come to pass.

In one sense this is a far-fetched and rather childish objection, for so much of the history of the finite is as formidably foreign to us as the static absolute can possibly be — in fact that entity derives its own foreignness largely from the bad character of the finite which it simultaneously is — that this sentimental reason for preferring the pluralistic view seems small.[1] I shall return to the subject in my final lecture, and meanwhile, with your permission, I will say no more about this objection. The more so as the necessary foreignness of the absolute is cancelled emotionally by its attribute of *totality*, which is universally considered to carry the further attribute of *perfection* in its train. 'Philosophy,' says a recent american philosopher, 'is humanity's hold on totality,' and there is no doubt that most of us find

50

that the bare notion of an absolute all-one is
inspiring. 'I yielded myself to the perfect
whole,' writes Emerson; and where can you
find a more mind-dilating object? A certain
loyalty is called forth by the idea; even if not
proved actual, it must be believed in somehow.
Only an enemy of philosophy can speak lightly
of it. Rationalism starts from the idea of such
a whole and builds downward. Movement and
change are absorbed into its immutability as
forms of mere appearance. When you accept
this beatific vision of what *is*, in contrast with
what *goes on*, you feel as if you had fulfilled
an intellectual duty. 'Reality is not in its
truest nature a process,' Mr. McTaggart tells
us, 'but a stable and timeless state.'[2] 'The
true knowledge of God begins,' Hegel writes,
'when we know that things as they immediately are have no truth.'[3] 'The consummation of the infinite aim,' he says elsewhere,
'consists merely in removing the illusion which
makes it seem yet unaccomplished. Good and
absolute goodness is eternally accomplishing
itself in the world: and the result is that it needs

not wait upon *us*, but is already . . . accomplished. It is an illusion under which we live.
. . . In the course of its process the Idea makes itself that illusion, by setting an antithesis to confront it, and its action consists in getting rid of the illusion which it has created.' ⁴

But abstract emotional appeals of any kind sound amateurish in the business that concerns us. Impressionistic philosophizing, like impressionistic watchmaking or land-surveying, is intolerable to experts. Serious discussion of the alternative before us forces me, therefore, to become more technical. The great *claim* of the philosophy of the absolute is that the absolute is no hypothesis, but a presupposition implicated in all thinking, and needing only a little effort of analysis to be seen as a logical necessity. I will therefore take it in this more rigorous character and see whether its claim is in effect so coercive.

It has seemed coercive to an enormous number of contemporaneous thinkers. Professor Henry Jones thus describes the range and influence of it upon the social and political life of the present time: [5] 'For many years adherents of this way of thought have deeply interested the british public by their writings. Almost more important than their writings is the fact that they have occupied philosophical chairs in almost every university in the kingdom. Even the professional critics of idealism are for the most part idealists — after a fashion. And when they are not, they are as a rule more occupied with the refutation of idealism than with the construction of a better theory. It follows from their position of academic authority, were it from nothing else, that idealism exercises an influence not easily measured upon the youth of the nation — upon those, that is, who from the educational opportunities they enjoy may naturally be expected to become the leaders of the nation's thought and practice. . . . Difficult as it is to measure the forces . . . it is hardly to be denied that the power exercised by Bentham and the utilitarian school has, for better or for worse, passed into the hands of the idealists. . . . "The Rhine has flowed into the Thames" is the warning note rung out by

Mr. Hobhouse. Carlyle introduced it, bringing it as far as Chelsea. Then Jowett and Thomas Hill Green, and William Wallace and Lewis Nettleship, and Arnold Toynbee and David Ritchie — to mention only those teachers whose voices now are silent — guided the waters into those upper reaches known locally as the Isis. John and Edward Caird brought them up the Clyde, Hutchison Stirling up the Firth of Forth. They have passed up the Mersey and up the Severn and Dee and Don. They pollute the bay of St. Andrews and swell the waters of the Cam, and have somehow crept overland into Birmingham. The stream of german idealism has been diffused over the academical world of Great Britain. The disaster is universal.'

Evidently if weight of authority were all, the truth of absolutism would be thus decided. But let us first pass in review the general style of argumentation of that philosophy.

As I read it, its favorite way of meeting pluralism and empiricism is by a *reductio ad absurdum* framed somewhat as follows: You contend, it says to the pluralist, that things, though

54

in some respects connected, are in other respects independent, so that they are not members of one all-inclusive individual fact. Well, your position is absurd on either point. For admit in fact the slightest modicum of independence, and you find (if you will only think accurately) that you have to admit more and more of it, until at last nothing but an absolute chaos, or the proved impossibility of any connexion whatever between the parts of the universe, remains upon your hands. Admit, on the other hand, the most incipient minimum of relation between any two things, and again you can't stop until you see that the absolute unity of all things is implied.

If we take the latter *reductio ad absurdum* first, we find a good example of it in Lotze's well-known proof of monism from the fact of interaction between finite things. Suppose, Lotze says in effect, and for simplicity's sake I have to paraphrase him, for his own words are too long to quote — many distinct beings a, b, c, etc., to exist independently of each other: *can a in that case ever act on b?*

What is it to act? Is it not to exert an influence? Does the influence detach itself from a and find b? If so, it is a third fact, and the problem is not how a acts, but how its 'influence' acts on b. By another influence perhaps? And how in the end does the chain of influences find b rather than c unless b is somehow prefigured in them already? And when they have found b, how do they make b respond, if b has nothing in common with them? Why don't they go right through b? The change in b is a *response*, due to b's capacity for taking account of a's influence, and that again seems to prove that b's nature is somehow fitted to a's nature in advance. A and b, in short, are not really as distinct as we at first supposed them, not separated by a void. Were this so they would be mutually impenetrable, or at least mutually irrelevant. They would form two universes each living by itself, making no difference to each other, taking no account of each other, much as the universe of your day dreams takes no account of mine. They must therefore belong together beforehand, be co-implicated already, their natures must have an inborn mutual reference each to each.

Lotze's own solution runs as follows: The multiple independent things supposed cannot be real in that shape, but all of them, if reciprocal action is to be possible between them, must be regarded as parts of a single real being, M. The pluralism with which our view began has to give place to a monism; and the 'transeunt' interaction, being unintelligible as such, is to be understood as an immanent operation.[6]

The words 'immanent operation' seem here to mean that the single real being M, of which *a* and *b* are members, is the only thing that changes, and that when it changes, it changes inwardly and all over at once. When part *a* in it changes, consequently, part *b* must also change, but without the whole M changing this would not occur.

A pretty argument, but a purely verbal one, as I apprehend it. *Call* your *a* and *b* distinct, they can't interact; *call* them one, they can. For taken abstractly and without qualification

the words 'distinct' and 'independent' suggest
only disconnection. If this be the only property of your *a* and *b* (and it is the only property
your words imply), then of course, since you
can't deduce their mutual influence from *it*,
you can find no ground of its occurring between
them. Your bare word 'separate,' contradicting your bare word 'joined,' seems to exclude
connexion.

Lotze's remedy for the impossibility thus
verbally found is to change the first word. If,
instead of calling *a* and *b* independent, we now
call them 'interdependent,' 'united,' or 'one,'
he says, *these* words do not contradict any sort
of mutual influence that may be proposed. If
a and *b* are 'one,' and the one changes, *a* and *b*
of course must co-ordinately change. What
under the old name they could n't do, they now
have license to do under the new name.

But I ask you whether giving the name of
'one' to the former 'many' makes us really understand the modus operandi of interaction any
better. We have now given verbal permission
to the many to change all together, if they can;

we have removed a verbal impossibility and substituted a verbal possibility, but the new name, with the possibility it suggests, tells us nothing of the actual process by which real things that are one can and do change at all. In point of fact abstract oneness as such *does n't* change, neither has it parts — any more than abstract independence as such interacts. But then neither abstract oneness nor abstract independence *exists;* only concrete real things exist, which add to these properties the other properties which they possess, to make up what we call their total nature. To construe any one of their abstract names as *making their total nature impossible* is a misuse of the function of naming. The real way of rescue from the abstract consequences of one name is not to fly to an opposite name, equally abstract, but rather to correct the first name by qualifying adjectives that restore some concreteness to the case. Don't take your 'independence' *simpliciter*, as Lotze does, take it *secundum quid*. Only when we know what the process of interaction literally and concretely *consists* in can

59

we tell whether beings independent *in definite respects*, distinct, for example, in origin, separate in place, different in kind, etc., can or cannot interact.

The treating of a name as excluding from the fact named what the name's definition fails positively to include, is what I call 'vicious intellectualism.' Later I shall have more to say about this intellectualism, but that Lotze's argument is tainted by it I hardly think we can deny. As well might you contend (to use an instance from Sigwart) that a person whom you have once called an 'equestrian' is thereby forever made unable to walk on his own feet.

I almost feel as if I should apologize for criticising such subtle arguments in rapid lectures of this kind. The criticisms have to be as abstract as the arguments, and in exposing their unreality, take on such an unreal sound themselves that a hearer not nursed in the intellectualist atmosphere knows not which of them to accuse. But *le vin est versé, il faut le boire,* and I must cite a couple more instances before I stop.

II. MONISTIC IDEALISM

If we are empiricists and go from parts to wholes, we believe that beings may first exist and feed so to speak on their own existence, and then secondarily become known to one another. But philosophers of the absolute tell us that such independence of being from being known would, if once admitted, disintegrate the universe beyond all hope of mending. The argument is one of Professor Royce's proofs that the only alternative we have is to choose the complete disunion of all things or their complete union in the absolute One.

Take, for instance, the proverb 'a cat may look at a king' and adopt the realistic view that the king's being is independent of the cat's witnessing. This assumption, which amounts to saying that it need make no essential difference to the royal object whether the feline subject cognizes him or not, that the cat may look away from him or may even be annihilated, and the king remain unchanged,—this assumption, I say, is considered by my ingenious colleague to lead to the absurd practical consequence that the two beings *can* never later acquire any possible linkages or connexions, but must remain eternally as if in different worlds. For suppose any connexion whatever to ensue, this connexion would simply be a third being additional to the cat and the king, which would itself have to be linked to both by additional links before it could connect them, and so on *ad infinitum*, the argument, you see, being the same as Lotze's about how *a*'s influence does its influencing when it influences *b*.

In Royce's own words, if the king can be without the cat knowing him, then king and cat 'can have no common features, no ties, no true relations; they are separated, each from the other, by absolutely impassable chasms. They can never come to get either ties or community of nature; they are not in the same space, nor in the same time, nor in the same natural or spiritual order.' [7] They form in short two unrelated universes,—which is the *reductio ad absurdum* required.

To escape this preposterous state of things we must accordingly revoke the original hypothesis. The king and the cat are not indifferent to each other in the way supposed. But if not in that way, then in no way, for connexion in that way carries connexion in other ways; so that, pursuing the reverse line of reasoning, we end with the absolute itself as the smallest fact that can exist. Cat and king are co-involved, they are a single fact in two names, they can never have been absent from each other, and they are both equally co-implicated with all the other facts of which the universe consists.

Professor Royce's proof that whoso admits the cat's witnessing the king at all must thereupon admit the integral absolute, may be briefly put as follows:—

First, to know the king, the cat must intend *that* king, must somehow pass over and lay hold of him individually and specifically. The cat's idea, in short, must transcend the cat's own separate mind and somehow include the king, for were the king utterly outside and independent of the cat, the cat's pure other, the beast's mind could touch the king in no wise. This makes the cat much less distinct from the king than we had at first naïvely supposed.

There must be some prior continuity between them, which continuity Royce interprets ideal- istically as meaning a higher mind that owns them both as objects, and owning them can also own any relation, such as the supposed wit- nessing, that may obtain between them. Taken purely pluralistically, neither of them can own any part of a *between*, because, so taken, each is supposed shut up to itself: the fact of a *between* thus commits us to a higher knower.

But the higher knower that knows the two beings we start with proves to be the same knower that knows everything else. For as- sume any third being, the queen, say, and as the cat knew the king, so let the king know his queen, and let this second knowledge, by the same reasoning, require a higher knower as its presupposition. That knower of the king's knowing must, it is now contended, be the same higher knower that was required for the cat's knowing; for if you suppose otherwise, you have no longer the *same king*. This may not seem immediately obvious, but if you fol- low the intellectualistic logic employed in all these reasonings, I don't see how you can escape the admission. If it be true that the independent or indifferent cannot be related, for the abstract words 'independent' or 'indifferent' as such imply no relation, then it is just as true that the king known by the cat cannot be the king that knows the queen, for taken merely 'as such,' the abstract term 'what the cat knows' and the abstract term 'what knows the queen' are logically distinct. The king thus logically breaks into two kings, with nothing to connect them, until a higher knower is introduced to recognize them as the self-same king concerned in any previous acts of knowledge which he may have brought about. This he can do because he possesses all the terms as his own objects and can treat them as he will. Add any fourth or fifth term, and you get a like result, and so on, until at last an all-owning knower, otherwise called the absolute, is reached. The co-implicated 'through-and-through' world of monism thus stands proved by irrefutable logic, and all pluralism appears as absurd.

The reasoning is pleasing from its ingenuity,

and it is almost a pity that so straight a bridge from abstract logic to concrete fact should not bear our weight. To have the alternative forced upon us of admitting either finite things each cut off from all relation with its environment, or else of accepting the integral absolute with no environment and all relations packed within itself, would be too delicious a simplification. But the purely verbal character of the operation is undisguised. Because the *names* of finite things and their relations are disjoined, it does n't follow that the realities named need a *deus ex machina* from on high to conjoin them. The same things disjoined in one respect *appear* as conjoined in another. Naming the disjunction does n't debar us from also naming the conjunction in a later modifying statement, for the two are absolutely co-ordinate elements in the finite tissue of experience. When at Athens it was found self-contradictory that a boy could be both tall and short (tall namely in respect of a child, short in respect of a man), the absolute had not yet been thought of, but it might just as well have been invoked

by Socrates as by Lotze or Royce, as a relief
from his peculiar intellectualistic difficulty.

Everywhere we find rationalists using the
same kind of reasoning. The primal whole
which is their vision must be there not only as a
fact but as a logical necessity. It must be the
minimum that can exist — either that absolute
whole is there, or there is absolutely nothing.
The logical proof alleged of the irrationality of
supposing otherwise, is that you can deny the
whole only in words that implicitly assert it.
If you say 'parts,' of *what* are they parts? If
you call them a 'many,' that very word unifies
them. If you suppose them unrelated in any
particular respect, that 'respect' connects
them; and so on. In short you fall into hope-
less contradiction. You must stay either at one
extreme or the other.[8] 'Partly this and partly
that,' partly rational, for instance, and partly
irrational, is no admissible description of the
world. If rationality be in it at all, it must be
in it throughout; if irrationality be in it anywhere, that also must pervade it throughout.
It must be wholly rational or wholly irrational,

pure universe or pure multiverse or nulliverse; and reduced to this violent alternative, no one's choice ought long to remain doubtful. The individual absolute, with its parts co-implicated through and through, so that there is nothing in any part by which any other part can remain inwardly unaffected, is the only rational supposition. Connexions of an external sort, by which the many became merely continuous instead of being consubstantial, would be an irrational supposition.

Mr. Bradley is the pattern champion of this philosophy *in extremis*, as one might call it, for he shows an intolerance to pluralism so extreme that I fancy few of his readers have been able fully to share it. His reasoning exemplifies everywhere what I call the vice of intellectualism, for abstract terms are used by him as positively excluding all that their definition fails to include. Some Greek sophists could deny that we may say that man is good, for man, they said, means only man, and good means only good, and the word *is* can't be construed to identify such disparate meanings.

II. MONISTIC IDEALISM

Mr. Bradley revels in the same type of argument. No adjective can rationally qualify a substantive, he thinks, for if distinct from the substantive, it can't be united with it; and if not distinct, there is only one thing there, and nothing left to unite. Our whole pluralistic procedure in using subjects and predicates as we do is fundamentally irrational, an example of the desperation of our finite intellectual estate, infected and undermined as that is by the separatist discursive forms which are our only categories, but which absolute reality must somehow absorb into its unity and overcome.

Readers of 'Appearance and reality' will remember how Mr. Bradley suffers from a difficulty identical with that to which Lotze and Royce fall a prey — how shall an influence influence? how shall a relation relate? Any conjunctive relation between two phenomenal experiences a and b must, in the intellectualist philosophy of these authors, be itself a third entity; and as such, instead of bridging the one original chasm, it can only create two smaller chasms, each to be freshly bridged. Instead of hooking *a* to *b*, it needs itself to be hooked by a fresh relation *r′* to *a* and by another *r″* to *b*. These new relations are but two more entities which themselves require to be hitched in turn by four still newer relations — so behold the vertiginous *regressus ad infinitum* in full career.

Since a *regressus ad infinitum* is deemed absurd, the notion that relations come 'between' their terms must be given up. No mere external go-between can logically connect. What occurs must be more intimate. The hooking must be a penetration, a possession. The relation must *involve* the terms, each term must involve *it*, and merging thus their being in it, they must somehow merge their being in each other, tho, as they seem still phenomenally so separate, we can never conceive exactly how it is that they are inwardly one. The absolute, however, must be supposed able to perform the unifying feat in his own inscrutable fashion.

In old times, whenever a philosopher was assailed for some particularly tough absurdity

in his system, he was wont to parry the attack
by the argument from the divine omnipotence.
'Do you mean to limit God's power?' he
would reply: 'do you mean to say that God
could not, if he would, do this or that?' This
retort was supposed to close the mouths of all
objectors of properly decorous mind. The
functions of the bradleian absolute are in this
particular identical with those of the theistic
God. Suppositions treated as too absurd to
pass muster in the finite world which we inhabit, the absolute must be able to make good
'somehow' in his ineffable way. First we hear
Mr. Bradley convicting things of absurdity;
next, calling on the absolute to vouch for them
quand même. Invoked for no other duty, that
duty it must and shall perform.

The strangest discontinuity of our world of
appearance with the supposed world of absolute reality is asserted both by Bradley and by
Royce; and both writers, the latter with great
ingenuity, seek to soften the violence of the jolt.
But it remains violent all the same, and is felt
to be so by most readers. Whoever feels the

violence strongly sees as on a diagram in just what the peculiarity of all this philosophy of the absolute consists. First, there is a healthy faith that the world must be rational and self-consistent. 'All science, all real knowledge, all experience presuppose,' as Mr. Ritchie writes, 'a coherent universe.' Next, we find a loyal clinging to the rationalist belief that sense-data and their associations are incoherent, and that only in substituting a conceptual order for their order can truth be found. Third, the substituted conceptions are treated intellectualistically, that is as mutually exclusive and discontinuous, so that the first innocent continuity of the flow of sense-experience is shattered for us without any higher conceptual continuity taking its place. Finally, since this broken state of things is intolerable, the absolute *deus ex machina* is called on to mend it in his own way, since we cannot mend it in ours.

Any other picture than this of post-kantian absolutism I am unable to frame. I see the intellectualistic criticism destroying the immediately given coherence of the phenomenal world, but unable to make its own conceptual substitutes cohere, and I see the resort to the absolute for a coherence of a higher type. The situation has dramatic liveliness, but it is inwardly incoherent throughout, and the question inevitably comes up whether a mistake may not somewhere have crept in in the process that has brought it about. May not the remedy lie rather in revising the intellectualist criticism than in first adopting it and then trying to undo its consequences by an arbitrary act of faith in an unintelligible agent. May not the flux of sensible experience itself contain a rationality that has been overlooked, so that the real remedy would consist in harking back to it more intelligently, and not in advancing in the opposite direction away from it and even away beyond the intellectualist criticism that disintegrates it, to the pseudo-rationality of the supposed absolute point of view. I myself believe that this is the real way to keep rationality in the world, and that the traditional rationalism has always been facing in the wrong direction. I hope in the end to make you share, or at any rate respect, this belief, but there is much to talk of before we get to that point.

I employed the word 'violent' just now in describing the dramatic situation in which it pleases the philosophy of the absolute to make its camp. I don't see how any one can help being struck in absolutist writings by that curious tendency to fly to violent extremes of which I have already said a word. The universe must be rational; well and good; but *how* rational? in what sense of that eulogistic but ambiguous word? — this would seem to be the next point to bring up. There are surely degrees in rationality that might be discriminated and described. Things can be consistent or coherent in very diverse ways. But no more in its conception of rationality than in its conception of relations can the monistic mind suffer the notion of more or less. Rationality is one and indivisible: if not rational thus indivisibly, the universe must be completely irrational, and no shadings or mixtures or compromises can obtain. Mr. McTaggart writes, in discussing the notion of a mixture: 'The two principles, of rationality and irrationality, to which the universe is then referred, will have to be absolutely separate and independent. For if there were any common unity to which they should be referred, it would be that unity and not its two manifestations which would be the ultimate explanation . . . and the theory, having thus become monistic,'[9] would resolve itself into the same alternative once more: is the single principle rational through and through or not?

'Can a plurality of reals be possible?' asks Mr. Bradley, and answers, 'No, impossible.' For it would mean a number of beings not dependent on each other, and this independence their plurality would contradict. For to be 'many' is to be related, the word having no meaning unless the units are somehow taken together, and it is impossible to take them in a sort of unreal void, so they must belong to a larger reality, and so carry the essence of the units beyond their proper selves, into a whole which possesses unity and is a larger system.[10]

Either absolute independence or absolute mutual dependence — this, then, is the only alternative allowed by these thinkers. Of course 'independence,' if absolute, would be preposterous, so the only conclusion allowable is that, in Ritchie's words, 'every single event is ultimately related to every other, and determined by the whole to which it belongs.' The whole complete block-universe through-and-through, therefore, or no universe at all!

Professor Taylor is so *naïf* in this habit of thinking only in extremes that he charges the pluralists with cutting the ground from under their own feet in not consistently following it themselves. What pluralists say is that a universe really connected loosely, after the pattern of our daily experience, is possible, and that for certain reasons it is the hypothesis to be preferred. What Professor Taylor thinks they naturally must or should say is that any other sort of universe is logically impossible, and that a totality of things interrelated like the world of the monists is not an hypothesis that can be seriously thought out at all.[11]

II. MONISTIC IDEALISM

Meanwhile no sensible pluralist ever flies or wants to fly to this dogmatic extreme.

If chance is spoken of as an ingredient of the universe, absolutists interpret it to mean that double sevens are as likely to be thrown out of a dice box as double sixes are. If free-will is spoken of, that must mean that an english general is as likely to eat his prisoners to-day as a Maori chief was a hundred years ago. It is as likely — I am using Mr. McTaggart's examples — that a majority of Londoners will burn themselves alive to-morrow as that they will partake of food, as likely that I shall be hanged for brushing my hair as for committing a murder,[12] and so forth, through various suppositions that no indeterminist ever sees real reason to make.

This habit of thinking only in the most violent extremes reminds me of what Mr. Wells says of the current objections to socialism, in his wonderful little book, 'New worlds for old.' The commonest vice of the human mind is its disposition to see everything as yes or no, as black or white, its incapacity for discrimination of intermediate shades. So the critics agree to some hard and fast impossible definition of socialism, and extract absurdities from it as a conjurer gets rabbits from a hat. Socialism abolishes property, abolishes the family, and the rest. The method, Mr. Wells continues, is always the same: It is to assume that whatever the socialist postulates as desirable is wanted without limit of qualification, — for socialist read pluralist and the parallel holds good, — it is to imagine that whatever proposal is made by him is to be carried out by uncontrolled monomaniacs, and so to make a picture of the socialist dream which can be presented to the simple-minded person in doubt —'This is socialism'—or pluralism, as the case may be. 'Surely! — SURELY! you don't want *this!*'

How often have I been replied to, when expressing doubts of the logical necessity of the absolute, of flying to the opposite extreme: 'But surely, SURELY there must be *some* connexion among things!' As if I must necessarily be an uncontrolled monomanic insanely denying any connexion whatever. The whole question revolves in very truth about the word 'some.' Radical empiricism and pluralism stand out for the legitimacy of the notion of *some:* each part of the world is in some ways connected, in some other ways not connected with its other parts, and the ways can be discriminated, for many of them are obvious, and their differences are obvious to view. Absolutism, on its side, seems to hold that 'some' is a category ruinously infected with self-contradictoriness, and that the only categories inwardly consistent and therefore pertinent to reality are 'all' and 'none.'

The question runs into the still more general one with which Mr. Bradley and later writers of the monistic school have made us abundantly familiar — the question, namely, whether all the relations with other things, possible to a being, are pre-included in its intrinsic nature and enter into its essence, or whether, in respect to some of these relations, it can *be* without reference to them, and, if it ever does enter into them, do so adventitiously and as it were by an after-thought. This is the great question as to whether 'external' relations can exist. They seem to, undoubtedly. My manuscript, for example, is ' on' the desk. The relation of being ' on' does n't seem to implicate or involve in any way the inner meaning of the manuscript or the inner structure of the desk — these objects engage in it only by their outsides, it seems only a temporary accident in their respective histories. Moreover, the ' on' fails to appear to our senses as one of those unintelligible 'betweens' that have to be separately hooked on the terms they pretend to connect. All this innocent sense-appearance, however, we are told, cannot pass muster in the eyes of reason. It is a tissue of self-contradiction which only the complete absorption of the desk and the manuscript into the higher unity of a more absolute reality can overcome.

The reasoning by which this conclusion is supported is too subtle and complicated to be properly dealt with in a public lecture, and you will thank me for not inviting you to consider it at all.[13] I feel the more free to pass it by now as I think that the cursory account of the absolutistic attitude which I have already given is sufficient for our present purpose, and that my own verdict on the philosophy of the absolute as 'not proven'—please observe that I go no farther now—need not be backed by argument at every special point. Flanking operations are less costly and in some ways more effective than frontal attacks. Possibly you will yourselves think after hearing my remaining lectures that the alternative of an universe absolutely rational or absolutely irrational is forced and strained, and that a *via media* exists which some of you may agree with me is to be preferred. *Some* rationality certainly does characterize our universe; and, weighing one kind with another, we may deem that the incomplete kinds that appear are on the whole as acceptable as the through-and-through sort of rationality on which the monistic systematizers insist.

All the said systematizers who have written since Hegel have owed their inspiration largely to him. Even when they have found no use for his particular triadic dialectic, they have drawn confidence and courage from his authoritative and conquering tone. I have said nothing about Hegel in this lecture, so I must repair the omission in the next.

III

HEGEL AND HIS METHOD

LECTURE III

HEGEL AND HIS METHOD

DIRECTLY or indirectly, that strange and powerful genius Hegel has done more to strengthen idealistic pantheism in thoughtful circles than all other influences put together. I must talk a little about him before drawing my final conclusions about the cogency of the arguments for the absolute. In no philosophy is the fact that a philosopher's vision and the technique he uses in proof of it are two different things more palpably evident than in Hegel. The vision in his case was that of a world in which reason holds all things in solution and accounts for all the irrationality that superficially appears by taking it up as a 'moment' into itself. This vision was so intense in Hegel, and the tone of authority with which he spoke from out of the midst of it was so weighty, that the impression he made has never been effaced. Once dilated to the scale of the master's eye, the disciples' sight could not contract to any lesser prospect. The technique which Hegel used to prove his vision was the so-called dialectic method, but here his fortune has been quite contrary. Hardly a recent disciple has felt his particular applications of the method to be satisfactory. Many have let them drop entirely, treating them rather as a sort of provisional stop-gap, symbolic of what might some day prove possible of execution, but having no literal cogency or value now. Yet these very same disciples hold to the vision itself as a revelation that can never pass away. The case is curious and worthy of our study.

It is still more curious in that these same disciples, altho they are usually willing to abandon any particular instance of the dialectic method to its critics, are unshakably sure that in some shape the dialectic method is the key to truth. What, then, is the dialectic method? It is itself a part of the hegelian vision or intuition, and a part that finds the strongest echo in empiricism and common sense. Great injustice is done to Hegel by treating him as primarily a reasoner. He is in reality a naïvely observant man, only beset with a perverse preference for the use of technical and logical jargon. He plants himself in the empirical flux of things and gets the impression of what happens. His mind is in very truth *impressionistic;* and his thought, when once you put yourself at the animating centre of it, is the easiest thing in the world to catch the pulse of and to follow.

Any author is easy if you can catch the centre of his vision. From the centre in Hegel come those towering sentences of his that are comparable only to Luther's, as where, speaking of the ontological proof of God's existence from the concept of him as the *ens perfectissimum* to which no attribute can be lacking, he says: 'It would be strange if the Notion, the very heart of the mind, or, in a word, the concrete totality we call God, were not rich enough to embrace so poor a category as Being, the very poorest and most abstract of all — for nothing can be more insignificant than Being.' But if Hegel's central thought is easy to catch, his abominable habits of speech make his application of it to details exceedingly difficult to follow. His passion for the slipshod in the way of sentences, his unprincipled playing fast and loose with terms; his dreadful vocabulary, calling what completes a thing its 'negation,' for example; his systematic refusal to let you know whether he is talking logic or physics or psychology, his whole deliberately adopted policy of ambiguity and vagueness, in short: all these things make his present-day readers wish to tear their hair—or his — out in desperation. Like Byron's corsair, he has left a name 'to other times, linked with one virtue and a thousand crimes.'

The virtue was the vision, which was really in two parts. The first part was that reason is all-inclusive, the second was that things are 'dialectic.' Let me say a word about this second part of Hegel's vision.

The impression that any *naïf* person gets who plants himself innocently in the flux of things is that things are off their balance. Whatever equilibriums our finite experiences attain to are but provisional. Martinique vol-

canoes shatter our wordsworthian equilibrium
with nature. Accidents, either moral, mental,
or physical, break up the slowly built-up equilibriums men reach in family life and in their
civic and professional relations. Intellectual
enigmas frustrate our scientific systems, and
the ultimate cruelty of the universe upsets our
religious attitudes and outlooks. Of no special
system of good attained does the universe
recognize the value as sacred. Down it tumbles,
over it goes, to feed the ravenous appetite for
destruction, of the larger system of history in
which it stood for a moment as a landing-
place and stepping-stone. This dogging of
everything by its negative, its fate, its undoing,
this perpetual moving on to something future
which shall supersede the present, this is the
hegelian intuition of the essential provision-
ality, and consequent unreality, of everything
empirical and finite. Take any concrete finite
thing and try to hold it fast. You cannot, for
so held, it proves not to be concrete at all, but
an arbitrary extract or abstract which you
have made from the remainder of empirical

reality. The rest of things invades and over-flows both it and you together, and defeats your rash attempt. Any partial view whatever of the world tears the part out of its relations, leaves out some truth concerning it, is untrue of it, falsifies it. The full truth about anything involves more than that thing. In the end nothing less than the whole of everything can be the truth of anything at all.

Taken so far, and taken in the rough, Hegel is not only harmless, but accurate. There is a dialectic movement in things, if such it please you to call it, one that the whole constitution of concrete life establishes; but it is one that can be described and accounted for in terms of the pluralistic vision of things far more naturally than in the monistic terms to which Hegel finally reduced it. Pluralistic empiricism knows that everything is in an environment, a surrounding world of other things, and that if you leave it to work there it will inevitably meet with friction and opposition from its neighbors. Its rivals and enemies will destroy it unless it can buy them off by com-

promising some part of its original pretensions.

But Hegel saw this undeniable characteristic of the world we live in in a non-empirical
light. Let the *mental idea* of the thing work
in your thought all alone, he fancied, and just
the same consequences will follow. It will be
negated by the opposite ideas that dog it, and
can survive only by entering, along with them,
into some kind of treaty. This treaty will be
an instance of the so-called 'higher synthesis'
of everything with its negative; and Hegel's
originality lay in transporting the process from
the sphere of percepts to that of concepts and
treating it as the universal method by which
every kind of life, logical, physical, or psychological, is mediated. Not to the sensible facts
as such, then, did Hegel point for the secret of
what keeps existence going, but rather to the
conceptual way of treating them. Concepts
were not in his eyes the static self-contained
things that previous logicians had supposed,
but were germinative, and passed beyond themselves into each other by what he called their

immanent dialectic. In ignoring each other as they do, they virtually exclude and deny each other, he thought, and thus in a manner introduce each other. So the dialectic logic, according to him, had to supersede the 'logic of identity' in which, since Aristotle, all Europe had been brought up.

This view of concepts is Hegel's revolutionary performance; but so studiously vague and ambiguous are all his expressions of it that one can hardly tell whether it is the concepts as such, or the sensible experiences and elements conceived, that Hegel really means to work with. The only thing that is certain is that whatever you may say of his procedure, some one will accuse you of misunderstanding it. I make no claim to understanding it, I treat it merely impressionistically.

So treating it, I regret that he should have called it by the name of logic. Clinging as he did to the vision of a really living world, and refusing to be content with a chopped-up intellectualist picture of it, it is a pity that he should have adopted the very word that intellectualism had already pre-empted. But he clung fast to the old rationalist contempt for the immediately given world of sense and all its squalid particulars, and never tolerated the notion that the form of philosophy might be empirical only. His own system had to be a product of eternal reason, so the word 'logic,' with its suggestions of coercive necessity, was the only word he could find natural. He pretended therefore to be using the *a priori* method, and to be working by a scanty equipment of ancient logical terms—position, negation, reflection, universal, particular, individual, and the like. But what he really worked by was his own empirical perceptions, which exceeded and overflowed his miserably insufficient logical categories in every instance of their use.

What he did with the category of negation was his most original stroke. The orthodox opinion is that you can advance logically through the field of concepts only by going from the same to the same. Hegel felt deeply the sterility of this law of conceptual thought;

he saw that in a fashion negation also relates things; and he had the brilliant idea of transcending the ordinary logic by treating advance from the different to the different as if it were also a necessity of thought. 'The so-called maxim of identity,' he wrote, 'is supposed to be accepted by the consciousness of every one. But the language which such a law demands, "a planet is a planet, magnetism is magnetism, mind is mind," deserves to be called silliness. No mind either speaks or thinks or forms conceptions in accordance with this law, and no existence of any kind whatever conforms to it. We must never view identity as abstract identity, to the exclusion of all difference. That is the touchstone for distinguishing all bad philosophy from what alone deserves the name of philosophy. If thinking were no more than registering abstract identities, it would be a most superfluous performance. Things and concepts are identical with themselves only in so far as at the same time they involve distinction.' [1]

The distinction that Hegel has in mind here

is naturally in the first instance distinction from all other things or concepts. But in his hands this quickly develops into contradiction of them, and finally, reflected back upon itself, into self-contradiction; and the immanent self-contradictoriness of all finite concepts thenceforth becomes the propulsive logical force that moves the world.[2] 'Isolate a thing from all its relations,' says Dr. Edward Caird,[3] expounding Hegel, 'and try to assert it by itself; you find that it has negated itself as well as its relations. The thing in itself is nothing.' Or, to quote Hegel's own words: 'When we suppose an existent A, and another, B, B is at first defined as the other. But A is just as much the other of B. Both are others in the same fashion. . . . "Other" is the other by itself, therefore the other of every other, consequently the other of itself, the simply unlike itself, the self-negator, the self-alterer,' etc.[4] Hegel writes elsewhere: 'The finite, as implicitly other than what it is, is forced to surrender its own immediate or natural being, and to turn suddenly into its opposite. . . . Dialectic is the universal and irresistible power before which nothing can stay. . . . *Summum jus, summa injuria* — to drive an abstract right to excess is to commit injustice. . . . Extreme anarchy and extreme despotism lead to one another. Pride comes before a fall. Too much wit outwits itself. Joy brings tears, melancholy a sardonic smile.'[5] To which one well might add that most human institutions, by the purely technical and professional manner in which they come to be administered, end by becoming obstacles to the very purposes which their founders had in view.

Once catch well the knack of this scheme of thought and you are lucky if you ever get away from it. It is all you can see. Let any one pronounce anything, and your feeling of a contradiction being implied becomes a habit, almost a motor habit in some persons who symbolize by a stereotyped gesture the position, sublation, and final reinstatement involved. If you say 'two' or 'many,' your speech bewrayeth you, for the very name collects them into one. If you express doubt, your expression contradicts its content, for the doubt itself is not doubted but affirmed. If you say 'disorder,' what is that but a certain bad kind of order? if you say 'indetermination,' you are determining just *that*. If you say 'nothing but the unexpected happens,' the unexpected becomes what you expect. If you say 'all things are relative,' to what is the all of them itself relative? If you say 'no more,' you have said more already, by implying a region in which no more is found; to know a limit as such is consequently already to have got beyond it; and so forth, throughout as many examples as one cares to cite.

Whatever you posit appears thus as one-sided, and negates its other, which, being equally one-sided, negates *it;* and, since this situation remains unstable, the two contradictory terms have together, according to Hegel, to engender a higher truth of which they both appear as indispensable members, mutually mediating aspects of that higher concept or situation in thought.

Every higher total, however provisional and relative, thus reconciles the contradictions which its parts, abstracted from it, prove implicitly to contain. Rationalism, you remember, is what I called the way of thinking that methodically subordinates parts to wholes, so Hegel here is rationalistic through and through. The only whole by which *all* contradictions are reconciled is for him the absolute whole of wholes, the all-inclusive reason to which Hegel himself gave the name of the absolute Idea, but which I shall continue to call 'the absolute' purely and simply, as I have done hitherto.

Empirical instances of the way in which higher unities reconcile contradictions are innumerable, so here again Hegel's vision, taken merely impressionistically, agrees with countless facts. Somehow life does, out of its total resources, find ways of satisfying opposites at once. This is precisely the paradoxical aspect which much of our civilization presents. Peace we secure by armaments, liberty by laws and constitutions; simplicity and naturalness are the consummate result of artificial breeding and training; health, strength, and wealth are increased only by lavish use, expense, and wear.

III. HEGEL AND HIS METHOD

Our mistrust of mistrust engenders our commercial system of credit; our tolerance of anarchistic and revolutionary utterances is the only way of lessening their danger; our charity has to say no to beggars in order not to defeat its own desires; the true epicurean has to observe great sobriety; the way to certainty lies through radical doubt; virtue signifies not innocence but the knowledge of sin and its overcoming; by obeying nature, we command her, etc. The ethical and the religious life are full of such contradictions held in solution. You hate your enemy? — well, forgive him, and thereby heap coals of fire on his head; to realize yourself, renounce yourself; to save your soul, first lose it; in short, die to live.

From such massive examples one easily generalizes Hegel's vision. Roughly, his 'dialectic' picture is a fair account of a good deal of the world. It sounds paradoxical, but whenever you once place yourself at the point of view of any higher synthesis, you see exactly how it does in a fashion take up opposites into itself. As an example, consider the conflict between our carnivorous appetites and hunting instincts and the sympathy with animals which our refinement is bringing in its train. We have found how to reconcile these opposites most effectively by establishing game-laws and close seasons and by keeping domestic herds. The creatures preserved thus are preserved for the sake of slaughter, truly, but if not preserved for that reason, not one of them would be alive at all. Their will to live and our will to kill them thus harmoniously combine in this peculiar higher synthesis of domestication.

Merely as a reporter of certain empirical aspects of the actual, Hegel, then, is great and true. But he aimed at being something far greater than an empirical reporter, so I must say something about that essential aspect of his thought. Hegel was dominated by the notion of a truth that should prove incontrovertible, binding on every one, and certain, which should be *the* truth, one, indivisible, eternal, objective, and necessary, to which all our particular thinking must lead as to its consummation. This is the dogmatic ideal, the postulate, uncriticised, undoubted, and unchallenged, of all rationalizers in philosophy. '*I have never doubted*,' a recent Oxford writer says, that truth is universal and single and timeless, a single content or significance, one and whole and complete.⁶ Advance in thinking, in the hegelian universe, has, in short, to proceed by the apodictic words *must be* rather than by those inferior hypothetic words *may be*, which are all that empiricists can use.

Now Hegel found that his idea of an immanent movement through the field of concepts by way of 'dialectic' negation played most beautifully into the hands of this rationalistic demand for something absolute and *inconcussum* in the way of truth. It is easy to see how. If you affirm anything, for example that A is, and simply leave the matter thus, you leave it at the mercy of any one who may supervene and say 'not A, but B is.' If he does say so, your statement does n't refute him, it simply contradicts him, just as his contradicts you. The only way of making your affirmation about A *self-securing* is by getting it into a form which will by

101

implication negate all possible negations in advance. The mere absence of negation is not enough; it must be present, but present with its fangs drawn. What you posit as A must already have cancelled the alternative or made it innocuous, by having negated it in advance. Double negation is the only form of affirmation that fully plays into the hands of the dogmatic ideal. Simply and innocently affirmative statements are good enough for empiricists, but unfit for rationalist use, lying open as they do to every accidental contradictor, and exposed to every puff of doubt. The *final* truth must be something to which there is no imaginable alternative, because it contains all its possible alternatives inside of itself as moments already taken account of and overcome. Whatever involves its own alternatives as elements of itself is, in a phrase often repeated, its 'own other,' made so by the *methode der absoluten negativität.*

Formally, this scheme of an organism of truth that has already fed as it were on its own liability to death, so that, death once dead for it,

there 's no more dying then, is the very fulfilment of the rationalistic aspiration. That one
and only whole, with all its parts involved in it,
negating and making one another impossible if
abstracted and taken singly, but necessitating
and holding one another in place if the whole
of them be taken integrally, is the literal ideal
sought after; it is the very diagram and picture
of that notion of *the* truth with no outlying
alternative, to which nothing can be added, nor
from it anything withdrawn, and all variations
from which are absurd, which so dominates
the human imagination. Once we have taken
in the features of this diagram that so successfully solves the world-old problem, the older
ways of proving the necessity of judgments
cease to give us satisfaction. Hegel's way we
think must be the right way. The true must be
essentially the self-reflecting self-contained re-
current, that which secures itself by including
its own other and negating it; that makes a
spherical system with no loose ends hanging
out for foreignness to get a hold upon; that is
forever rounded in and closed, not strung along

rectilinearly and open at its ends like that universe of simply collective or additive form which Hegel calls the world of the bad infinite, and which is all that empiricism, starting with simply posited single parts and elements, is ever able to attain to.

No one can possibly deny the sublimity of this hegelian conception. It is surely in the grand style, if there be such a thing as a grand style in philosophy. For us, however, it remains, so far, a merely formal and diagrammatic conception; for with the actual content of absolute truth, as Hegel materially tries to set it forth, few disciples have been satisfied, and I do not propose to refer at all to the concreter parts of his philosophy. The main thing now is to grasp the generalized vision, and feel the authority of the abstract scheme of a statement self-secured by involving double negation. Absolutists who make no use of Hegel's own technique are really working by his method. You remember the proofs of the absolute which I instanced in my last lecture, Lotze's and Royce's proofs by *reductio ad absurdum*, to the effect that any smallest connexion rashly supposed in things will logically work out into absolute union, and any minimal disconnexion into absolute disunion, —these are really arguments framed on the hegelian pattern. The truth is that which you implicitly affirm in the very attempt to deny it; it is that from which every variation refutes itself by proving self-contradictory. This is the supreme insight of rationalism, and to-day the best *must-be's* of rationalist argumentation are but so many attempts to communicate it to the hearer.

Thus, you see, my last lecture and this lecture make connexion again and we can consider Hegel and the other absolutists to be supporting the same system. The next point I wish to dwell on is the part played by what I have called vicious intellectualism in this wonderful system's structure.

Rationalism in general thinks it gets the fulness of truth by turning away from sensation to conception, conception obviously giving the more universal and immutable picture. Intellectualism in the vicious sense I have already defined as the habit of assuming that a concept *ex*cludes from any reality conceived by its means everything not included in the concept's definition. I called such intellectualism illegitimate as I found it used in Lotze's, Royce's, and Bradley's proofs of the absolute (which absolute I consequently held to be non-proven by their arguments), and I left off by asserting my own belief that a pluralistic and incompletely integrated universe, describable only by the free use of the word 'some,' is a legitimate hypothesis.

Now Hegel himself, in building up his method of double negation, offers the vividest possible example of this vice of intellectualism. Every idea of a finite thing is of course a concept of *that* thing and not a concept of anything else. But Hegel treats this not being a concept of anything else as if it were *equivalent to the concept of anything else not being*, or in other words as if it were a denial or negation of everything else. Then, as the other things, thus implicitly contradicted by the thing first conceived, also by the same law contradict *it*, the pulse of dialectic commences to beat and the famous triads begin to grind out the cosmos. If any one finds the process here to be a luminous one, he must be left to the illumination, he must remain an undisturbed hegelian. What others feel as the intolerable ambiguity, verbosity, and unscrupulousness of the master's way of deducing things, he will probably ascribe — since divine oracles are notoriously hard to interpret — to the 'difficulty' that habitually accompanies profundity. For my own part, there seems something grotesque and *saugrenu* in the pretension of a style so disobedient to the first rules of sound communication between minds, to be the authentic mother-tongue of reason, and to keep step more accurately than any other style does with the absolute's own ways of thinking. I do not therefore take Hegel's technical apparatus seriously at all. I regard him rather as one of those numerous original seers who can never learn how to articulate. His would-be coercive logic counts for nothing in my eyes; but that does not in the least impugn the philosophic importance of his conception of the absolute, if we take it merely hypothetically as one of the great types of cosmic vision.

Taken thus hypothetically, I wish to discuss it briefly. But before doing so I must call your attention to an odd peculiarity in the hegelian procedure. The peculiarity is one which will come before us again for a final judgment in my seventh lecture, so at present I only note it in passing. Hegel, you remember, considers that the immediate finite data of experience are 'untrue' because they are not their own others. They are negated by what is external to them. The absolute is true because it and it only has no external environment, and has attained to being its own other. (These words sound queer enough, but those of you who know something of Hegel's text will follow them.) Granting his premise that to be true a thing must in some sort be its own other, everything hinges on whether he is right in holding that the several pieces of finite experience themselves cannot be said to be in any wise *their* own others. When conceptually or intellectualistically treated, they of course cannot be their own others. Every abstract concept as such excludes what it does n't include, and if such concepts are adequate substitutes for reality's concrete pulses, the latter must square themselves with intellectualistic logic, and no one of them in any sense can claim to be its own other. If, however, the conceptual treatment of the flow of reality should prove for any good reason to be inadequate and to have a practical rather than a theoretical or speculative value, then an independent empirical look into the constitution of reality's pulses might possibly show that some of them *are* their own others, and indeed are so in the self-same sense in which the absolute is maintained to be so by Hegel. When we come to my sixth lecture, on Professor Bergson, I shall in effect defend this very view, strengthening my thesis by his authority. I am unwilling to say anything more about the point at this time, and what I have just said of it is only a sort of surveyor's note of where our present position lies in the general framework of these lectures.

Let us turn now at last to the great question

of fact, *Does the absolute exist or not?* to which all our previous discussion has been preliminary. I may sum up that discussion by saying that whether there really be an absolute or not, no one makes himself absurd or self-contradictory by doubting or denying it. The charges of self-contradiction, where they do not rest on purely verbal reasoning, rest on a vicious intellectualism. I will not recapitulate my criticisms. I will simply ask you to change the *venue*, and to discuss the absolute now as if it were only an open hypothesis. As such, is it more probable or more improbable?

But first of all I must parenthetically ask you to distinguish the notion of the absolute carefully from that of another object with which it is liable to become heedlessly entangled. That other object is the 'God' of common people in their religion, and the creator-God of orthodox christian theology. Only thoroughgoing monists or pantheists believe in the absolute. The God of our popular Christianity is but one member of a pluralistic system. He and we stand outside of each other, just as

the devil, the saints, and the angels stand outside of both of us. I can hardly conceive of
anything more different from the absolute than
the God, say, of David or of Isaiah. *That* God
is an essentially finite being *in* the cosmos, not
with the cosmos in him, and indeed he has a
very local habitation there, and very one-sided
local and personal attachments. If it should
prove probable that the absolute does not exist,
it will not follow in the slightest degree that a
God like that of David, Isaiah, or Jesus may
not exist, or may not be the most important existence in the universe for us to acknowledge.
I pray you, then, not to confound the two ideas
as you listen to the criticisms I shall have to
proffer. I hold to the finite God, for reasons
which I shall touch on in the seventh of these
lectures; but I hold that his rival and compet-
itor —I feel almost tempted to say his enemy
— the absolute, is not only not forced on us by
logic, but that it is an improbable hypothesis.

The great claim made for the absolute is that
by supposing it we make the world appear
more rational. Any hypothesis that does that

will always be accepted as more probably true than an hypothesis that makes the world appear irrational. Men are once for all so made that they prefer a rational world to believe in and to live in. But rationality has at least four dimensions, intellectual, æsthetical, moral, and practical; and to find a world rational to the maximal degree *in all these respects simultaneously* is no easy matter. Intellectually, the world of mechanical materialism is the most rational, for we subject its events to mathematical calculation. But the mechanical world is ugly, as arithmetic is ugly, and it is nonmoral. Morally, the theistic world is rational enough, but full of intellectual frustrations. The practical world of affairs, in its turn, so supremely rational to the politician, the military man, or the man of conquering business-faculty that he never would vote to change the type of it, is irrational to moral and artistic temperaments; so that whatever demand for rationality we find satisfied by a philosophic hypothesis, we are liable to find some other demand for rationality unsatisfied by the same hypothesis.

III. HEGEL AND HIS METHOD

The rationality we gain in one coin we thus pay for in another; and the problem accordingly seems at first sight to resolve itself into that of getting a conception which will yield the largest *balance* of rationality rather than one which will yield perfect rationality of every description. In general, it may be said that if a man's conception of the world lets loose any action in him that is easy, or any faculty which he is fond of exercising, he will deem it rational in so far forth, be the faculty that of computing, fighting, lecturing, classifying, framing schematic tabulations, getting the better end of a bargain, patiently waiting and enduring, preaching, joke-making, or what you like. Albeit the absolute is defined as being necessarily an embodiment of objectively perfect rationality, it is fair to its english advocates to say that those who have espoused the hypothesis most concretely and seriously have usually avowed the irrationality to their own minds of certain elements in it.

Probably the weightiest contribution to our feeling of the rationality of the universe which the notion of the absolute brings is the assurance that however disturbed the surface may be, at bottom all is well with the cosmos — central peace abiding at the heart of endless agitation. This conception is rational in many ways, beautiful æsthetically, beautiful intellectually (could we only follow it into detail), and beautiful morally, if the enjoyment of security can be accounted moral. Practically it is less beautiful; for, as we saw in our last lecture, in representing the deepest reality of the world as static and without a history, it loosens the world's hold upon our sympathies and leaves the soul of it foreign. Nevertheless it does give *peace*, and that kind of rationality is so paramountly demanded by men that to the end of time there will be absolutists, men who choose belief in a static eternal, rather than admit that the finite world of change and striving, even with a God as one of the strivers, is itself eternal. For such minds Professor Royce's words will always be the truest: ' The very presence of ill in the temporal order is the condition of the perfection of the eternal order. . . . We

114

long for the absolute only in so far as in us the
absolute also longs, and seeks through our very
temporal striving, the peace that is nowhere in
time, but only, and yet absolutely, in eternity.
Were there no longing in time there would be
no peace in eternity. . . . God [*i. e.* the abso-
lute] who here in me aims at what I now temporally miss, not only possesses in the eternal
world the goal after which I strive, but comes
to possess it even through and because of
my sorrow. Through this my tribulation the
absolute triumph then is won. . . . In the
absolute I am fulfilled. Yet my very fulfilment
demands and therefore can transcend this sorrow.'[7] Royce is particularly felicitous in his
ability to cite parts of finite experience to
which he finds his picture of this absolute experience analogous. But it is hard to portray the
absolute at all without rising into what might
be called the 'inspired' style of language —
I use the word not ironically, but prosaically
and descriptively, to designate the only literary form that goes with the kind of emotion
that the absolute arouses. One can follow the

pathway of reasoning soberly enough,[8] but the picture itself has to be effulgent. This admirable faculty of transcending, whilst inwardly preserving, every contrariety, is the absolute's characteristic form of rationality. We are but syllables in the mouth of the Lord; if the whole sentence is divine, each syllable is absolutely what it should be, in spite of all appearances. In making up the balance for or against absolutism, this emotional value weights heavily the credit side of the account.

The trouble is that we are able to see so little into the positive detail of it, and that if once admitted not to be coercively proven by the intellectualist arguments, it remains only a hypothetic possibility.

On the debit side of the account the absolute, taken seriously, and not as a mere name for our right occasionally to drop the strenuous mood and take a moral holiday, introduces all those tremendous irrationalities into the universe which a frankly pluralistic theism escapes, but which have been flung as a reproach at every form of monistic theism or pantheism.

It introduces a speculative 'problem of evil'
namely, and leaves us wondering why the perfection of the absolute should require just such
particular hideous forms of life as darken the
day for our human imaginations. If they were
forced on it by something alien, and to 'overcome' them the absolute had still to keep hold
of them, we could understand its feeling of triumph, though we, so far as we were ourselves
among the elements overcome, could acqui-
esce but sullenly in the resultant situation, and
would never just have chosen it as the most
rational one conceivable. But the absolute is
represented as a being without environment,
upon which nothing alien can be forced, and
which has spontaneously chosen from within
to give itself the spectacle of all that evil rather
than a spectacle with less evil in it. [9] Its perfection is represented as the source of things,
and yet the first effect of that perfection is the
tremendous imperfection of all finite experience. In whatever sense the word 'rationality'
may be taken, it is vain to contend that the
impression made on our finite minds by such

117

a way of representing things is altogether rational. Theologians have felt its irrationality acutely, and the 'fall,' the predestination, and the election which the situation involves have given them more trouble than anything else in their attempt to pantheize Christianity. The whole business remains a puzzle, both intellectually and morally.

Grant that the spectacle or world-romance offered to itself by the absolute is in the absolute's eyes perfect. Why would not the world be more perfect by having the affair remain in just those terms, and by not having any finite spectators to come in and add to what was perfect already their innumerable imperfect manners of seeing the same spectacle? Suppose the entire universe to consist of one superb copy of a book, fit for the ideal reader. Is that universe improved or deteriorated by having myriads of garbled and misprinted separate leaves and chapters also created, giving false impressions of the book to whoever looks at them? To say the least, the balance of rationality is not obviously in favor of such added

mutilations. So this question becomes urgent:
Why, the absolute's own total vision of things
being so rational, was it necessary to com-
minute it into all these coexisting inferior
fragmentary visions?

Leibnitz in his theodicy represents God as
limited by an antecedent reason in things
which makes certain combinations logically
incompatible, certain goods impossible. He
surveys in advance all the universes he might
create, and by an act of what Leibnitz calls his
antecedent will he chooses our actual world as
the one in which the evil, unhappily necessary
anyhow, is at its minimum. It is the best of all
the worlds that are possible, therefore, but by
no means the most abstractly desirable world.
Having made this mental choice, God next
proceeds to what Leibnitz calls his act of consequent or decretory will: he says '*Fiat*' and
the world selected springs into objective being,
with all the finite creatures in it to suffer from
its imperfections without sharing in its creator's atoning vision.

Lotze has made some penetrating remarks

119

on this conception of Leibnitz's, and they exactly fall in with what I say of the absolutist conception. The world projected out of the creative mind by the *fiat*, and existing in detachment from its author, is a sphere of being where the parts realize themselves only singly. If the divine value of them is evident only when they are collectively looked at, then, Lotze rightly says, the world surely becomes poorer and not richer for God's utterance of the *fiat*. He might much better have remained contented with his merely antecedent choice of the scheme, without following it up by a creative decree. The scheme *as such* was admirable; it could only lose by being translated into reality.[10] Why, I similarly ask, should the absolute ever have lapsed from the perfection of its own integral experience of things, and refracted itself into all our finite experiences?

It is but fair to recent english absolutists to say that many of them have confessed the imperfect rationality of the absolute from this point of view. Mr. McTaggart, for example, writes: 'Does not our very failure to perceive

the perfection of the universe destroy it? . . .
In so far as we do not see the perfection of the
universe, we are not perfect ourselves. And as
we are parts of the universe, that cannot be
perfect.'[11]

And Mr. Joachim finds just the same difficulty. Calling the hypothesis of the absolute
by the name of the 'coherence theory of truth,'
he calls the problem of understanding how the
complete coherence of all things in the absolute
should involve as a necessary moment in its
self-maintenance the self-assertion of the finite
minds, a self-assertion which in its extreme
form is error, — he calls this problem, I say,
an insoluble puzzle. If truth be the universal
fons et origo, how does error slip in? 'The coherence theory of truth,' he concludes, 'may
thus be said to suffer shipwreck at the very
entrance of the harbor.'[12] Yet in spite of this
rather bad form of irrationality, Mr. Joachim
stoutly asserts his 'immediate certainty'[13] of the
theory shipwrecked, the correctness of which
he says he has 'never doubted.' This candid confession of a fixed attitude of faith in

the absolute, which even one's own criticisms and perplexities fail to disturb, seems to me very significant. Not only empiricists, but absolutists also, would all, if they were as candid as this author, confess that the prime thing in their philosophy is their vision of a truth possible, which they then employ their reasoning to convert, as best it can, into a certainty or probability.

I can imagine a believer in the absolute retorting at this point that *he* at any rate is not dealing with mere probabilities, but that the nature of things logically requires the multitudinous erroneous copies, and that therefore the universe cannot be the absolute's book alone. For, he will ask, is not the absolute defined as the total consciousness of everything that is? Must not its field of view consist of parts? And what can the parts of a total consciousness be unless they be fractional consciousnesses? Our finite minds *must* therefore coexist with the absolute mind. We are its constituents, and it cannot live without us. — But if any one of you feels tempted to retort

122

in this wise, let me remind you that you are frankly employing pluralistic weapons, and thereby giving up the absolutist cause. The notion that the absolute is made of constituents on which its being depends is the rankest empiricism. The absolute as such has *objects*, not constituents, and if the objects develop selfhoods upon their own several accounts, those selfhoods must be set down as facts additional to the absolute consciousness, and not as elements implicated in its definition. The absolute is a rationalist conception. Rationalism goes from wholes to parts, and always assumes wholes to be self-sufficing.[14]

My conclusion, so far, then, is this, that altho the hypothesis of the absolute, in yielding a certain kind of religious peace, performs a most important rationalizing function, it nevertheless, from the intellectual point of view, remains decidedly irrational. The *ideally* perfect whole is certainly that whole of which the *parts also are perfect*—if we can depend on logic for anything, we can depend on it for that definition. The absolute is defined as the ideally perfect whole, yet most of its parts, if not all, are admittedly imperfect. Evidently the conception lacks internal consistency, and yields us a problem rather than a solution. It creates a speculative puzzle, the so-called mystery of evil and of error, from which a pluralistic metaphysic is entirely free.

In any pluralistic metaphysic, the problems that evil presents are practical, not speculative. Not why evil should exist at all, but how we can lessen the actual amount of it, is the sole question we need there consider. 'God,' in the religious life of ordinary men, is the name not of the whole of things, heaven forbid, but only of the ideal tendency in things, believed in as a superhuman person who calls us to co-operate in his purposes, and who furthers ours if they are worthy. He works in an external environment, has limits, and has enemies. When John Mill said that the notion of God's omnipotence must be given up, if God is to be kept as a religious object, he was surely accurately right; yet so prevalent is the lazy monism that idly haunts the region of God's name, that so simple and truthful a saying was generally treated as a paradox: God, it was said, *could* not be finite. I believe that the only God worthy of the name *must* be finite, and I shall return to this point in a later lecture. If the absolute exist in addition — and the hypothesis must, in spite of its irrational features, still be left open — then the absolute is only the wider cosmic whole of which our God is but the most ideal portion, and which in the more usual human sense is hardly to be termed a religious hypothesis at all. 'Cosmic emotion' is the better name for the reaction it may awaken.

Observe that all the irrationalities and puzzles which the absolute gives rise to, and from which the finite God remains free, are due to the fact that the absolute has nothing, absolutely nothing, outside of itself. The finite God whom I contrast with it may conceivably have *almost* nothing outside of himself; he may already have triumphed over and absorbed all but the minutest fraction of the universe; but that fraction, however small, reduces him to the status of a relative being, and in principle the universe is saved from all the irrationalities incidental to absolutism. The only irrationality left would be the irrationality of which pluralism as such is accused, and of this I hope to say a word more later.

I have tired you with so many subtleties in this lecture that I will add only two other counts to my indictment.

First, then, let me remind you that *the absolute is useless for deductive purposes*. It gives us absolute safety if you will, but it is compatible with every relative danger. You cannot enter the phenomenal world with the notion of it in your grasp, and name beforehand any detail which you are likely to meet there. Whatever the details of experience may prove to be, *after the fact of them* the absolute will adopt them. It is an hypothesis that functions retrospectively only, not prospectively. *That*, whatever it may be, will have been in point of fact the sort of world which the absolute was pleased to offer to itself as a spectacle.

Again, the absolute is always represented

126

idealistically, as the all-knower. Thinking this view consistently out leads one to frame an almost ridiculous conception of the absolute mind, owing to the enormous mass of unprofitable information which it would then seem obliged to carry. One of the many *reductiones ad absurdum* of pluralism by which idealism thinks it proves the absolute One is as follows: Let there be many facts; but since on idealist principles facts exist only by being known, the many facts will therefore mean many knowers. But that there are so many knowers is itself a fact, which in turn requires *its* knower, so the one absolute knower has eventually to be brought in. *All* facts lead to him. If it be a fact that this table is not a chair, not a rhinoceros, not a logarithm, not a mile away from the door, not worth five hundred pounds sterling, not a thousand centuries old, the absolute must even now be articulately aware of all these negations. Along with what everything is it must also be conscious of everything which it is not. This infinite atmosphere of explicit negativity—observe that it has to be explicit—

around everything seems to us so useless an encumbrance as to make the absolute still more foreign to our sympathy. Furthermore, if it be a fact that certain ideas are silly, the absolute has to have already thought the silly ideas to establish them in silliness. The rubbish in its mind would thus appear easily to outweigh in amount the more desirable material. One would expect it fairly to burst with such an obesity, plethora, and superfœtation of useless information.[15]

I will spare you further objections. The sum of it all is that the absolute is not forced on our belief by logic, that it involves features of irrationality peculiar to itself, and that a thinker to whom it does not come as an 'immediate certainty' (to use Mr. Joachim's words), is in no way bound to treat it as anything but an emotionally rather sublime hypothesis. As such, it might, with all its defects, be, on account of its peace-conferring power and its formal grandeur, more rational than anything else in the field. But meanwhile the strung-along unfinished world in time is its rival: *reality MAY exist in distributive form, in the shape not of an all but of a set of eaches, just as it seems to*—this is the anti-absolutist hypothesis. *Prima facie* there is this in favor of the eaches, that they are at any rate real enough to have made themselves at least *appear* to every one, whereas the absolute has as yet appeared immediately to only a few mystics, and indeed to them very ambiguously. The advocates of the absolute assure us that any distributive form of being is infected and undermined by self-contradiction. If we are unable to assimilate their arguments, and we have been unable, the only course we can take, it seems to me, is to let the absolute bury the absolute, and to seek reality in more promising directions, even among the details of the finite and the immediately given.

If these words of mine sound in bad taste to some of you, or even sacrilegious, I am sorry. Perhaps the impression may be mitigated by what I have to say in later lectures.

IV

CONCERNING FECHNER

LECTURE IV

CONCERNING FECHNER

THE prestige of the absolute has rather crumbled in our hands. The logical proofs of it miss fire; the portraits which its best court-painters show of it are featureless and foggy in the extreme; and, apart from the cold comfort of assuring us that with *it* all is well, and that to see that all is well with us also we need only rise to its eternal point of view, it yields us no relief whatever. It introduces, on the contrary, into philosophy and theology certain poisonous difficulties of which but for its intrusion we never should have heard.

But if we drop the absolute out of the world, must we then conclude that the world contains nothing better in the way of consciousness than our consciousness? Is our whole instinctive belief in higher presences, our persistent inner turning towards divine companionship, to count for nothing? Is it but the pathetic illusion of beings with incorrigibly social and imaginative minds?

Such a negative conclusion would, I believe, be desperately hasty, a sort of pouring out of the child with the bath. Logically it is possible to believe in superhuman beings without identifying them with the absolute at all. The treaty of offensive and defensive alliance which certain groups of the christian clergy have recently made with our transcendentalist philosophers seems to me to be based on a well-meaning but baleful mistake. Neither the Jehovah of the old testament nor the heavenly father of the new has anything in common with the absolute except that they are all three greater than man; and if you say that the notion of the absolute is what the gods of Abraham, of David, and of Jesus, after first developing into each other, were inevitably destined to develop into in more reflective and modern minds, I reply that although in certain specifically philosophical minds this may have been the case, in minds more properly to be termed religious the development has followed quite another path. The whole history of evangelical Christianity is there to prove it. I propose in these lectures to plead for that other line of development. To set the doctrine of the absolute in its proper framework, so that it shall not fill the whole welkin and exclude all alternative possibilities of higher thought — as it seems to do for many students who approach it with a limited previous acquaintance with philosophy — I will contrast it with a system which, abstractly considered, seems at first to have much in common with absolutism, but which, when taken concretely and temperamentally, really stands at the opposite pole. I refer to the philosophy of Gustav Theodor Fechner, a writer but little known as yet to English readers, but destined, I am persuaded, to wield more and more influence as time goes on.

It is the intense concreteness of Fechner, his fertility of detail, which fills me with an admiration which I should like to make this audience share. Among the philosophic cranks of my acquaintance in the past was a lady all the tenets of whose system I have forgotten except one. Had she been born in the Ionian Archipelago some three thousand years ago, that one

doctrine would probably have made her name
sure of a place in every university curriculum
and examination paper. The world, she said,
is composed of only two elements, the Thick,
namely, and the Thin. No one can deny the
truth of this analysis, as far as it goes (though
in the light of our contemporary knowledge of
nature it has itself a rather 'thin' sound), and
it is nowhere truer than in that part of the world
called philosophy. I am sure, for example, that
many of you, listening to what poor account I
have been able to give of transcendental idealism, have received an impression of its arguments being strangely thin, and of the terms it
leaves us with being shiveringly thin wrappings
for so thick and burly a world as this. Some
of you of course will charge the thinness to my
exposition; but thin as that has been, I believe
the doctrines reported on to have been thinner.
From Green to Haldane the absolute proposed
to us to straighten out the confusions of the
thicket of experience in which our life is passed
remains a pure abstraction which hardly any
one tries to make a whit concreter. If we open

Green, we get nothing but the transcendental ego of apperception (Kant's name for the fact that to be counted in experience a thing has to be witnessed), blown up into a sort of timeless soap-bubble large enough to mirror the whole universe. Nature, Green keeps insisting, consists only in relations, and these imply the action of a mind that is eternal; a self-distinguishing consciousness which itself escapes from the relations by which it determines other things. Present to whatever is in succession, it is not in succession itself. If we take the Cairds, they tell us little more of the principle of the universe — it is always a return into the identity of the self from the difference of its objects. It separates itself from them and so becomes conscious of them in their separation from one another, while at the same time it binds them together as elements in one higher self-consciousness.

This seems the very quintessence of thinness; and the matter hardly grows thicker when we gather, after enormous amounts of reading, that the great enveloping self in question is absolute reason as such, and that as such it is characterized by the habit of using certain jejune 'categories' with which to perform its eminent relating work. The whole active material of natural fact is tried out, and only the barest intellectualistic formalism remains.

Hegel tried, as we saw, to make the system concreter by making the relations between things 'dialectic,' but if we turn to those who use his name most worshipfully, we find them giving up all the particulars of his attempt, and simply praising his intention — much as in our manner we have praised it ourselves. Mr. Haldane, for example, in his wonderfully clever Gifford lectures, praises Hegel to the skies, but what he tells of him amounts to little more than this, that 'the categories in which the mind arranges its experiences, and gives meaning to them, the universals in which the particulars are grasped in the individual, are a logical chain, in which the first presupposes the last, and the last is its presupposition and its truth.' He hardly tries at all to thicken this thin logical scheme. He says indeed that absolute mind in

138

itself, and absolute mind in its hetereity or otherness, under the distinction which it sets up of itself from itself, have as their real *prius* absolute mind in synthesis; and, this being absolute mind's true nature, its dialectic character must show itself in such concrete forms as Goethe's and Wordsworth's poetry, as well as in religious forms. 'The nature of God, the nature of absolute mind, is to exhibit the triple movement of dialectic, and so the nature of God as presented in religion must be a triplicity, a trinity.' But beyond thus naming Goethe and Wordsworth and establishing the trinity, Mr. Haldane's Hegelianism carries us hardly an inch into the concrete detail of the world we actually inhabit.

Equally thin is Mr. Taylor, both in his principles and in their results. Following Mr. Bradley, he starts by assuring us that reality cannot be self-contradictory, but to be related to anything really outside of one's self is to be self-contradictory, so the ultimate reality must be a single all-inclusive systematic whole. Yet all he can say of this whole at the end of his excellently written book is that the notion of it 'can make no addition to our information and can of itself supply no motives for practical endeavor.'

Mr. McTaggart treats us to almost as thin a fare. 'The main practical interest of Hegel's philosophy,' he says, 'is to be found in the abstract certainty which the logic gives us that all reality is rational and righteous, even when we cannot see in the least how it is so. . . . Not that it shows us how the facts around us are good, not that it shows us how we can make them better, but that it proves that they, like other reality, are *sub specie eternitatis*, perfectly good, and *sub specie temporis*, destined to become perfectly good.'

Here again, no detail whatever, only the abstract certainty that whatever the detail may prove to be, it will be good. Common non-dialectical men have already this certainty as a result of the generous vital enthusiasm about the universe with which they are born. The peculiarity of transcendental philosophy is its sovereign contempt for merely vital functions

like enthusiasm, and its pretension to turn our
simple and immediate trusts and faiths into the
form of logically mediated certainties, to question which would be absurd. But the whole
basis on which Mr. McTaggart's own certainty
so solidly rests, settles down into the one nutshell of an assertion into which he puts Hegel's
gospel, namely, that in every bit of experience and thought, however finite, the whole of
reality (the absolute idea, as Hegel calls it) is
'implicitly present.'

This indeed is Hegel's *vision*, and Hegel
thought that the details of his dialectic proved
its truth. But disciples who treat the details of
the proof as unsatisfactory and yet cling to the
vision, are surely, in spite of their pretension to
a more rational consciousness, no better than
common men with their enthusiasms or deliberately adopted faiths. We have ourselves seen
some of the weakness of the monistic proofs.
Mr. McTaggart picks plenty of holes of his own
in Hegel's logic, and finally concludes that 'all
true philosophy must be mystical, not indeed
in its methods but in its final conclusions,'

which is as much as to say that the rationalistic methods leave us in the lurch, in spite of all their superiority, and that in the end vision and faith must eke them out. But how abstract and thin is here the vision, to say nothing of the faith! The whole of reality, explicitly absent from our finite experiences, must nevertheless be present in them all implicitly, altho no one of us can ever see how — the bare word 'implicit' here bearing the whole pyramid of the monistic system on its slender point. Mr. Joachim's monistic system of truth rests on an even slenderer point. —'*I have never doubted,*' he says, 'that universal and timeless truth is a single content or significance, one and whole and complete,' and he candidly confesses the failure of rationalistic attempts 'to raise this immediate certainty' to the level of reflective knowledge. There is, in short, no mediation for him between the Truth in capital letters and all the little 'lower-case' truths — and errors — which life presents. The psychological fact that he never has 'doubted' is enough.

The whole monistic pyramid, resting on

points as thin as these, seems to me to be a *machtspruch*, a product of will far more than one of reason. Unity is good, therefore things *shall* cohere; they *shall* be one; there *shall* be categories to make them one, no matter what empirical disjunctions may appear. In Hegel's own writings, the *shall-be* temper is ubiquitous and towering; it overrides verbal and logical resistances alike. Hegel's error, as Professor Royce so well says, 'lay not in introducing logic into passion,' as some people charge, 'but in conceiving the logic of passion as the only logic. . . . He is [thus] suggestive,' Royce says, 'but never final. His system as a system has crumbled, but his vital comprehension of our life remains forever.'[1]

That vital comprehension we have already seen. It is that there is a sense in which real things are not merely their own bare selves, but may vaguely be treated as also their own others, and that ordinary logic, since it denies this, must be overcome. Ordinary logic denies this because it substitutes concepts for real things, and concepts *are* their own bare selves and nothing else. What Royce calls Hegel's 'system' was Hegel's attempt to make us believe that he was working by concepts and grinding out a higher style of logic, when in reality sensible experiences, hypotheses, and passion furnished him with all his results.

What I myself may mean by things being their own others, we shall see in a later lecture. It is now time to take our look at Fechner, whose thickness is a refreshing contrast to the thin, abstract, indigent, and threadbare appearance, the starving, school-room aspect, which the speculations of most of our absolutist philosophers present.

There is something really weird and uncanny in the contrast between the abstract pretensions of rationalism and what rationalistic methods concretely can do. If the 'logical prius' of our mind were really the 'implicit presence' of the whole 'concrete universal,' the whole of reason, or reality, or spirit, or the absolute idea, or whatever it may be called, in all our finite thinking, and if this reason worked (for example) by the dialectical method, does n't it seem odd that in the greatest instance of rationalization mankind has known, in 'science,' namely, the dialectical method should never once have been tried? Not a solitary instance of the use of it in science occurs to my mind. Hypotheses, and deductions from these, controlled by sense-observations and analogies with what we know elsewhere, are to be thanked for all of science's results.

Fechner used no methods but these latter ones in arguing for his metaphysical conclusions about reality — but let me first rehearse a few of the facts about his life.

Born in 1801, the son of a poor country pastor in Saxony, he lived from 1817 to 1887, when he died, seventy years therefore, at Leipzig, a typical *gelehrter* of the old-fashioned german stripe. His means were always scanty, so his only extravagances could be in the way of thought, but these were gorgeous ones. He passed his medical examinations at Leipzig University at the age of twenty-one, but decided, instead of becoming a doctor, to devote himself to physical science. It was ten years before he was made professor of physics, although he soon was authorized to lecture. Meanwhile, he had to make both ends meet, and this he did by voluminous literary labors. He translated, for example, the four volumes of Biot's treatise on physics, and the six of Thénard's work on chemistry, and took care of their enlarged editions later. He edited repertories of chemistry and physics, a pharmaceutical journal, and an encyclopædia in eight volumes, of which he wrote about one third. He published physical treatises and experimental investigations of his own, especially in electricity. Electrical measurements, as you know, are the basis of electrical science, and Fechner's measurements in galvanism, performed with the simplest self-made apparatus, are classic to this day. During this time he also published a number of half-philosophical, half-humorous writings, which have gone through several editions, under the name of Dr. Mises, besides poems, literary and artistic essays, and other occasional articles.

146

But overwork, poverty, and an eye-trouble
produced by his observations on after-images
in the retina (also a classic piece of investiga-
tion) produced in Fechner, then about thirty-
eight years old, a terrific attack of nervous
prostration with painful hyperæsthesia of all
the functions, from which he suffered three
years, cut off entirely from active life. Present-
day medicine would have classed poor Fechner's malady quickly enough, as partly a habit-
neurosis, but its severity was such that in his
day it was treated as a visitation incomprehen-
sible in its malignity; and when he suddenly
began to get well, both Fechner and others
treated the recovery as a sort of divine miracle.
This illness, bringing Fechner face to face with
inner desperation, made a great crisis in his
life. 'Had I not then clung to the faith,' he
writes, 'that clinging to faith would somehow
or other work its reward, *so hätte ich jene zeit
nicht ausgehalten.*' His religious and cosmo-
logical faiths saved him — thenceforward one
great aim with him was to work out and communicate these faiths to the world. He did so

on the largest scale; but he did many other things too ere he died.

A book on the atomic theory, classic also; four elaborate mathematical and experimental volumes on what he called psychophysics — many persons consider Fechner to have practically founded scientific psychology in the first of these books; a volume on organic evolution, and two works on experimental æsthetics, in which again Fechner is considered by some judges to have laid the foundations of a new science, must be included among these other performances. Of the more religious and philosophical works, I shall immediately give a further account.

All Leipzig mourned him when he died, for he was the pattern of the ideal german scholar, as daringly original in his thought as he was homely in his life, a modest, genial, laborious slave to truth and learning, and withal the owner of an admirable literary style of the vernacular sort. The materialistic generation, that in the fifties and sixties called his speculations fantastic, had been replaced by one with greater liberty of imagination, and a Preyer, a Wundt, a Paulsen, and a Lasswitz could now speak of Fechner as their master.

His mind was indeed one of those multitudinously organized cross-roads of truth which are occupied only at rare intervals by children of men, and from which nothing is either too far or too near to be seen in due perspective. Patientest observation, exactest mathematics, shrewdest discrimination, humanest feeling, flourished in him on the largest scale, with no apparent detriment to one another. He was in fact a philosopher in the 'great' sense, altho he cared so much less than most philosophers care for abstractions of the 'thin' order. For him the abstract lived in the concrete, and the hidden motive of all he did was to bring what he called the daylight view of the world into ever greater evidence, that daylight view being this, that the whole universe in its different spans and wave-lengths, exclusions and envelopments, is everywhere alive and conscious. It has taken fifty years for his chief book, 'Zend-avesta,' to pass into a sec-

149

ond edition (1901). 'One swallow,' he cheerfully writes, 'does not make a summer. But the first swallow would not come unless the summer were coming; and for me that summer means my daylight view some time prevailing.'

The original sin, according to Fechner, of both our popular and our scientific thinking, is our inveterate habit of regarding the spiritual not as the rule but as an exception in the midst of nature. Instead of believing our life to be fed at the breasts of the greater life, our individuality to be sustained by the greater individuality, which must necessarily have more consciousness and more independence than all that it brings forth, we habitually treat whatever lies outside of our life as so much slag and ashes of life only; or if we believe in a Divine Spirit, we fancy him on the one side as bodiless, and nature as soulless on the other. What comfort, or peace, Fechner asks, can come from such a doctrine? The flowers wither at its breath, the stars turn into stone; our own body grows unworthy of our spirit and sinks to a tenement for carnal senses only. The book of nature turns into a volume on mechanics, in which whatever has life is treated as a sort of anomaly; a great chasm of separation yawns between us and all that is higher than ourselves; and God becomes a thin nest of abstractions.

Fechner's great instrument for vivifying the daylight view is analogy; not a rationalistic argument is to be found in all his many pages — only reasonings like those which men continually use in practical life. For example: My house is built by some one, the world too is built by some one. The world is greater than my house, it must be a greater some one who built the world. My body moves by the influence of my feeling and will; the sun, moon, sea, and wind, being themselves more powerful, move by the influence of some more powerful feeling and will. I live now, and change from one day to another; I shall live hereafter, and change still more, etc.

Bain defines genius as the power of seeing analogies. The number that Fechner could perceive was prodigious; but he insisted on the differences as well. Neglect to make allowance for these, he said, is the common fallacy in analogical reasoning. Most of us, for example, reasoning justly that, since all the minds we know are connected with bodies, therefore God's mind should be connected with a body, proceed to suppose that that body must be just an animal body over again, and paint an altogether human picture of God. But all that the analogy comports is *a* body — the particular features of *our* body are adaptations to a habitat so different from God's that if God have a physical body at all, it must be utterly different from ours in structure. Throughout his writings Fechner makes difference and analogy walk abreast, and by his extraordinary power of noticing both, he converts what would ordinarily pass for objections to his conclusions into factors of their support.

The vaster orders of mind go with the vaster orders of body. The entire earth on which we live must have, according to Fechner, its own collective consciousness. So must each sun, moon, and planet; so must the whole solar system have its own wider consciousness, in which the consciousness of our earth plays one part. So has the entire starry system as such its consciousness; and if that starry system be not the sum of all that *is*, materially considered, then that whole system, along with whatever else may be, is the body of that absolutely totalized consciousness of the universe to which men give the name of God.

Speculatively Fechner is thus a monist in his theology; but there is room in his universe for every grade of spiritual being between man and the final all-inclusive God; and in suggesting what the positive content of all this super-humanity may be, he hardly lets his imagination fly beyond simple spirits of the planetary order. The earth-soul he passionately believes in; he treats the earth as our special human guardian angel; we can pray to the earth as men pray to their saints; but I think that in his system, as in so many of the actual historic theologies, the supreme God marks only a sort of limit of enclosure of the worlds above man. He is left thin and abstract in his majesty, men preferring to carry on their personal transactions with the many less remote and abstract messengers and mediators whom the divine order provides.

I shall ask later whether the abstractly monistic turn which Fechner's speculations took was necessitated by logic. I believe it not to have been required. Meanwhile let me lead you a little more into the detail of his thought. Inevitably one does him miserable injustice by summarizing and abridging him. For altho the type of reasoning he employs is almost childlike for simplicity, and his bare conclusions can be written on a single page, the *power* of the man is due altogether to the profuseness of his concrete imagination, to the multitude of the points which he considers successively, to the cumulative effect of his learning, of his thoroughness, and of the ingenuity of his detail, to his admirably homely style, to the sincerity with which his pages glow, and finally to the impression he gives of a man who doesn't live at second-hand, but who *sees*, who in fact speaks as one having authority, and not as if he were

one of the common herd of professorial philosophic scribes.

Abstractly set down, his most important
conclusion for my purpose in these lectures is
that the constitution of the world is identical
throughout. In ourselves, visual consciousness
goes with our eyes, tactile consciousness with
our skin. But altho neither skin nor eye knows
aught of the sensations of the other, they come
together and figure in some sort of relation and
combination in the more inclusive consciousness which each of us names his *self*. Quite
similarly, then, says Fechner, we must suppose
that my consciousness of myself and yours of
yourself, altho in their immediacy they keep
separate and know nothing of each other, are
yet known and used together in a higher consciousness, that of the human race, say, into
which they enter as constituent parts. Similarly, the whole human and animal kingdoms
come together as conditions of a consciousness of still wider scope. This combines in the
soul of the earth with the consciousness of the
vegetable kingdom, which in turn contributes

its share of experience to that of the whole solar system, and so on from synthesis to synthesis and height to height, till an absolutely universal consciousness is reached.

A vast analogical series, in which the basis of the analogy consists of facts directly observable in ourselves.

The supposition of an earth-consciousness meets a strong instinctive prejudice which Fechner ingeniously tries to overcome. Man's mind is the highest consciousness upon the earth, we think — the earth itself being in all ways man's inferior. How should its consciousness, if it have one, be superior to his?

What are the marks of superiority which we are tempted to use here? If we look more carefully into them, Fechner points out that the earth possesses each and all of them more perfectly than we. He considers in detail the points of difference between us, and shows them all to make for the earth's higher rank. I will touch on only a few of these points.

One of them of course is independence of other external beings. External to the earth are only the other heavenly bodies. All the things on which we externally depend for life —air, water, plant and animal food, fellow men, etc.—are included in her as her constituent parts. She is self-sufficing in a million respects in which we are not so. We depend on her for almost everything, she on us for but a small portion of her history. She swings us in her orbit from winter to summer and revolves us from day into night and from night into day.

Complexity in unity is another sign of superiority. The total earth's complexity far exceeds that of any organism, for she includes all our organisms in herself, along with an infinite number of things that our organisms fail to include. Yet how simple and massive are the phases of her own proper life! As the total bearing of any animal is sedate and tranquil compared with the agitation of its blood corpuscles, so is the earth a sedate and tranquil being compared with the animals whom she supports.

To develop from within, instead of being fashioned from without, is also counted as something superior in men's eyes. An egg is a higher style of being than a piece of clay which an external modeler makes into the image of a bird. Well, the earth's history develops from within. It is like that of a wonderful egg which the sun's heat, like that of a mother-hen, has stimulated to its cycles of evolutionary change.

Individuality of type, and difference from other beings of its type, is another mark of rank. The earth differs from every other planet, and as a class planetary beings are extraordinarily distinct from other beings.

Long ago the earth was called an animal; but a planet is a higher class of being than either man or animal; not only quantitatively greater, like a vaster and more awkward whale or elephant, but a being whose enormous size requires an altogether different plan of life. Our animal organization comes from our inferiority. Our need of moving to and fro, of stretching our limbs and bending our bodies, shows only our defect. What are our legs but crutches, by means of which, with restless efforts, we go hunting after the things we have not inside of ourselves. But the earth is no such cripple; why should she who already possesses within herself the things we so painfully pursue, have limbs analogous to ours? Shall she mimic a small part of herself? What need has she of arms, with nothing to reach for? of a neck, with no head to carry? of eyes or nose when she finds her way through space without either, and has the millions of eyes of all her animals to guide their movements on her surface, and all their noses to smell the flowers that grow? For, as we are ourselves a part of the earth, so our organs are her organs. She is, as it were, eye and ear over her whole extent — all that we see and hear in separation she sees and hears at once. She brings forth living beings of countless kinds upon her surface, and their multitudinous conscious relations with each other she takes up into her higher and more general conscious life.

Most of us, considering the theory that the whole terrestrial mass is animated as our bodies are, make the mistake of working the analogy too literally, and allowing for no differences. If the earth be a sentient organism, we say, where are her brain and nerves? What corresponds to her heart and lungs? In other words, we expect functions which she already performs through us, to be performed outside of us again, and in just the same way. But we see perfectly well how the earth performs some of these functions in a way unlike our way. If you speak of circulation, what need has she of a heart when the sun keeps all the showers of rain that fall upon her and all the springs and brooks and rivers that irrigate her, going? What need has she of internal lungs, when her whole sensitive surface is in living commerce with the atmosphere that clings to it?

The organ that gives us most trouble is the brain. All the consciousness we directly know seems tied to brains. — Can there be consciousness, we ask, where there is no brain? But our brain, which primarily serves to correlate our muscular reactions with the external objects on which we depend, performs a function which the earth performs in an entirely different way. She has no proper muscles or limbs of her own, and the only objects external to her are the other stars. To these her whole mass reacts by most exquisite alterations in its total gait, and by still more exquisite vibratory responses in its substance. Her ocean reflects the lights of heaven as in a mighty mirror, her atmosphere refracts them like a monstrous lens, the clouds and snow-fields combine them into white, the woods and flowers disperse them into colors. Polarization, interference, absorption, awaken sensibilities in matter of which our senses are too coarse to take any note.

For these cosmic relations of hers, then, she no more needs a special brain than she needs eyes or ears. *Our* brains do indeed unify and correlate innumerable functions. Our eyes know nothing of sound, our ears nothing of light, but, having brains, we can feel sound and light together, and compare them. We account for this by the fibres which in the brain connect the optical with the acoustic centre, but just how these fibres bring together not only the sensations, but the centres, we fail to see. But if fibres are indeed all that is needed to do that trick, has not the earth pathways, by which you and I are physically continuous, more than enough to do for our two minds what the brain-fibres do for the sounds and sights in a single mind? Must every higher means of unification between things be a literal *brain*-fibre, and go by that name? Cannot the earth-mind know otherwise the contents of our minds together?

Fechner's imagination, insisting on the differences as well as on the resemblances, thus tries to make our picture of the whole earth's life more concrete. He revels in the thought of its perfections. To carry her precious freight through the hours and seasons what form could be more excellent than hers — being as it is horse, wheels, and wagon all in one. Think of her beauty — a shining ball, sky-blue and sun-lit over one half, the other bathed in starry night, reflecting the heavens from all her waters, myriads of lights and shadows in the folds of her mountains and windings of her valleys, she would be a spectacle of rainbow glory,

could one only see her from afar as we see
parts of her from her own mountain-tops.
Every quality of landscape that has a name
would then be visible in her at once—all that
is delicate or graceful, all that is quiet, or wild,
or romantic, or desolate, or cheerful, or luxu-
riant, or fresh. That landscape is her face —
a peopled landscape, too, for men's eyes would
appear in it like diamonds among the dew-
drops. Green would be the dominant color,
but the blue atmosphere and the clouds would
enfold her as a bride is shrouded in her veil —
a veil the vapory transparent folds of which the
earth, through her ministers the winds, never
tires of laying and folding about herself anew.

Every element has its own living denizens.
Can the celestial ocean of ether, whose waves
are light, in which the earth herself floats,
not have hers, higher by as much as their element is higher, swimming without fins, flying
without wings, moving, immense and tranquil,
as by a half-spiritual force through the half-
spiritual sea which they inhabit, rejoicing in
the exchange of luminous influence with one

another, following the slightest pull of one another's attraction, and harboring, each of them, an inexhaustible inward wealth?

Men have always made fables about angels, dwelling in the light, needing no earthly food or drink, messengers between ourselves and God. Here are actually existent beings, dwelling in the light and moving through the sky, needing neither food nor drink, intermediaries between God and us, obeying his commands. So, if the heavens really are the home of angels, the heavenly bodies must be those very angels, for other creatures *there* are none. Yes! the earth is our great common guardian angel, who watches over all our interests combined.

In a striking page Fechner relates one of his moments of direct vision of this truth.

'On a certain spring morning I went out to walk. The fields were green, the birds sang, the dew glistened, the smoke was rising, here and there a man appeared; a light as of transfiguration lay on all things. It was only a little bit of the earth; it was only one moment of her existence; and yet as my look embraced her

164

more and more it seemed to me not only so beautiful an idea, but so true and clear a fact, that she is an angel, an angel so rich and fresh and flower-like, and yet going her round in the skies so firmly and so at one with herself, turning her whole living face to Heaven, and carrying me along with her into that Heaven, that I asked myself how the opinions of men could ever have so spun themselves away from life so far as to deem the earth only a dry clod, and to seek for angels above it or about it in the emptiness of the sky,—only to find them nowhere. . . . But such an experience as this passes for fantastic. The earth is a globular body, and what more she may be, one can find in mineralogical cabinets.'[2]

Where there is no vision the people perish. Few professorial philosophers have any vision. Fechner had vision, and that is why one can read him over and over again, and each time bring away a fresh sense of reality.

His earliest book was a vision of what the inner life of plants may be like. He called it 'Nanna.' In the development of animals the nervous system is the central fact. Plants develop centrifugally, spread their organs abroad. For that reason people suppose that they can have no consciousness, for they lack the unity which the central nervous system provides. But the plant's consciousness may be of another type, being connected with other structures. Violins and pianos give out sounds because they have strings. Does it follow that nothing but strings can give out sound ? How then about flutes and organ-pipes ? Of course their sounds are of a different quality, and so may the consciousness of plants be of a quality correlated exclusively with the kind of organization that they possess. Nutrition, respiration, propagation take place in them without nerves. In us these functions are conscious only in unusual states, normally their consciousness is eclipsed by that which goes with the brain. No such eclipse occurs in plants, and their lower consciousness may therefore be all the more lively. With nothing to do but to drink the light and air with their leaves, to let their cells proliferate, to feel their rootlets draw the sap, is it conceivable that they should not consciously suffer if water, light, and air are suddenly withdrawn? or that when the flowering and fertilization which are the culmination of their life take place, they should not feel their own existence more intensely and enjoy something like what we call pleasure in ourselves? Does the water-lily, rocking in her triple bath of water, air, and light, relish in no wise her own beauty? When the plant in our room turns to the light, closes her blossoms in the dark, responds to our watering or pruning by increase of size or change of shape and bloom, who has the right to say she does not feel, or that she plays a purely passive part? Truly plants can foresee nothing, neither the scythe of the mower, nor the hand extended to pluck their flowers. They can neither run away nor cry out. But this only proves how different their modes of feeling life must be from those of animals that live by eyes and ears and locomotive organs, it does not prove that they have no mode of feeling life at all.

How scanty and scattered would sensation

be on our globe, if the feeling-life of plants were blotted from existence. Solitary would consciousness move through the woods in the shape of some deer or other quadruped, or fly about the flowers in that of some insect, but can we really suppose that the Nature through which God's breath blows is such a barren wilderness as this?

I have probably by this time said enough to acquaint those of you who have never seen these metaphysical writings of Fechner with their more general characteristics, and I hope that some of you may now feel like reading them yourselves.[3] The special thought of Fechner's with which in these lectures I have most practical concern, is his belief that the more inclusive forms of consciousness are in part *constituted* by the more limited forms. Not that they are the mere sum of the more limited forms. As our mind is not the bare sum of our sights plus our sounds plus our pains, but in adding these terms together also finds relations among them and weaves them into schemes and forms and objects of which no one sense in its separate estate knows anything, so the earth-soul traces relations between the contents of my mind and the contents of yours of which neither of our separate minds is conscious. It has schemes, forms, and objects proportionate to its wider field, which our mental fields are far too narrow to cognize. By ourselves we are simply out of relation with each other, for it we are both of us there, and *different* from each other, which is a positive relation. What we are without knowing, it knows that we are. We are closed against its world, but that world is not closed against us. It is as if the total universe of inner life had a sort of grain or direction, a sort of valvular structure, permitting knowledge to flow in one way only, so that the wider might always have the narrower under observation, but never the narrower the wider.

Fechner's great analogy here is the relation of the senses to our individual minds. When our eyes are open their sensations enter into our general mental life, which grows incessantly by the addition of what they see. Close

the eyes, however, and the visual additions
stop, nothing but thoughts and memories of
the past visual experiences remain — in combination of course with the enormous stock of
other thoughts and memories, and with the
data coming in from the senses not yet closed.
Our eye-sensations of themselves know nothing of this enormous life into which they fall.
Fechner thinks, as any common man would
think, that they are taken into it directly when
they occur, and form part of it just as they are.
They don't stay outside and get represented
inside by their copies. It is only the memories and concepts of them that are copies;
the sensible perceptions themselves are taken
in or walled out in their own proper persons
according as the eyes are open or shut.

Fechner likens our individual persons on
the earth unto so many sense-organs of the
earth's soul. We add to its perceptive life so
long as our own life lasts. It absorbs our perceptions, just as they occur, into its larger
sphere of knowledge, and combines them with
the other data there. When one of us dies, it

is as if an eye of the world were closed, for all *perceptive* contributions from that particular quarter cease. But the memories and conceptual relations that have spun themselves round the perceptions of that person remain in the larger earth-life as distinct as ever, and form new relations and grow and develop throughout all the future, in the same way in which our own distinct objects of thought, once stored in memory, form new relations and develop throughout our whole finite life. This is Fechner's theory of immortality, first published in the little 'Büchlein des lebens nach dem tode,' in 1836, and re-edited in greatly improved shape in the last volume of his 'Zend-avesta.'

We rise upon the earth as wavelets rise upon the ocean. We grow out of her soil as leaves grow from a tree. The wavelets catch the sunbeams separately, the leaves stir when the branches do not move. They realize their own events apart, just as in our own consciousness, when anything becomes emphatic, the background fades from observation. Yet the event works back upon the background, as the wave-let works upon the waves, or as the leaf's movements work upon the sap inside the branch. The whole sea and the whole tree are registers of what has happened, and are different for the wave's and the leaf's action having occurred. A grafted twig may modify its stock to the roots:—so our outlived private experiences, impressed on the whole earth-mind as memories, lead the immortal life of ideas there, and become parts of the great system, fully distinguished from one another, just as we ourselves when alive were distinct, realizing themselves no longer isolatedly, but along with one another as so many partial systems, entering thus into new combinations, being affected by the perceptive experiences of those living then, and affecting the living in their turn — altho they are so seldom recognized by living men to do so.

If you imagine that this entrance after the death of the body into a common life of higher type means a merging and loss of our distinct personality, Fechner asks you whether a visual sensation of our own exists in any sense *less for itself* or *less distinctly*, when it enters into our higher relational consciousness and is there distinguished and defined.

— But here I must stop my reporting and send you to his volumes. Thus is the universe alive, according to this philosopher! I think you will admit that he makes it more *thickly* alive than do the other philosophers who, following rationalistic methods solely, gain the same results, but only in the thinnest outlines. Both Fechner and Professor Royce, for example, believe ultimately in one all-inclusive mind. Both believe that we, just as we stand here, are constituent parts of that mind. No other *content* has it than us, with all the other creatures like or unlike us, and the relations which it finds between us. Our eaches, collected into one, are substantively identical with its all, tho the all is perfect while no each is perfect, so that we have to admit that new qualities as well as unperceived relations accrue from the collective form. It is thus superior to the distributive form. But having reached this result, Royce (tho his treatment of the subject on its moral side seems to me infinitely richer and thicker than that of any other contemporary idealistic philosopher) leaves us very much to our own devices. Fechner, on the contrary, tries to trace the superiorities due to the more collective form in as much detail as he can. He marks the various intermediary stages and halting places of collectivity, — as we are to our separate senses, so is the earth to us, so is the solar system to the earth, etc., — and if, in order to escape an infinitely long summation, he posits a complete God as the all-container and leaves him about as indefinite in feature as the idealists leave their absolute, he yet provides us with a very definite gate of approach to him in the shape of the earth-soul, through which in the nature of things we must first make connexion with all the more enveloping superhuman realms, and with which our more immediate religious commerce at any rate has to be carried on.

Ordinary monistic idealism leaves everything intermediary out. It recognizes only the extremes, as if, after the first rude face of the phenomenal world in all its particularity, nothing but the supreme in all its perfection could be found. First, you and I, just as we are in this room; and the moment we get below that surface, the unutterable absolute itself! Does n't this show a singularly indigent imagination? Is n't this brave universe made on a richer pattern, with room in it for a long hierarchy of beings? Materialistic science makes it infinitely richer in terms, with its molecules, and ether, and electrons, and what not. Absolute idealism, thinking of reality only under intellectual forms, knows not what to do with *bodies* of any grade, and can make no use of any psychophysical analogy or correspondence. The resultant thinness is startling when compared with the thickness and articulation of such a universe as Fechner paints. May not satisfaction with the rationalistic absolute as the alpha and omega, and treatment of it in all its abstraction as an adequate religious object, argue a certain native poverty of mental demand? Things reveal themselves soonest to those who most passionately want them, for our need sharpens our wit. To a mind content with little, the much in the universe may always remain hid.

To be candid, one of my reasons for saying so much about Fechner has been to make the thinness of our current transcendentalism appear more evident by an effect of contrast. Scholasticism ran thick; Hegel himself ran thick; but english and american transcendentalisms run thin. If philosophy is more a matter of passionate vision than of logic, — and I believe it is, logic only finding reasons for the vision afterwards, — must not such thinness come either from the vision being defective in the disciples, or from their passion, matched with Fechner's or with Hegel's own passion, being as moonlight unto sunlight or as water unto wine? [4]

But I have also a much deeper reason for making Fechner a part of my text. His *assumption that conscious experiences freely compound and separate themselves*, the same assumption

176

by which absolutism explains the relation of
our minds to the eternal mind, and the same
by which empiricism explains the composition
of the human mind out of subordinate mental elements, is not one which we ought to let
pass without scrutiny. I shall scrutinize it in
the next lecture.

V

THE COMPOUNDING OF
CONSCIOUSNESS

LECTURE V

THE COMPOUNDING OF CONSCIOUSNESS

In my last lecture I gave a miserably scanty outline of the way of thinking of a philosopher remarkable for the almost unexampled richness of his imagination of details. I owe to Fechner's shade an apology for presenting him in a manner so unfair to the most essential quality of his genius; but the time allotted is too short to say more about the particulars of his work, so I proceed to the programme I suggested at the end of our last hour. I wish to discuss the assumption that states of consciousness, so-called, can separate and combine themselves freely, and keep their own identity unchanged while forming parts of simultaneous fields of experience of wider scope.

Let me first explain just what I mean by this. While you listen to my voice, for example, you are perhaps inattentive to some bodily sensation due to your clothing or your posture.

Yet that sensation would seem probably to be there, for in an instant, by a change of attention, you can have it in one field of consciousness with the voice. It seems as if it existed first in a separate form, and then as if, without itself changing, it combined with your other co-existent sensations. It is after this analogy that pantheistic idealism thinks that we exist in the absolute. The absolute, it thinks, makes the world by knowing the whole of it at once in one undivided eternal act.[1] To 'be,' *really* to be, is to be as it knows us to be, along with everything else, namely, and clothed with the fulness of our meaning. Meanwhile we *are* at the same time not only really and as it knows us, but also apparently, for to our separate single selves we appear *without* most other things and unable to declare with any fulness what our own meaning is. Now the classic doctrine of pantheistic idealism, from the Upanishads down to Josiah Royce, is that the finite knowers, in spite of their apparent ignorance, are one with the knower of the all. In the most limited moments of our private experience, the absolute idea, as Dr. McTaggart told us, is implicitly contained. The moments, as Royce says, exist only in relation to it. They are true or erroneous only through its overshadowing presence. Of the larger self that alone eternally is, they are the organic parts. They *are*, only inasmuch as they are implicated in its being.

There is thus in reality but this one self, consciously inclusive of all the lesser selves, *logos*, problem-solver, and all-knower; and Royce ingeniously compares the ignorance that in our persons breaks out in the midst of its complete knowledge and isolates me from you and both of us from it, to the inattention into which our finite minds are liable to fall with respect to such implicitly present details as those corporeal sensations to which I made allusion just now. Those sensations stand to our total private minds in the same relation in which our private minds stand to the absolute mind. Privacy means ignorance — I still quote Royce — and ignorance means inattention. We are finite because our wills, as such, are only fragments

183

of the absolute will; because will means interest, and an incomplete will means an incomplete interest; and because incompleteness of
interest means inattention to much that a fuller
interest would bring us to perceive.[2]

In this account Royce makes by far the
manliest of the post-hegelian attempts to read
some empirically apprehensible content into
the notion of our relation to the absolute mind.

I have to admit, now that I propose to you
to scrutinize this assumption rather closely,
that trepidation seizes me. The subject is a
subtle and abstruse one. It is one thing to
delve into subtleties by one's self with pen in
hand, or to study out abstruse points in books,
but quite another thing to make a popular lecture out of them. Nevertheless I must not
flinch from my task here, for I think that this
particular point forms perhaps the vital knot
of the present philosophic situation, and I
imagine that the times are ripe, or almost ripe,
for a serious attempt to be made at its untying.

It may perhaps help to lessen the arduous-
ness of the subject if I put the first part of what

184

V. COMPOUNDING OF CONSCIOUSNESS

I have to say in the form of a direct personal confession.

In the year 1890 I published a work on psychology in which it became my duty to discuss the value of a certain explanation of our higher mental states that had come into favor among the more biologically inclined psychologists. Suggested partly by the association of ideas, and partly by the analogy of chemical compounds, this opinion was that complex mental states are resultants of the self-compounding of simpler ones. The Mills had spoken of mental chemistry; Wundt of a 'psychic synthesis,' which might develop properties not contained in the elements; and such writers as Spencer, Taine, Fiske, Barratt, and Clifford had propounded a great evolutionary theory in which, in the absence of souls, selves, or other principles of unity, primordial units of mind-stuff or mind-dust were represented as summing themselves together in successive stages of compounding and re-compounding, and thus engendering our higher and more complex states of mind. The elementary feeling of A, let us say, and the elementary feeling of B, when they occur in certain conditions, combine, according to this doctrine, into a feeling of A-plus-B, and this in turn combines with a similarly generated feeling of C-plus-D, until at last the whole alphabet may appear together in one field of awareness, without any other witnessing principle or principles beyond the feelings of the several letters themselves, being supposed to exist. What each of them witnesses separately, 'all' of them are supposed to witness in conjunction. But their distributive knowledge does n't *give rise* to their collective knowledge by any act, it *is* their collective knowledge. The lower forms of consciousness 'taken together' *are* the higher. It, 'taken apart,' consists of nothing and *is* nothing but them. This, at least, is the most obvious way of understanding the doctrine, and is the way I understood it in the chapter in my psychology.

Superficially looked at, this seems just like the combination of H_2 and O into water, but looked at more closely, the analogy halts badly.

186

V. COMPOUNDING OF CONSCIOUSNESS

When a chemist tells us that two atoms of hydrogen and one of oxygen combine themselves of their own accord into the new compound substance 'water,' he knows (if he believes in the mechanical view of nature) that this is only an elliptical statement for a more complex fact. That fact is that when H_2 and O, instead of keeping far apart, get into closer quarters, say into the position H-O-H, they *affect surrounding bodies differently*: they now wet our skin, dissolve sugar, put out fire, etc., which they didn't in their former positions. 'Water' is but *our name* for what acts thus peculiarly. But if the skin, sugar, and fire were absent, no witness would speak of water at all. He would still talk of the H and O distributively, merely noting that they acted now in the new position H-O-H.

In the older psychologies the soul or self took the place of the sugar, fire, or skin. The lower feelings produced *effects on it*, and their apparent compounds were only its reactions. As you tickle a man's face with a feather, and he laughs, so when you tickle his intellectual principle with a retinal feeling, say, and a muscular feeling at once, it laughs responsively by its category of 'space,' but it would be false to treat the space as simply made of those simpler feelings. It is rather a new and unique psychic creation which their combined action on the mind is able to evoke.

I found myself obliged, in discussing the mind-dust theory, to urge this last alternative view. The so-called mental compounds are simple psychic reactions of a higher type. The form itself of them, I said, is something new. We can't say that awareness of the alphabet as such is nothing more than twenty-six awarenesses, each of a separate letter; for those are twenty-six distinct awarenesses, of single letters *without* others, while their so-called sum is one awareness, of every letter *with* its comrades. There is thus something new in the collective consciousness. It knows the same letters, indeed, but it knows them in this novel way. It is safer, I said (for I fought shy of admitting a self or soul or other agent of combination), to treat the consciousness of the alphabet as a twenty-seventh fact, the substitute and not the sum of the twenty-six simpler consciousnesses, and to say that while under certain physiological conditions they alone are produced, other more complex physiological conditions result in its production instead. Do not talk, therefore, I said, of the higher states *consisting* of the simpler, or *being* the same with them; talk rather of their *knowing the same things*. They are different mental facts, but they apprehend, each in its own peculiar way, the same objective A, B, C, and D.

The theory of combination, I was forced to conclude, is thus untenable, being both logically nonsensical and practically unnecessary. Say what you will, twelve thoughts, each of a single word, are not the self-same mental thing as one thought of the whole sentence. The higher thoughts, I insisted, are psychic units, not compounds; but for all that, they may know together as a collective multitude the very same objects which under other conditions are known separately by as many simple thoughts.

For many years I held rigorously to this view,[3] and the reasons for doing so seemed to me during all those years to apply also to the opinion that the absolute mind stands to our minds in the relation of a whole to its parts. If untenable in finite psychology, that opinion ought to be untenable in metaphysics also. The great transcendentalist metaphor has always been, as I lately reminded you, a grammatical sentence. Physically such a sentence is of course composed of clauses, these of words, the words of syllables, and the syllables of letters. We may take each word in, yet not understand the sentence; but if suddenly the meaning of the whole sentence flashes, the sense of each word is taken up into that whole meaning. Just so, according to our transcendentalist teachers, the absolute mind thinks the whole sentence, while we, according to our rank as thinkers, think a clause, a word, a syllable, or a letter. Most of us are, as I said, mere syllables in the mouth of Allah. And as Allah comes first in the order of being, so comes first the entire sentence, the *logos* that

190

forms the eternal absolute thought. Students
of language tell us that speech began with
men's efforts to make *statements*. The rude
synthetic vocal utterances first used for this
effect slowly got stereotyped, and then much
later got decomposed into grammatical parts.
It is not as if men had first invented letters
and made syllables of them, then made words
of the syllables and sentences of the words; —
they actually followed the reverse order. So,
the transcendentalists affirm, the complete
absolute thought is the pre-condition of our
thoughts, and we finite creatures *are* only in
so far as it owns us as its verbal fragments.

The metaphor is so beautiful, and applies,
moreover, so literally to such a multitude of
the minor wholes of experience, that by merely
hearing it most of us are convinced that it must
apply universally. We see that no smallest
raindrop can come into being without a whole
shower, no single feather without a whole bird,
neck and crop, beak and tail, coming into being
simultaneously: so we unhesitatingly lay down
the law that no part of anything can be except

so far as the whole also is. And then, since everything whatever is part of the whole universe, and since (if we are idealists) nothing, whether part or whole, exists except for a witness, we proceed to the conclusion that the unmitigated absolute as witness of the whole is the one sole ground of being of every partial fact, the fact of our own existence included. We think of ourselves as being only a few of the feathers, so to speak, which help to constitute that absolute bird. Extending the analogy of certain wholes, of which we have familiar experience, to the whole of wholes, we easily become absolute idealists.

But if, instead of yielding to the seductions of our metaphor, be it sentence, shower, or bird, we analyze more carefully the notion suggested by it that we are constituent parts of the absolute's eternal field of consciousness, we find grave difficulties arising. First, the difficulty I found with the mind-dust theory. If the absolute makes us by knowing us, how can we exist otherwise than *as* it knows us? But it knows each of us indivisibly from everything else. Yet

V. COMPOUNDING OF CONSCIOUSNESS

if to exist means nothing but to be experienced, as idealism affirms, we surely exist otherwise, for we experience *ourselves* ignorantly and in division. We indeed differ from the absolute not only by defect, but by excess. Our ignorances, for example, bring curiosities and doubts by which it cannot be troubled, for it owns eternally the solution of every problem. Our impotence entails pains, our imperfection sins, which its perfection keeps at a distance. What I said of the alphabet-form and the letters holds good of the absolute experience and our experiences. Their relation, whatever it may be, seems not to be that of identity.

It is impossible to reconcile the peculiarities of our experience with our being only the absolute's mental objects. A God, as distinguished from the absolute, creates things by projecting them beyond himself as so many substances, each endowed with *perseity*, as the scholastics call it. But objects of thought are not things *per se*. They are there only *for* their thinker, and only *as* he thinks them. How, then, can they become severally alive on their own ac-

counts and think themselves quite otherwise
than as he thinks them? It is as if the characters in a novel were to get up from the pages,
and walk away and transact business of their
own outside of the author's story.

A third difficulty is this: The bird-metaphor
is physical, but we see on reflection that in the
physical world there is no real compounding.
'Wholes' are not realities there, parts only are
realities. 'Bird' is only our *name* for the physical fact of a certain grouping of organs, just
as 'Charles's Wain' is our name for a certain
grouping of stars. The 'whole,' be it bird or
constellation, is nothing but our vision, nothing
but an effect on our sensorium when a lot of
things act on it together. It is not realized by
any organ or any star, or experienced apart
from the consciousness of an onlooker.[4] In
the physical world taken by itself there *is* thus
no 'all,' there are only the 'eaches' — at least
that is the 'scientific' view.

In the mental world, on the contrary, wholes
do in point of fact realize themselves *per se*. The
meaning of the whole sentence is just as much a

real experience as the feeling of each word is; the absolute's experience *is* for itself, as much as yours is for yourself or mine for myself. So the feather-and-bird analogy won't work unless you make the absolute into a distinct sort of mental agent with a vision produced in it *by* our several minds analogous to the 'bird'-vision which the feathers, beak, etc., produce *in* those same minds. The 'whole,' which is *its* experience, would then be its unifying reaction on our experiences, and not those very experiences self-combined. Such a view as this would go with theism, for the theistic God is a separate being; but it would not go with pantheistic idealism, the very essence of which is to insist that we are literally *parts* of God, and he only ourselves in our totality — the word 'ourselves' here standing of course for all the universe's finite facts.

I am dragging you into depths unsuitable, I fear, for a rapid lecture. Such difficulties as these have to be teased out with a needle, so to speak, and lecturers should take only bird's-eye views. The practical upshot of the matter, however, so far as I am concerned, is this, that if I had been lecturing on the absolute a very few years ago, I should unhesitatingly have urged these difficulties, and developed them at still greater length, to show that the hypothesis of the absolute was not only non-coercive from the logical point of view, but self-contradictory as well, its notion that parts and whole are only two names for the same thing not bearing critical scrutiny. If you stick to purely physical terms like stars, there *is* no whole. If you call the whole mental, then the so-called whole, instead of being one fact with the parts, appears rather as the integral reaction on those parts of an independent higher witness, such as the theistic God is supposed to be.

So long as this was the state of my own mind, I could accept the notion of self-compounding in the supernal spheres of experience no more easily than in that chapter on mind-dust I had accepted it in the lower spheres. I found myself compelled, therefore, to call the absolute impossible ; and the untrammelled freedom with which pantheistic or monistic idealists stepped over the logical barriers which Lotze

V. COMPOUNDING OF CONSCIOUSNESS

and others had set down long before I had—I had done little more than quote these previous critics in my chapter—surprised me not a little, and made me, I have to confess, both resentful and envious. Envious because in the bottom of my heart I wanted the same freedom myself, for motives which I shall develop later; and resentful because my absolutist friends seemed to me to be stealing the privilege of blowing both hot and cold. To establish their absolute they used an intellectualist type of logic which they disregarded when employed against it. It seemed to me that they ought at least to have mentioned the objections that had stopped me so completely. I had yielded to them against my 'will to believe,' out of pure logical scrupulosity. They, professing to loathe the will to believe and to follow purest rationality, had simply ignored them. The method was easy, but hardly to be called candid. Fechner indeed was candid enough, for he had never thought of the objections, but later writers, like Royce, who should presumably have heard them, had passed them by in silence. I felt as if these philosophers were granting their will to believe in monism too easy a license. My own conscience would permit me no such license.

So much for the personal confession by which you have allowed me to introduce the subject. Let us now consider it more objectively.

The fundamental difficulty I have found is the number of contradictions which idealistic monists seem to disregard. In the first place they attribute to all existence a mental or experiential character, but I find their simultaneous belief that the higher and the lower in the universe are entitatively identical, incompatible with this character. Incompatible in consequence of the generally accepted doctrine that, whether Berkeley were right or not in saying of material existence that its *esse* is *sentiri*, it is undoubtedly right to say of *mental* existence that its *esse* is *sentiri* or *experiri*. If I feel pain, it is just pain that I feel, however I may have come by the feeling. No one pretends that pain as such only appears like pain, but in itself is different, for to be as a mental experience *is* only to appear to some one.

The idealists in question ought then to do one of two things, but they do neither. They ought either to refute the notion that as mental states appear, so they are; or, still keeping that notion, they ought to admit a distinct agent of unification to do the work of the all-knower, just as our respective souls or selves in popular philosophy do the work of partial knowers. Otherwise it is like a joint-stock company all shareholders and no treasurer or director. If our finite minds formed a billion facts, then its mind, knowing our billion, would make a universe composed of a billion and one facts. But transcendental idealism is quite as unfriendly to active principles called souls as physiological psychology is, Kant having, as it thinks, definitively demolished them. And altho some disciples speak of the transcendental ego of apperception (which they celebrate as Kant's most precious legacy to posterity) as if it were a combining agent, the drift of monistic authority is certainly in the direction of treating it as only an all-witness, whose field of vision we finite witnesses do not cause, but constitute rather. We are the letters, it is the alphabet; we are the features, it is the face; not indeed as if either alphabet or face were something additional to the letters or the features, but rather as if it were only another name for the very letters or features themselves. The all-form assuredly differs from the each-form, but the *matter* is the same in both, and the each-form only an unaccountable appearance.

But this, as you see, contradicts the other idealist principle, of a mental fact being just what it appears to be. If their forms of appearance are so different, the all and the eaches cannot be identical.

The way out (unless, indeed, we are willing to discard the logic of identity altogether) would seem to be frankly to write down the all and the eaches as two distinct orders of witness, each minor witness being aware of its own 'content' solely, while the greater witness knows the minor witnesses, knows their whole content pooled together, knows their relations to one another, and knows of just how much each one of them is ignorant.

The two types of witnessing are here palpably non-identical. We get a pluralism, not a monism, out of them. In my psychology-chapter I had resorted openly to such pluralism, treating each total field of consciousness as a distinct entity, and maintaining that the higher fields merely supersede the lower functionally by knowing more about the same objects.

The monists themselves writhe like worms on the hook to escape pluralistic or at least dualistic language, but they cannot escape it. They speak of the eternal and the temporal 'points of view'; of the universe in its infinite 'aspect' or in its finite 'capacity'; they say that '*quâ* absolute' it is one thing, '*quâ* relative' another; they contrast its 'truth' with its 'appearances'; they distinguish the total from the partial way of 'taking' it, etc.; but they forget that, on idealistic principles, to make such distinctions is tantamount to making different beings, or at any rate that varying points of view, aspects, appearances, ways of taking,

201

and the like, are meaningless phrases unless we suppose outside of the unchanging content of reality a diversity of witnesses who experience or take it variously, the absolute mind being just the witness that takes it most completely.

For consider the matter one moment longer, if you can. Ask what this notion implies, of appearing differently from different points of view. If there be no outside witness, a thing can appear only to itself, the eaches or parts to their several selves temporally, the all or whole to itself eternally. Different 'selves' thus break out inside of what the absolutist insists to be intrinsically one fact. But how can what is *actually* one be *effectively* so many? Put your witnesses anywhere, whether outside or inside of what is witnessed, in the last resort your witnesses must on idealistic principles be distinct, for what is witnessed is different.

I fear that I am expressing myself with terrible obscurity — some of you, I know, are groaning over the logic-chopping. Be a pluralist or be a monist, you say, for heaven's sake, no matter which, so long as you stop arguing. It reminds one of Chesterton's epigram that the only thing that ever drives human beings insane is logic. But whether I be sane or insane, you cannot fail, even tho you be transcendentalists yourselves, to recognize to some degree by my trouble the difficulties that beset monistic idealism. What boots it to call the parts and the whole the same body of experience, when in the same breath you have to say that the all 'as such' means one sort of experience and each part 'as such' means another?

Difficulties, then, so far, but no stable solution as yet, for I have been talking only critically. You will probably be relieved to hear, then, that having rounded this corner, I shall begin to consider what may be the possibilities of getting farther.

To clear the path, I beg you first to note one point. What has so troubled my logical conscience is not so much the absolute by itself as the whole class of suppositions of which it is the supreme example, collective experiences namely, claiming identity with their constituent parts, yet experiencing things quite differently from these latter. If *any* such collective experience can be, then of course, so far as the mere logic of the case goes, the absolute may be. In a previous lecture I have talked against the absolute from other points of view. In this lecture I have meant merely to take it as the example most prominent at Oxford of the thing which has given me such logical perplexity. I don't logically see how a collective experience of any grade whatever can be treated as logically identical with a lot of distributive experiences. They form two different concepts. The absolute happens to be the only collective experience concerning which Oxford idealists have urged the identity, so I took it as my prerogative instance. But Fechner's earth-soul, or any stage of being below or above that, would have served my purpose just as well: the same logical objection applies to these collective experiences as to the absolute.

So much, then, in order that you may not be confused about my strategical objective. The real point to defend against the logic that I have used is the identity of the collective and distributive anyhow, not the particular example of such identity known as the absolute.

So now for the directer question. Shall we say that every complex mental fact is a separate psychic entity succeeding upon a lot of other psychic entities which are erroneously called its parts, and superseding them in function, but not literally being composed of them? This was the course I took in my psychology; and if followed in theology, we should have to deny the absolute as usually conceived, and replace it by the 'God' of theism. We should also have to deny Fechner's 'earth-soul' and all other superhuman collections of experience of every grade, so far at least as these are held to be compounded of our simpler souls in the way which Fechner believed in; and we should have to make all these denials in the name of the incorruptible logic of self-identity, teaching us that to call a thing and its other the same is to commit the crime of self-contradiction.

But if we realize the whole philosophic situation thus produced, we see that it is almost intolerable. Loyal to the logical kind of rationality, it is disloyal to every other kind. It makes the universe discontinuous. These fields of experience that replace each other so punctually, each knowing the same matter, but in ever-widening contexts, from simplest feeling up to absolute knowledge, *can* they have no *being* in common when their cognitive function is so manifestly common? The regular succession of them is on such terms an unintelligible miracle. If you reply that their common *object* is of itself enough to make the many witnesses continuous, the same implacable logic follows you — how *can* one and the same object appear so variously? Its diverse appearances break it into a plurality; and our world of objects then falls into discontinuous pieces quite as much as did our world of subjects. The resultant irrationality is really intolerable.

I said awhile ago that I was envious of Fechner and the other pantheists because I myself wanted the same freedom that I saw them unscrupulously enjoying, of letting mental fields compound themselves and so make the universe more continuous, but that my conscience held me prisoner. In my heart of hearts, however, I knew that my situation was absurd and could be only provisional. That secret of a continuous life which the universe knows by heart and acts on every instant cannot be a contradiction incarnate. If logic says it is one, so much the worse for logic. Logic being the lesser thing, the static incomplete abstraction, must succumb to reality, not reality to logic. Our intelligence cannot wall itself up alive, like a pupa in its chrysalis. It must at any cost keep on speaking terms with the universe that engendered it. Fechner, Royce, and Hegel seem on the truer path. Fechner has never heard of logic's veto, Royce hears the voice but cannily ignores the utterances, Hegel hears them but to spurn them — and all go on their way rejoicing. Shall we alone obey the veto?

Sincerely, and patiently as I could, I struggled with the problem for years, covering hundreds of sheets of paper with notes and memoranda and discussions with myself over the difficulty. How can many consciousnesses be at the same time one consciousness? How can one and the same identical fact experience itself so diversely? The struggle was vain; I found myself in an *impasse*. I saw that I must either forswear that 'psychology without a soul' to which my whole psychological and kantian education had committed me, — I must, in short, bring back distinct spiritual agents to know the mental states, now singly and now in combination, in a word bring back scholasticism and common sense — or else I must squarely confess the solution of the problem impossible, and then either give up my intellectualistic logic, the logic of identity, and adopt some higher (or lower) form of rationality, or, finally, face the fact that life is logically irrational.

Sincerely, this is the actual trilemma that confronts every one of us. Those of you who are scholastic-minded, or simply common-sense minded, will smile at the elaborate groans of my parturient mountain resulting in nothing but this mouse. Accept the spiritual agents, for heaven's sake, you will say, and leave off your ridiculous pedantry. Let but our 'souls' combine our sensations by their intellectual faculties, and let but 'God' replace the pantheistic world-soul, and your wheels will go round again — you will enjoy both life and logic together.

This solution is obvious and I know that many of you will adopt it. It is comfortable, and all our habits of speech support it. Yet it is not for idle or fantastical reasons that the notion of the substantial soul, so freely used by common men and the more popular philosophies, has fallen upon such evil days, and has no prestige in the eyes of critical thinkers. It only shares the fate of other unrepresentable substances and principles. They are without exception all so barren that to sincere inquirers they appear as little more than names masquerading — Wo die begriffe fehlen da stellt ein wort zur rechten zeit sich ein. You see no deeper into the fact that a hundred sensations get compounded or known together by thinking that a 'soul' does the compounding than you see into a man's living eighty years by thinking of him as an octogenarian, or into our having five fingers by calling us pentadactyls. Souls have worn out both themselves and their welcome, that is the plain truth. Philosophy ought to get the manifolds of experience unified on principles less empty. Like the word 'cause,' the word 'soul' is but a theoretic stop-gap — it marks a place and claims it for a future explanation to occupy.

This being our post-humian and post-kantian state of mind, I will ask your permission to leave the soul wholly out of the present discussion and to consider only the residual dilemma. Some day, indeed, souls may get their innings again in philosophy — I am quite ready to admit that possibility — they form a category of thought too natural to the human mind to expire without prolonged resistance. But if the belief in the soul ever does come to life after the many funeral-discourses which humian and kantian criticism have preached over it, I am sure it will be only when some one has found in the term a pragmatic significance that has hitherto eluded observation.

V. COMPOUNDING OF CONSCIOUSNESS

When that champion speaks, as he well may speak some day, it will be time to consider souls more seriously.

Let us leave out the soul, then, and confront what I just called the residual dilemma. Can we, on the one hand, give up the logic of identity? — can we, on the other, believe human experience to be fundamentally irrational? Neither is easy, yet it would seem that we must do one or the other.

Few philosophers have had the frankness fairly to admit the necessity of choosing between the 'horns' offered. Reality must be rational, they have said, and since the ordinary intellectualist logic is the only usual test of rationality, reality and logic must agree 'somehow.' Hegel was the first non-mystical writer to face the dilemma squarely and throw away the ordinary logic, saving a pseudo-rationality for the universe by inventing the higher logic of the 'dialectic process.' Bradley holds to the intellectualist logic, and by dint of it convicts the human universe of being irrationality incarnate. But what must be and can be, is, he says; there must and can be relief from *that* irrationality; and the absolute must already have got the relief in secret ways of its own, impossible for us to guess at. *We* of course get no relief, so Bradley's is a rather ascetic doctrine. Royce and Taylor accept similar solutions, only they emphasize the irrationality of our finite universe less than Bradley does; and Royce in particular, being unusually 'thick' for an idealist, tries to bring the absolute's secret forms of relief more sympathetically home to our imagination.

Well, what must we do in this tragic predicament? For my own part, I have finally found myself compelled to *give up the logic*, fairly, squarely, and irrevocably. It has an imperishable use in human life, but that use is not to make us theoretically acquainted with the essential nature of reality — just what it is I can perhaps suggest to you a little later. Reality, life, experience, concreteness, immediacy, use what word you will, exceeds our logic, overflows and surrounds it. If you like to employ words eulogistically, as most men do, and so

212

encourage confusion, you may say that reality obeys a higher logic, or enjoys a higher rationality. But I think that even eulogistic words should be used rather to distinguish than to commingle meanings, so I prefer bluntly to call reality if not irrational then at least non-rational in its constitution, — and by reality here I mean reality where things *happen*, all temporal reality without exception. I myself find no good warrant for even suspecting the existence of any reality of a higher denomination than that distributed and strung-along and flowing sort of reality which we finite beings swim in. That is the sort of reality given us, and that is the sort with which logic is so incommensurable. If there be any higher sort of reality — the 'absolute,' for example — that sort, by the confession of those who believe in it, is still less amenable to ordinary logic; it transcends logic and is therefore still less rational in the intellectualist sense, so it cannot help us to save our logic as an adequate definer and confiner of existence.

These sayings will sound queer and dark,

probably they will sound quite wild or childish in the absence of explanatory comment.
Only the persuasion that I soon can explain
them, if not satisfactorily to all of you, at least
intelligibly, emboldens me to state them thus
baldly as a sort of programme. Please take
them as a thesis, therefore, to be defended
by later pleading.

I told you that I had long and sincerely
wrestled with the dilemma. I have now to
confess (and this will probably re-animate
your interest) that I should not now be eman-
cipated, not now subordinate logic with so very
light a heart, or throw it out of the deeper
regions of philosophy to take its rightful and
respectable place in the world of simple human
practice, if I had not been influenced by a
comparatively young and very original french
writer, Professor Henri Bergson. Reading his
works is what has made me bold. If I had not
read Bergson, I should probably still be black-
ening endless pages of paper privately, in the
hope of making ends meet that were never
meant to meet, and trying to discover some

mode of conceiving the behavior of reality which should leave no discrepancy between it and the accepted laws of the logic of identity. It is certain, at any rate, that without the confidence which being able to lean on Bergson's authority gives me I should never have ventured to urge these particular views of mine upon this ultra-critical audience.

I must therefore, in order to make my own views more intelligible, give some preliminary account of the bergsonian philosophy. But here, as in Fechner's case, I must confine myself only to the features that are essential to the present purpose, and not entangle you in collateral details, however interesting otherwise. For our present purpose, then, the essential contribution of Bergson to philosophy is his criticism of intellectualism. In my opinion he has killed intellectualism definitively and without hope of recovery. I don't see how it can ever revive again in its ancient platonizing rôle of claiming to be the most authentic, intimate, and exhaustive definer of the nature of reality. Others, as Kant for example, have denied intellectualism's pretensions to define reality *an sich* or in its absolute capacity; but Kant still leaves it laying down laws — and laws from which there is no appeal — to all our human experience; while what Bergson denies is that its methods give any adequate account of this human experience in its very finiteness. Just how Bergson accomplishes all this I must try to tell in my imperfect way in the next lecture; but since I have already used the words 'logic,' 'logic of identity,' 'intellectualistic logic,' and 'intellectualism' so often, and sometimes used them as if they required no particular explanation, it will be wise at this point to say at greater length than heretofore in what sense I take these terms when I claim that Bergson has refuted their pretension to decide what reality can or cannot be. Just what I mean by intellectualism is therefore what I shall try to give a fuller idea of during the remainder of this present hour.

In recent controversies some participants have shown resentment at being classed as intellectualists. I mean to use the word disparagingly, but shall be sorry if it works offence. Intellectualism has its source in the faculty which gives us our chief superiority to the brutes, our power, namely, of translating the crude flux of our merely feeling-experience into a conceptual order. An immediate experience, as yet unnamed or classed, is a mere *that* that we undergo, a thing that asks, '*What* am I ?' When we name and class it, we say for the first time what it is, and all these whats are abstract names or concepts. Each concept means a particular *kind* of thing, and as things seem once for all to have been created in kinds, a far more efficient handling of a given bit of experience begins as soon as we have classed the various parts of it. Once classed, a thing can be treated by the law of its class, and the advantages are endless. Both theoretically and practically this power of framing abstract concepts is one of the sublimest of our human prerogatives. We come back into the concrete from our journey into these abstractions, with an increase both of vision and of power. It is no wonder that earlier thinkers, forgetting that

217

concepts are only man-made extracts from the temporal flux, should have ended by treating them as a superior type of being, bright, changeless, true, divine, and utterly opposed in nature to the turbid, restless lower world. The latter then appears as but their corruption and falsification.

Intellectualism in the vicious sense began when Socrates and Plato taught that what a thing really is, is told us by its *definition*. Ever since Socrates we have been taught that reality consists of essences, not of appearances, and that the essences of things are known whenever we know their definitions. So first we identify the thing with a concept and then we identify the concept with a definition, and only then, inasmuch as the thing *is* whatever the definition expresses, are we sure of apprehending the real essence of it or the full truth about it.

So far no harm is done. The misuse of concepts begins with the habit of employing them privatively as well as positively, using them not merely to assign properties to things, but to deny the very properties with which the things sensibly present themselves. Logic can extract all its possible consequences from any definition, and the logician who is *unerbittlich consequent* is often tempted, when he cannot extract a certain property from a definition, to deny that the concrete object to which the definition applies can possibly possess that property. The definition that fails to yield it must exclude or negate it. This is Hegel's regular method of establishing his system.

It is but the old story, of a useful practice first becoming a method, then a habit, and finally a tyranny that defeats the end it was used for. Concepts, first employed to make things intelligible, are clung to even when they make them unintelligible. Thus it comes that when once you have conceived things as 'independent,' you must proceed to deny the possibility of any connexion whatever among them, because the notion of connexion is not contained in the definition of independence. For a like reason you must deny any possible forms or modes of unity among things which you have begun by defining as a 'many.' We have cast a glance at Hegel's and Bradley's use of this sort of reasoning, and you will remember Sigwart's epigram that according to it a horseman can never in his life go on foot, or a photographer ever do anything but photograph.

The classic extreme in this direction is the denial of the possibility of change, and the consequent branding of the world of change as unreal, by certain philosophers. The definition of A is changeless, so is the definition of B. The one definition cannot change into the other, so the notion that a concrete thing A should change into another concrete thing B is made out to be contrary to reason. In Mr. Bradley's difficulty in seeing how sugar can be sweet intellectualism outstrips itself and becomes openly a sort of verbalism. Sugar is just sugar and sweet is just sweet; neither is the other; nor can the word 'is' ever be understood to join any subject to its predicate rationally. Nothing 'between' things can connect them, for 'between' is just that third thing, 'between,' and would need itself to be connected to the

first and second things by two still finer betweens, and so on ad infinitum.

The particular intellectualistic difficulty that
had held my own thought so long in a vise was,
as we have seen at such tedious length, the impossibility of understanding how 'your' experience and 'mine,' which 'as such' are defined as
not conscious of each other, can nevertheless
at the same time be members of a world-expe-
rience defined expressly as having all its parts
co-conscious, or known together. The definitions are contradictory, so the things defined
can in no way be united. You see how unintelligible intellectualism here seems to make the
world of our most accomplished philosophers.
Neither as they use it nor as we use it does it
do anything but make nature look irrational
and seem impossible.

In my next lecture, using Bergson as my
principal topic, I shall enter into more concrete
details and try, by giving up intellectualism
frankly, to make, if not the world, at least my
own general thesis, less unintelligible.

VI

BERGSON AND HIS CRITIQUE OF INTELLECTUALISM

LECTURE VI

BERGSON AND HIS CRITIQUE OF INTELLECTUALISM

I GAVE you a very stiff lecture last time, and I fear that this one can be little less so. The best way of entering into it will be to begin immediately with Bergson's philosophy, since I told you that that was what had led me personally to renounce the intellectualistic method and the current notion that logic is an adequate measure of what can or cannot be.

Professor Henri Bergson is a young man, comparatively, as influential philosophers go, having been born at Paris in 1859. His career has been the perfectly routine one of a successful french professor. Entering the école normale supérieure at the age of twenty-two, he spent the next seventeen years teaching at *lycées*, provincial or parisian, until his fortieth year, when he was made professor at the said école normale. Since 1900 he has been professor at the Collège de France, and member of the Institute since 1900.

So far as the outward facts go, Bergson's career has then been commonplace to the utmost. Neither one of Taine's famous principles of explanation of great men, *the race, the environment, or the moment,* no, nor all three together, will explain that peculiar way of looking at things that constitutes his mental individuality. Originality in men dates from nothing previous, other things date from it, rather. I have to confess that Bergson's originality is so profuse that many of his ideas baffle me entirely. I doubt whether any one understands him all over, so to speak; and I am sure that he would himself be the first to see that this must be, and to confess that things which he himself has not yet thought out clearly, had yet to be mentioned and have a tentative place assigned them in his philosophy. Many of us are profusely original, in that no man can understand us — violently peculiar ways of looking at things are no great rarity. The rarity is when great peculiarity of vision is allied with great lucidity and unusual command of all the classic expository apparatus. Bergson's resources in the way of erudition are remarkable, and in the way of expression they are simply phenomenal. This is why in France, where *l'art de bien dire* counts for so much and is so sure of appreciation, he has immediately taken so eminent a place in public esteem. Old-fashioned professors, whom his ideas quite fail to satisfy, nevertheless speak of his talent almost with bated breath, while the youngsters flock to him as to a master.

If anything can make hard things easy to follow, it is a style like Bergson's. A 'straightforward' style, an american reviewer lately called it; failing to see that such straightforwardness means a flexibility of verbal resource that follows the thought without a crease or wrinkle, as elastic silk underclothing follows the movements of one's body. The lucidity of Bergson's way of putting things is what all readers are first struck by. It seduces you and bribes you in advance to become his disciple. It is a miracle, and he a real magician.

M. Bergson, if I am rightly informed, came into philosophy through the gateway of mathematics. The old antinomies of the infinite were, I imagine, the irritant that first woke his faculties from their dogmatic slumber. You all remember Zeno's famous paradox, or sophism, as many of our logic books still call it, of Achilles and the tortoise. Give that reptile ever so small an advance and the swift runner Achilles can never overtake him, much less get ahead of him; for if space and time are infinitely divisible (as our intellects tell us they must be), by the time Achilles reaches the tortoise's starting-point, the tortoise has already got ahead of *that* starting-point, and so on *ad infinitum*, the interval between the pursuer and the pursued growing endlessly minuter, but never becoming wholly obliterated. The common way of showing up the sophism here is by pointing out the ambiguity of the expression 'never can overtake.' What the word 'never' falsely suggests, it is said, is an infinite duration of time; what it really means is the inexhaustible number of the steps of which the overtaking must consist. But if these steps are infinitely short, a finite time will suffice for them; and in point of fact they do rapidly converge, whatever be the original interval or the contrasted speeds, toward infinitesimal shortness. This proportionality of the shortness of the times to that of the spaces required frees us, it is claimed, from the sophism which the word 'never' suggests.

But this criticism misses Zeno's point entirely. Zeno would have been perfectly willing to grant that if the tortoise can be overtaken at all, he can be overtaken in (say) twenty seconds, but he would still have insisted that he can't be overtaken at all. Leave Achilles and the tortoise out of the account altogether, he would have said — they complicate the case unnecessarily. Take any single process of change whatever, take the twenty seconds themselves elapsing. If time be infinitely divisible, and it must be so on intellectualist principles, they simply cannot elapse, their end cannot be reached; for no matter how much of them has already elapsed, before the remainder, however minute, can have wholly elapsed, the earlier half of it must first have elapsed. And this ever re-arising need of making the earlier half elapse *first* leaves time with always something to do *before* the last thing is done, so that the last thing never gets done. Expressed in bare numbers, it is like the convergent series ½ plus ¼ plus ⅛ . . . , of which the limit is one. But this limit, simply because it is a limit, stands outside the series, the value of which approaches it indefinitely but never touches it. If in the natural world there were no other way of getting things save by such successive addition of their logically involved fractions, no complete units or whole things would ever come into being, for the fractions' sum would always leave a remainder. But in point of fact nature does n't make eggs by making first half an egg, then a quarter, then an eighth, etc., and adding them together. She either makes a whole egg at once or none at all, and so of all her other units. It is only in the sphere of change, then, where one phase of a thing must needs come into being before another phase can come that Zeno's paradox gives trouble.

And it gives trouble then only if the succession of steps of change be infinitely divisible. If a bottle had to be emptied by an infinite number of successive decrements, it is mathematically impossible that the emptying should ever positively terminate. In point of fact, however, bottles and coffee-pots empty themselves by a finite number of decrements, each of definite amount. Either a whole drop emerges or nothing emerges from the spout. If all change went thus drop-wise, so to speak, if real time sprouted or grew by units of duration of determinate amount, just as our perceptions of it grow by pulses, there would be no zenonian paradoxes or kantian antinomies to trouble us. All our sensible experiences, as we get them immediately, do thus change by discrete pulses of perception, each of which keeps us saying 'more, more, more,' or 'less, less, less,' as the definite increments or diminutions make themselves felt. The discreteness is still more obvious when, instead of old things changing, they cease, or when altogether new things come. Fechner's term of the 'threshold,' which has played such a part in the psychology of perception, is only one way of naming the quantitative discreteness in the change of all our sensible experiences. They come to us in drops. Time itself comes in drops.

Our ideal decomposition of the drops which are all that we feel into still finer fractions is but an incident in that great transformation of the perceptual order into a conceptual order of which I spoke in my last lecture. It is made in the interest of our rationalizing intellect solely. The times directly *felt* in the experiences of living subjects have originally no common measure. Let a lump of sugar melt in a glass, to use one of M. Bergson's instances. We feel the time to be long while waiting for the process to end, but who knows how long or how short it feels to the sugar? All *felt* times coexist and overlap or compenetrate each other thus vaguely, but the artifice of plotting them on a common scale helps us to reduce their aboriginal confusion, and it helps us still more to plot, against the same scale, the successive possible steps into which nature's various changes may be resolved, either sensibly or conceivably. We thus straighten out the aboriginal privacy and vagueness, and can date things publicly, as it were, and by each other. The notion of one objective and 'evenly flowing' time, cut into numbered instants, applies itself as a common measure to all the steps and phases, no matter how many, into which we cut the processes of nature. They are now definitely contemporary, or later or earlier one than another, and we can handle them mathematically, as we say, and far better, practically as well as theoretically, for having thus correlated them one to one with each other on the common schematic or conceptual time-scale.

Motion, to take a good example, is originally a turbid sensation, of which the native shape is perhaps best preserved in the phenomenon of vertigo. In vertigo we feel that movement *is*, and is more or less violent or rapid, more or less in this direction or that, more or less alarming or sickening. But a man subject to vertigo may gradually learn to co-ordinate his felt motion with his real position and that of other things, and intellectualize it enough to succeed at last in walking without staggering. The mathematical mind similarly organizes motion in its way, putting it into a logical definition: motion is now conceived as 'the occupancy of serially successive points of space at serially successive instants of time.' With such a definition we escape wholly from the turbid privacy of sense. But do we not also escape from sense-reality altogether? Whatever motion really may be, it surely is not static; but the definition we have gained is of the absolutely static. It gives a set of one-to-one relations between space-points and time-points, which relations themselves are as fixed as the points are. It gives *positions* assignable ad infinitum, but how the body gets from one position to another it omits to mention. The body gets there by moving, of course; but the conceived positions, however numerously multiplied, contain no element of movement, so Zeno, using nothing but them in his discussion, has no alternative but to say that our intellect repudiates motion as a non-reality. Intellectualism here does what I said it does — it makes experience less instead of more intelligible.

We of course need a stable scheme of concepts, stably related with one another, to lay hold of our experiences and to co-ordinate them withal. When an experience comes with sufficient saliency to stand out, we keep the thought of it for future use, and store it in our conceptual system. What does not of itself stand out, we learn to *cut* out; so the system grows completer, and new reality, as it comes, gets named after and conceptually strung upon this or that element of it which we have already established. The immutability of such an abstract system is its great practical merit; the same identical terms and relations in it can always be recovered and referred to — change itself is just such an unalterable concept. But all these abstract concepts are but as flowers gathered, they are only moments dipped out from the stream of time, snap-shots taken, as by a kinetoscopic camera, at a life that in its original coming is continuous. Useful as they are as samples of the garden, or to re-enter the stream with, or to insert in our revolving lantern, they have no value but these practical values.

You cannot explain by them what makes any single phenomenon be or go — you merely dot out the path of appearances which it traverses. For you cannot make continuous being out of discontinuities, and your concepts are discontinuous. The stages into which you analyze a change are *states*, the change itself goes on between them. It lies along their intervals, inhabits what your definition fails to gather up, and thus eludes conceptual explanation altogether.

'When the mathematician,' Bergson writes, 'calculates the state of a system at the end of a time *t*, nothing need prevent him from supposing that betweenwhiles the universe vanishes, in order suddenly to appear again at the due moment in the new configuration. It is only the *t*-th moment that counts — that which flows throughout the intervals, namely real time, plays no part in his calculation. . . . In short, the world on which the mathematician operates is a world which dies and is born anew at every instant, like the world which Descartes thought of when he spoke of a continued creation.' To know adequately what really *happens* we ought, Bergson insists, to see into the intervals, but the mathematician sees only their extremities. He fixes only a few results, he dots a curve and then interpolates, he substitutes a tracing for a reality.

This being so undeniably the case, the history of the way in which philosophy has dealt with it is curious. The ruling tradition in philosophy has always been the platonic and aristotelian belief that fixity is a nobler and worthier thing than change. Reality must be one and unalterable. Concepts, being themselves fixities, agree best with this fixed nature of truth, so that for any knowledge of ours to be quite true it must be knowledge by universal concepts rather than by particular experiences, for these notoriously are mutable and corruptible. This is the tradition known as rationalism in philosophy, and what I have called intellectualism is only the extreme application of it. In spite of sceptics and empiricists, in spite of Protagoras, Hume, and James Mill, rationalism has never been seriously questioned, for its sharpest critics have always had a tender place in their hearts for it, and have obeyed some of its mandates. They have not been consistent; they have played fast and loose with the enemy; and Bergson alone has been radical.

To show what I mean by this, let me contrast his procedure with that of some of the transcendentalist philosophers whom I have lately mentioned. Coming after Kant, these pique themselves on being 'critical,' on building in fact upon Kant's 'critique' of pure reason. What that critique professed to establish was this, that concepts do not apprehend reality, but only such appearances as our senses feed out to them. They give immutable intellectual forms to these appearances, it is true, but the reality *an sich* from which in ultimate resort the sense-appearances have to come remains forever unintelligible to our intellect. Take motion, for example. Sensibly, motion comes in drops, waves, or pulses; either some actual amount of it, or none, being apprehended. This amount is the datum or *gabe* which reality feeds out to our intellectual faculty; but our intellect makes of it a task or *aufgabe* — this pun is one of the most memorable of Kant's formulas — and insists that in every pulse of it an infinite number of successive minor pulses shall be ascertainable. These minor pulses *we* can indeed *go on* to ascertain or to compute indefinitely if we have patience; but it would contradict the definition of an infinite number to suppose the endless series of them to have actually counted *themselves* out piecemeal. Zeno made this manifest; so the infinity which our intellect requires of the sense-datum is thus a future and potential rather than a past and actual infinity of structure. The datum after it has made itself must be decompos*able* ad infinitum by our conception, but of the steps by which that structure actually got composed we know nothing. Our intellect casts, in short, no ray of light on the processes by which experiences *get made*.

Kant's monistic successors have in general found the data of immediate experience even more self-contradictory, when intellectually treated, than Kant did. Not only the character of infinity involved in the relation of various empirical data to their 'conditions,' but the very notion that empirical things should be related to one another at all, has seemed to them, when the intellectualistic fit was upon them, full of paradox and contradiction. We saw in a former lecture numerous instances of this from Hegel, Bradley, Royce, and others. We saw also where the solution of such an intolerable state of things was sought for by these authors. Whereas Kant had placed it outside of and *before* our experience, in the *dinge an sich* which are the causes of the latter, his monistic successors all look for it either *after* experience, as its absolute completion, or else consider it to be even now implicit within experience as its ideal signification. Kant and his successors look, in short, in diametrically opposite directions. Do not be misled by Kant's admission of theism into his system. His God is the ordinary dualistic God of Christianity, to whom his philosophy simply opens the door; he has nothing whatsoever in common with the 'absolute spirit' set up by his successors. So far as this absolute spirit is logically derived from Kant, it is not from his God, but from entirely different elements of his philosophy. First from his notion that an unconditioned totality of the conditions of any experience must be assignable; and then from his other notion that the presence of some witness, or ego of apperception, is the most universal of all the conditions in question. The post-kantians make of the witness-condition what is called a concrete universal, an individualized all-witness or world-self, which shall imply in its rational constitution each and all of the other conditions put together, and therefore necessitate each and all of the conditioned experiences.

Abridgments like this of other men's opinions are very unsatisfactory, they always work injustice; but in this case those of you who are familiar with the literature will see immediately what I have in mind; and to the others, if there be any here, it will suffice to say that what I am trying so pedantically to point out is only the fact that monistic idealists after Kant have invariably sought relief from the supposed contradictions of our world of sense by looking forward toward an *ens rationis* conceived as its integration or logical completion, while he looked backward toward non-rational *dinge an sich* conceived as its cause. Pluralistic empiricists, on the other hand, have remained in the world of sense, either naïvely and because they overlooked the intellectualistic contradictions, or because, not able to ignore them, they thought they could refute them by a superior use of the same intellectualistic logic. Thus it is that John Mill pretends to refute the Achilles-tortoise fallacy.

The important point to notice here is the intellectualist logic. Both sides treat it as authoritative, but they do so capriciously: the absolutists smashing the world of sense by its means, the empiricists smashing the absolute — for the absolute, they say, is the quintessence of all logical contradictions. Neither side attains consistency. The Hegelians have to invoke a higher logic to supersede the purely

destructive efforts of their first logic. The
empiricists use their logic against the absolute,
but refuse to use it against finite experience.
Each party uses it or drops it to suit the
vision it has faith in, but neither impugns in
principle its general theoretic authority.

Bergson alone challenges its theoretic authority in principle. He alone denies that mere
conceptual logic can tell us what is impossible
or possible in the world of being or fact; and he
does so for reasons which at the same time that
they rule logic out from lordship over the whole
of life, establish a vast and definite sphere of
influence where its sovereignty is indisputable.
Bergson's own text, felicitous as it is, is too
intricate for quotation, so I must use my own
inferior words in explaining what I mean by
saying this.

In the first place, logic, giving primarily the
relations between concepts as such, and the
relations between natural facts only secondarily or so far as the facts have been already
identified with concepts and defined by them,
must of course stand or fall with the conceptual

method. But the conceptual method is a transformation which the flux of life undergoes at
our hands in the interests of practice essentially and only subordinately in the interests
of theory. We live forward, we understand
backward, said a danish writer; and to understand life by concepts is to arrest its movement,
cutting it up into bits as if with scissors, and
immobilizing these in our logical herbarium
where, comparing them as dried specimens,
we can ascertain which of them statically includes or excludes which other. This treatment
supposes life to have already accomplished
itself, for the concepts, being so many views
taken after the fact, are retrospective and post
mortem. Nevertheless we can draw conclusions from them and project them into the
future. We cannot learn from them how life
made itself go, or how it will make itself go;
but, on the supposition that its ways of making itself go are unchanging, we can calculate
what positions of imagined arrest it will exhibit
hereafter under given conditions. We can compute, for instance, at what point Achilles will

be, and where the tortoise will be, at the end of the twentieth minute. Achilles may then be at a point far ahead; but the full detail of how he will have managed practically to get there our logic never gives us — we have seen, indeed, that it finds that its results contradict the facts of nature. The computations which the other sciences make differ in no respect from those of mathematics. The concepts used are all of them dots through which, by interpolation or extrapolation, curves are drawn, while along the curves other dots are found as consequences. The latest refinements of logic dispense with the curves altogether, and deal solely with the dots and their correspondences each to each in various series. The authors of these recent improvements tell us expressly that their aim is to abolish the last vestiges of intuition, *videlicet* of concrete reality, from the field of reasoning, which then will operate literally on mental dots or bare abstract units of discourse, and on the ways in which they may be strung in naked series.

This is all very esoteric, and my own understanding of it is most likely misunderstanding.
So I speak here only by way of brief reminder
to those who know. For the rest of us it is
enough to recognize this fact, that altho by
means of concepts cut out from the sensible
flux of the past, we can re-descend upon the
future flux and, making another cut, say what
particular thing is likely to be found there; and
that altho in this sense concepts give us knowledge, and may be said to have some theoretic
value (especially when the particular thing
foretold is one in which we take no present
practical interest); yet in the deeper sense of
giving *insight* they have no theoretic value, for
they quite fail to connect us with the inner life
of the flux, or with the causes that govern its
direction. Instead of being interpreters of
reality, concepts negate the inwardness of reality altogether. They make the whole notion
of a causal influence between finite things in-
comprehensible. No real activities and indeed
no real connexions of any kind can obtain if we
follow the conceptual logic; for to be distin-

guishable, according to what I call intellectualism, is to be incapable of connexion. The
work begun by Zeno, and continued by Hume,
Kant, Herbart, Hegel, and Bradley, does not
stop till sensible reality lies entirely disinte-
grated at the feet of 'reason.'

Of the 'absolute' reality which reason pro-
poses to substitute for sensible reality I shall
have more to say presently. Meanwhile you
see what Professor Bergson means by insisting
that the function of the intellect is practical
rather than theoretical. Sensible reality is too
concrete to be entirely manageable—look at
the narrow range of it which is all that any
animal, living in it exclusively as he does, is
able to compass. To get from one point in it
to another we have to plough or wade through
the whole intolerable interval. No detail is
spared us; it is as bad as the barbed-wire com-
plications at Port Arthur, and we grow old
and die in the process. But with our faculty of
abstracting and fixing concepts we are there in
a second, almost as if we controlled a fourth
dimension, skipping the intermediaries as by a

divine winged power, and getting at the exact point we require without entanglement with any context. What we do in fact is to *harness up* reality in our conceptual systems in order to drive it the better. This process is practical because all the termini to which we drive are *particular* termini, even when they are facts of the mental order. But the sciences in which the conceptual method chiefly celebrates its triumphs are those of space and matter, where the transformations of external things are dealt with. To deal with moral facts conceptually, we have first to transform them, substitute brain-diagrams or physical metaphors, treat ideas as atoms, interests as mechanical forces, our conscious 'selves' as 'streams,' and the like. Paradoxical effect! as Bergson well remarks, if our intellectual life were not practical but destined to reveal the inner natures. One would then suppose that it would find itself most at home in the domain of its own intellectual realities. But it is precisely there that it finds itself at the end of its tether. We know the inner movements of our spirit only perceptually.

VI. BERGSON AND INTELLECTUALISM

We feel them live in us, but can give no distinct account of their elements, nor definitely predict their future; while things that lie along the world of space, things of the sort that we literally *handle*, are what our intellects cope with most successfully. Does not this confirm us in the view that the original and still surviving function of our intellectual life is to guide us in the practical adaptation of our expectancies and activities?

One can easily get into a verbal mess at this point, and my own experience with 'pragmatism' makes me shrink from the dangers that lie in the word 'practical,' and far rather than stand out against you for that word, I am quite willing to part company with Professor Bergson, and to ascribe a primarily theoretical function to our intellect, provided you on your part then agree to discriminate 'theoretic' or scientific knowledge from the deeper 'speculative' knowledge aspired to by most philosophers, and concede that theoretic knowledge, which is knowledge *about* things, as distinguished from living or sympathetic acquaintance with them, touches only the outer surface of reality.[1] The surface which theoretic knowledge taken in this sense covers may indeed be enormous in extent; it may dot the whole diameter of space and time with its conceptual creations; but it does not penetrate a millimeter into the solid dimension. That inner dimension of reality is occupied by the *activities* that keep it going, but the intellect, speaking through Hume, Kant & Co., finds itself obliged to deny, and persists in denying, that activities have any intelligible existence. What exists for *thought*, we are told, is at most the results that we illusorily ascribe to such activities, strung along the surfaces of space and time by *regeln der verknüpfung*, laws of nature which state only coexistences and successions.[1]

Thought deals thus solely with surfaces. It can name the thickness of reality, but it cannot fathom it, and its insufficiency here is essential and permanent, not temporary.

The only way in which to apprehend reality's thickness is either to experience it directly by

being a part of reality one's self, or to evoke
it in imagination by sympathetically divining
some one else's inner life. But what we thus
immediately experience or concretely divine is
very limited in duration, whereas abstractly we
are able to conceive eternities. Could we feel a
million years concretely as we now feel a passing
minute, we should have very little employment
for our conceptual faculty. We should know the
whole period fully at every moment of its passage, whereas we must now construct it labori-
ously by means of concepts which we project.
Direct acquaintance and conceptual knowledge
are thus complementary of each other; each
remedies the other's defects. If what we care
most about be the synoptic treatment of phenomena, the vision of the far and the gathering
of the scattered like, we must follow the conceptual method. But if, as metaphysicians, we
are more curious about the inner nature of
reality or about what really makes it go, we
must turn our backs upon our winged concepts
altogether, and bury ourselves in the thickness
of those passing moments over the surface of

which they fly, and on particular points of
which they occasionally rest and perch.

Professor Bergson thus inverts the traditional platonic doctrine absolutely. Instead of
intellectual knowledge being the profounder,
he calls it the more superficial. Instead of
being the only adequate knowledge, it is grossly
inadequate, and its only superiority is the practical one of enabling us to make short cuts
through experience and thereby to save time.
The one thing it cannot do is to reveal the
nature of things — which last remark, if not
clear already, will become clearer as I proceed.
Dive back into the flux itself, then, Bergson
tells us, if you wish to *know* reality, that flux
which Platonism, in its strange belief that only
the immutable is excellent, has always spurned;
turn your face toward sensation, that flesh-
bound thing which rationalism has always
loaded with abuse. — This, you see, is exactly
the opposite remedy from that of looking forward into the absolute, which our idealistic
contemporaries prescribe. It violates our mental habits, being a kind of passive and recep-

tive listening quite contrary to that effort to react noisily and verbally on everything, which is our usual intellectual pose.

What, then, are the peculiar features in the perceptual flux which the conceptual translation so fatally leaves out?

The essence of life is its continuously changing character; but our concepts are all discontinuous and fixed, and the only mode of making them coincide with life is by arbitrarily supposing positions of arrest therein. With such arrests our concepts may be made congruent. But these concepts are not *parts* of reality, not real positions taken by it, but *suppositions* rather, notes taken by ourselves, and you can no more dip up the substance of reality with them than you can dip up water with a net, however finely meshed.

When we conceptualize, we cut out and fix, and exclude everything but what we have fixed. A concept means a *that-and-no-other*. Conceptually, time excludes space; motion and rest exclude each other; approach excludes contact; presence excludes absence; unity excludes plurality; independence excludes relativity; 'mine' excludes 'yours'; this connexion excludes that connexion—and so on indefinitely; whereas in the real concrete sensible flux of life experiences compenetrate each other so that it is not easy to know just what is excluded and what not. Past and future, for example, conceptually separated by the cut to which we give the name of present, and defined as being the opposite sides of that cut, are to some extent, however brief, co-present with each other throughout experience. The literally present moment is a purely verbal supposition, not a position; the only present ever realized concretely being the 'passing moment' in which the dying rearward of time and its dawning future forever mix their lights. Say 'now' and it *was* even while you say it.

It is just intellectualism's attempt to substitute static cuts for units of experienced duration that makes real motion so unintelligible. The conception of the first half of the interval between Achilles and the tortoise excludes that of the last half, and the mathematical neces-

sity of traversing it separately before the last
half is traversed stands permanently in the way
of the last half ever being traversed. Meanwhile the living Achilles (who, for the purposes
of this discussion, is only the abstract name of
one phenomenon of impetus, just as the tortoise is of another) asks no leave of logic. The
velocity of his acts is an indivisible nature in
them like the expansive tension in a spring
compressed. We define it conceptually as $\frac{s}{t}$,
but the s and t are only artificial cuts made
after the fact, and indeed most artificial when
we treat them in both runners as the same
tracts of 'objective' space and time, for the
experienced spaces and times in which the
tortoise inwardly lives are probably as different as his velocity from the same things in
Achilles. The impetus of Achilles is one concrete fact, and carries space, time, and conquest
over the inferior creature's motion indivisibly
in it. He perceives nothing, while running, of
the mathematician's homogeneous time and
space, of the infinitely numerous succession
of cuts in both, or of their order. End and

beginning come for him in the one onrush, and all that he actually experiences is that, in the midst of a certain intense effort of his own, the rival is in point of fact outstripped.

We are so inveterately wedded to the conceptual decomposition of life that I know that this will seem to you like putting muddiest confusion in place of clearest thought, and relapsing into a molluscoid state of mind. Yet I ask you whether the absolute superiority of our higher thought is so very clear, if all that it can find is impossibility in tasks which sense-experience so easily performs.

What makes you call real life confusion is that it presents, as if they were dissolved in one another, a lot of differents which conception breaks life's flow by keeping apart. But *are* not differents actually dissolved in one another? Has n't every bit of experience its quality, its duration, its extension, its intensity, its urgency, its clearness, and many aspects besides, no one of which can exist in the isolation in which our verbalized logic keeps it? They exist only *durcheinander*. Reality always is, in M. Bergson's phrase, an endosmosis or conflux of the same with the different: they compenetrate and telescope. For conceptual logic, the same is nothing but the same, and all sames with a third thing are the same with each other. Not so in concrete experience. Two spots on our skin, each of which feels the same as a third spot when touched along with it, are felt as different from each other. Two tones, neither distinguishable from a third tone, are perfectly distinct from each other. The whole process of life is due to life's violation of our logical axioms. Take its continuity as an example. Terms like A and C appear to be connected by intermediaries, by B for example. Intellectualism calls this absurd, for 'B-connected-with-A' is, 'as such,' a different term from 'B-connected-with-C.' But real life laughs at logic's veto. Imagine a heavy log which takes two men to carry it. First A and B take it. Then C takes hold and A drops off; then D takes hold and B drops off, so that C and D now bear it; and so on. The log meanwhile never drops, and keeps its sameness throughout the journey. Even so it is with all our experiences. Their changes are not complete annihilations followed by complete creations of something absolutely novel. There is partial decay and partial growth, and all the while a nucleus of relative constancy from which what decays drops off, and which takes into itself whatever is grafted on, until at length something wholly different has taken its place. In such a process we are as sure, in spite of intellectualist logic with its 'as suches,' that it *is* the same nucleus which is able now to make connexion with what goes and again with what comes, as we are sure that the same point can lie on diverse lines that intersect there. Without being one throughout, such a universe is continuous. Its members interdigitate with their next neighbors in manifold directions, and there are no clean cuts between them anywhere.

The great clash of intellectualist logic with sensible experience is where the experience is that of influence exerted. Intellectualism denies (as we saw in lecture ii) that finite things can act on one another, for all things, once translated into concepts, remain shut up to themselves. To act on anything means to get into it somehow; but that would mean to get out of one's self and be one's other, which is self-contradictory, etc. Meanwhile each of us actually *is* his own other to that extent, livingly knowing how to perform the trick which logic tells us can't be done. My thoughts animate and actuate this very body which you see and hear, and thereby influence your thoughts. The dynamic current somehow does get from me to you, however numerous the intermediary conductors may have to be. Distinctions may be insulators in logic as much as they like, but in life distinct things can and do commune together every moment.

The conflict of the two ways of knowing is best summed up in the intellectualist doctrine that 'the same cannot exist in many relations.' This follows of course from the concepts of the two relations being so distinct that 'what-is-in-the-one' means 'as such' something distinct from what 'what-is-in-the-other' means.

259

It is like Mill's ironical saying, that we should not think of Newton as both an Englishman and a mathematician, because an Englishman as such is not a mathematician and a mathematician as such is not an Englishman. But the real Newton was somehow both things at once; and throughout the whole finite universe each real thing proves to be many differents without undergoing the necessity of breaking into disconnected editions of itself.

These few indications will perhaps suffice to put you at the bergsonian point of view. The immediate experience of life solves the problems which so baffle our conceptual intelligence: How can what is manifold be one? how can things get out of themselves? how be their own others? how be both distinct and connected? how can they act on one another? how be for others and yet for themselves? how be absent and present at once? The intellect asks these questions much as we might ask how anything can both separate and unite things, or how sounds can grow more alike by continuing to grow more different. If you already know space sensibly, you can answer the former question by pointing to any interval in it, long or short; if you know the musical scale, you can answer the latter by sounding an octave; but then you must first have the sensible knowledge of these realities. Similarly Bergson answers the intellectualist conundrums by pointing back to our various finite sensational experiences and saying, 'Lo, even thus; even so are these other problems solved livingly.'

When you have broken the reality into concepts you never can reconstruct it in its wholeness. Out of no amount of discreteness can you manufacture the concrete. But place yourself at a bound, or *d'emblée*, as M. Bergson says, inside of the living, moving, active thickness of the real, and all the abstractions and distinctions are given into your hand: you can now make the intellectualist substitutions to your heart's content. Install yourself in phenomenal movement, for example, and velocity, succession, dates, positions, and innumerable other things are given you in the bargain. But with only an abstract succession of dates and positions you can never patch up movement itself. It slips through their intervals and is lost.

So it is with every concrete thing, however complicated. Our intellectual handling of it is a retrospective patchwork, a post-mortem dissection, and can follow any order we find most expedient. We can make the thing seem self-contradictory whenever we wish to. But place yourself at the point of view of the thing's interior *doing*, and all these back-looking and conflicting conceptions lie harmoniously in your hand. Get at the expanding centre of a human character, the *élan vital* of a man, as Bergson calls it, by living sympathy, and at a stroke you see how it makes those who see it from without interpret it in such diverse ways. It is something that breaks into both honesty and dishonesty, courage and cowardice, stupidity and insight, at the touch of varying circumstances, and you feel exactly why and how it does this, and never seek to identify it stably with any of these single abstractions. Only your intellectualist does that, — and you now also feel why *he* must do it to the end.

VI. BERGSON AND INTELLECTUALISM

Place yourself similarly at the centre of a man's philosophic vision and you understand at once all the different things it makes him write or say. But keep outside, use your post-mortem method, try to build the philosophy up out of the single phrases, taking first one and then another and seeking to make them fit, and of course you fail. You crawl over the thing like a myopic ant over a building, tumbling into every microscopic crack or fissure, finding nothing but inconsistencies, and never suspecting that a centre exists. I hope that some of the philosophers in this audience may occasionally have had something different from this intellectualist type of criticism applied to their own works!

What really *exists* is not things made but things in the making. Once made, they are dead, and an infinite number of alternative conceptual decompositions can be used in defining them. But put yourself *in the making* by a stroke of intuitive sympathy with the thing and, the whole range of possible decompositions coming at once into your possession, you are no longer troubled with the question which of them is the more absolutely true. Reality *falls* in passing into conceptual analysis; it *mounts* in living its own undivided life—it buds and bourgeons, changes and creates. Once adopt the movement of this life in any given instance and you know what Bergson calls the *devenir réel* by which the thing evolves and grows. Philosophy should seek this kind of living understanding of the movement of reality, not follow science in vainly patching together fragments of its dead results.

Thus much of M. Bergson's philosophy is sufficient for my purpose in these lectures, so here I will stop, leaving unnoticed all its other constituent features, original and interesting tho they be. You may say, and doubtless some of you now are saying inwardly, that his re-manding us to sensation in this wise is only a regress, a return to that ultra-crude empiricism which your own idealists since Green have buried ten times over. I confess that it is indeed a return to empiricism, but I think that the return in such accomplished shape only proves the latter's immortal truth. What won't stay buried must have some genuine life. *Am anfang war die tat;* fact is a *first;* to which all our conceptual handling comes as an inadequate second, never its full equivalent. When I read recent transcendentalist literature — I must partly except my colleague Royce! — I get nothing but a sort of marking of time, champing of jaws, pawing of the ground, and resettling into the same attitude, like a weary horse in a stall with an empty manger. It is but turning over the same few threadbare categories, bringing the same objections, and urging the same answers and solutions, with never a new fact or a new horizon coming into sight. But open Bergson, and new horizons loom on every page you read. It is like the breath of the morning and the song of birds. It tells of reality itself, instead of merely reiterating what dusty-minded professors have written about what other previous professors have thought. Nothing in Bergson is shop-worn or at second hand.

That he gives us no closed-in system will of

course be fatal to him in intellectualist eyes. He only evokes and invites; but he first annuls the intellectualist veto, so that we now join step with reality with a philosophical conscience never quite set free before. As a french disciple of his well expresses it: 'Bergson claims of us first of all a certain inner catastrophe, and not every one is capable of such a logical revolution. But those who have once found themselves flexible enough for the execution of such a psychological change of front, discover somehow that they can never return again to their ancient attitude of mind. They are now Bergsonians . . . and possess the principal thoughts of the master all at once. They have understood in the fashion in which one loves, they have caught the whole melody and can thereafter admire at their leisure the originality, the fecundity, and the imaginative genius with which its author develops, transposes, and varies in a thousand ways by the orchestration of his style and dialectic, the original theme.'[2]

This, scant as it is, is all I have to say about

Bergson on this occasion — I hope it may send some of you to his original text. I must now turn back to the point where I found it advisable to appeal to his ideas. You remember my own intellectualist difficulties in the last lecture, about how a lot of separate consciousnesses can at the same time be one collective thing. How, I asked, can one and the same identical content of experience, of which on idealist principles the *esse* is to be felt, be felt so diversely if itself be the only feeler? The usual way of escape by 'quatenus' or 'as such' won't help us here if we are radical intellectualists, I said, for appearance-together is as such *not* appearance-apart, the world *quâ* many is not the world *quâ* one, as absolutism claims. If we hold to Hume's maxim, which later intellectualism uses so well, that whatever things are distinguished are as separate as if there were no manner of connexion between them, there seemed no way out of the difficulty save by stepping outside of experience altogether and invoking different spiritual agents, selves or souls, to realize the diversity required. But this rescue by 'scholastic entities' I was unwilling to accept any more than pantheistic idealists accept it.

Yet, to quote Fechner's phrase again, 'nichts wirkliches kann unmöglich sein,' the actual cannot be impossible, and what *is* actual at every moment of our lives is the sort of thing which I now proceed to remind you of. You can hear the vibration of an electric contact-maker, smell the ozone, see the sparks, and feel the thrill, co-consciously as it were or in one field of experience. But you can also isolate any one of these sensations by shutting out the rest. If you close your eyes, hold your nose, and remove your hand, you can get the sensation of sound alone, but it seems still the same sensation that it was; and if you restore the action of the other organs, the sound coalesces with the feeling, the sight, and the smell sensations again. Now the natural way of talking of all this[3] is to say that certain sensations are experienced, now singly, and now together with other sensations, in a common conscious field. Fluctuations of attention give analogous results. We let a sensation in or keep it out by changing our attention; and similarly we let an item of memory in or drop it out. [Please don't raise the question here of how these changes *come to pass*. The immediate condition is probably cerebral in every instance, but it would be irrelevant now to consider it, for now we are thinking only of results, and I repeat that the natural way of thinking of them is that which intellectualist criticism finds so absurd.]

The absurdity charged is that the self-same should function so differently, now with and now without something else. But this it sensibly seems to do. This very desk which I strike with my hand strikes in turn your eyes. It functions at once as a physical object in the outer world and as a mental object in our sundry mental worlds. The very body of mine that *my* thought actuates is the body whose gestures are *your* visual object and to which you give my name. The very log which John helped to carry is the log now borne by James. The very girl you love is simultane-

ously entangled elsewhere. The very place behind me is in front of you. Look where you
will, you gather only examples of the same amid
the different, and of different relations existing
as it were in solution in the same thing. *Quâ*
this an experience is not the same as it is *quâ*
that, truly enough; but the *quâs* are conceptual
shots of ours at its post-mortem remains, and
in its sensational immediacy everything is all
at once whatever different things it is at once
at all. It is before C and after A, far from
you and near to me, without this associate and
with that one, active and passive, physical and
mental, a whole of parts and part of a higher
whole, all simultaneously and without interference or need of doubling-up its being, so
long as we keep to what I call the 'immediate'
point of view, the point of view in which we
follow our sensational life's continuity, and to
which all living language conforms. It is only
when you try — to continue using the hegelian
vocabulary — to 'mediate' the immediate, or
to substitute concepts for sensational life, that
intellectualism celebrates its triumph and the

immanent - self - contradictoriness of all this smooth-running finite experience gets proved.

Of the oddity of inventing as a remedy for the inconveniences resulting from this situation a supernumerary conceptual object called an absolute, into which you pack the self-same contradictions unreduced, I will say something in the next lecture. The absolute is said to perform its feats by taking up its other into itself. But that is exactly what is done when every individual morsel of the sensational stream takes up the adjacent morsels by coalescing with them. This is just what we mean by the stream's sensible continuity. No element *there* cuts itself off from any other element, as concepts cut themselves from concepts. No part *there* is so small as not to be a place of conflux. No part there is not really *next* its neighbors; which means that there is literally nothing between; which means again that no part goes exactly so far and no farther; that no part absolutely excludes another, but that they compenetrate and are cohesive; that if you tear out one, its roots bring out more with them; that whatever is real is telescoped and diffused into other reals; that, in short, every minutest thing is already its hegelian 'own other,' in the fullest sense of the term.

Of course this *sounds* self-contradictory, but as the immediate facts don't sound at all, but simply *are*, until we conceptualize and name them vocally, the contradiction results only from the conceptual or discursive form being substituted for the real form. But if, as Bergson shows, that form is superimposed for practical ends only, in order to let us jump about over life instead of wading through it; and if it cannot even pretend to reveal anything of what life's inner nature is or ought to be; why then we can turn a deaf ear to its accusations. The resolve to turn the deaf ear is the inner crisis or 'catastrophe' of which M. Bergson's disciple whom I lately quoted spoke. We are so subject to the philosophic tradition which treats *logos* or discursive thought generally as the sole avenue to truth, that to fall back on raw unverbalized life as more of a revealer, and to think of concepts as the merely practical things which

Bergson calls them, comes very hard. It is putting off our proud maturity of mind and becoming again as foolish little children in the eyes of reason. But difficult as such a revolution is, there is no other way, I believe, to the possession of reality, and I permit myself to hope that some of you may share my opinion after you have heard my next lecture.

VII

THE CONTINUITY OF EXPERIENCE

LECTURE VII

THE CONTINUITY OF EXPERIENCE

I FEAR that few of you will have been able to obey Bergson's call upon you to look towards the sensational life for the fuller knowledge of reality, or to sympathize with his attempt to limit the divine right of concepts to rule our mind absolutely. It is too much like looking downward and not up. Philosophy, you will say, does n't lie flat on its belly in the middle of experience, in the very thick of its sand and gravel, as this Bergsonism does, never getting a peep at anything from above. Philosophy is essentially the vision of things from above. It does n't simply feel the detail of things, it comprehends their intelligible plan, sees their forms and principles, their categories and rules, their order and necessity. It takes the superior point of view of the architect. Is it conceivable that it should ever forsake that point of view and abandon itself to a slovenly life of immediate feeling? To say nothing of your traditional Oxford devotion to Aristotle and Plato, the leaven of T. H. Green probably works still too strongly here for his anti-sensationalism to be outgrown quickly. Green more than any one realized that knowledge *about* things was knowledge of their relations; but nothing could persuade him that our sensational life could contain any relational element. He followed the strict intellectualist method with sensations. What they were not expressly defined as including, they must exclude. Sensations are not defined as relations, so in the end Green thought that they could get related together only by the action on them from above of a 'self-distinguishing' absolute and eternal mind, present to that which is related, but not related itself. 'A relation,' he said, 'is not contingent with the contingency of feeling. It is permanent with the permanence of the combining and comparing thought which alone constitutes it.'[1] In other words, relations are purely conceptual objects, and the sensational life as such cannot relate itself together. Sensation in itself, Green wrote, is fleeting, momentary, unnameable (because, while we name it, it has become another), and for the same reason unknowable, the very negation of knowability. Were there no permanent objects of conception for our sensations to be 'referred to,' there would be no significant names, but only noises, and a consistent sensationalism must be speechless.[2] Green's intellectualism was so earnest that it produced a natural and an inevitable effect. But the atomistic and unrelated sensations which he had in mind were purely fictitious products of his rationalist fancy. The psychology of our own day disavows them utterly,[3] and Green's laborious belaboring of poor old Locke for not having first seen that his ideas of sensation were just that impracticable sort of thing, and then fled to transcendental idealism as a remedy, — his belaboring of poor old Locke for this, I say, is pathetic. Every examiner of the sensible life *in concreto* must see that relations of every sort, of time, space, difference, likeness, change, rate, cause, or what not, are just as integral members of the sensational flux as terms are, and that conjunctive relations are just as true members of the flux as disjunctive relations are.[4] This is what in some recent writings of mine I have called the 'radically empiricist' doctrine (in distinction from the doctrine of mental atoms which the name empiricism so often suggests). Intellectualistic critics of sensation insist that sensations are *dis*-joined only. Radical empiricism insists that conjunctions between them are just as immediately given as disjunctions are, and that relations, whether disjunctive or conjunctive, are in their original sensible givenness just as fleeting and momentary (in Green's words), and just as 'particular,' as terms are. Later, both terms and relations get universalized by being conceptualized and named.[5] But all the thickness, concreteness, and individuality of experience exists in the immediate and relatively unnamed stages of it, to the richness of which, and to the standing inadequacy of our conceptions to match it, Professor Bergson so emphatically calls our attention.

And now I am happy to say that we can begin

to gather together some of the separate threads of our argument, and see a little better the general kind of conclusion toward which we are tending. Pray go back with me to the lecture before the last, and recall what I said about the difficulty of seeing how states of consciousness can compound themselves. The difficulty seemed to be the same, you remember, whether we took it in psychology as the composition of finite states of mind out of simpler finite states, or in metaphysics as the composition of the absolute mind out of finite minds in general. It is the general conceptualist difficulty of any one thing being the same with many things, either at once or in succession, for the abstract concepts of oneness and manyness must needs exclude each other. In the particular instance that we have dwelt on so long, the one thing is the all-form of experience, the many things are the each-forms of experience in you and me. To call them the same we must treat them as if each were simultaneously its own other, a feat on conceptualist principles impossible of performance.

On the principle of going behind the conceptual function altogether, however, and looking to the more primitive flux of the sensational life for reality's true shape, a way is open to us, as I tried in my last lecture to show. Not only the absolute is its own other, but the simplest bits of immediate experience are their own others, if that hegelian phrase be once for all allowed. The concrete pulses of experience appear pent in by no such definite limits as our conceptual substitutes for them are confined by. They run into one another continuously and seem to interpenetrate. What in them is relation and what is matter related is hard to discern. You feel no one of them as inwardly simple, and no two as wholly without confluence where they touch. There is no datum so small as not to show this mystery, if mystery it be. The tiniest feeling that we can possibly have comes with an earlier and a later part and with a sense of their continuous procession. Mr. Shadworth Hodgson showed long ago that there is literally no such object as the present moment except as an unreal postulate of abstract thought.[6] The 'passing' moment is, as I already have reminded you, the minimal fact, with the 'apparition of difference' inside of it as well as outside. If we do not feel both past and present in one field of feeling, we feel them not at all. We have the same many-in-one in the matter that fills the passing time. The rush of our thought forward through its fringes is the everlasting peculiarity of its life. We realize this life as something always off its balance, something in transition, something that shoots out of a darkness through a dawn into a brightness that we feel to be the dawn fulfilled. In the very midst of the continuity our experience comes as an alteration. 'Yes,' we say at the full brightness, '*this* is what I just meant.' 'No,' we feel at the dawning, 'this is not yet the full meaning, there is more to come.' In every crescendo of sensation, in every effort to recall, in every progress towards the satisfaction of desire, this succession of an emptiness and fulness that have reference to each other and are one flesh is the essence of the phenomenon. In every hindrance of desire the sense of an ideal presence which is absent in fact, of an absent, in a word, which the only function of the present is to *mean*, is even more notoriously there. And in the movement of pure thought we have the same phenomenon. When I say *Socrates is mortal*, the moment *Socrates* is incomplete; it falls forward through the *is* which is pure movement, into the *mortal* which is indeed bare mortal on the tongue, but for the mind is *that mortal*, the *mortal Socrates*, at last satisfactorily disposed of and told off.[7]

Here, then, inside of the minimal pulses of experience, is realized that very inner complexity which the transcendentalists say only the absolute can genuinely possess. The gist of the matter is always the same — something ever goes indissolubly with something else. You cannot separate the same from its other, except by abandoning the real altogether and taking to the conceptual system. What is immediately given in the single and particular instance is always something pooled and mutual, something with no dark spot, no point of ignorance. No one elementary bit of reality is eclipsed from the next bit's point of view, if only we take reality sensibly and in small enough pulses—and by us it has to be taken pulse-wise, for our span of consciousness is too short to grasp the larger collectivity of things except nominally and abstractly. No more of reality collected together at once is extant anywhere, perhaps, than in my experience of reading this page, or in yours of listening; yet within those bits of experience as they come to pass we get a fulness of content that no conceptual description can equal. Sensational experiences *are* their 'own others,' then, both internally and externally. Inwardly they are one with their parts, and outwardly they pass continuously into their next neighbors, so that events separated by years of time in a man's life hang together unbrokenly by the intermediary events. Their *names*, to be sure, cut them into separate conceptual entities, but no cuts existed in the continuum in which they originally came.

If, with all this in our mind, we turn to our

own particular predicament, we see that our old objection to the self-compounding of states of consciousness, our accusation that it was impossible for purely logical reasons, is unfounded in principle. Every smallest state of consciousness, concretely taken, overflows its own definition. Only concepts are self-identical; only 'reason' deals with closed equations; nature is but a name for excess; every point in her opens out and runs into the more; and the only question, with reference to any point we may be considering, is how far into the rest of nature we may have to go in order to get entirely beyond its overflow. In the pulse of inner life immediately present now in each of us is a little past, a little future, a little awareness of our own body, of each other's persons, of these sublimities we are trying to talk about, of the earth's geography and the direction of history, of truth and error, of good and bad, and of who knows how much more? Feeling, however dimly and subconsciously, all these things, your pulse of inner life is continuous with them, belongs to them and they

to it. You can't identify it with either one of
them rather than with the others, for if you
let it develop into no matter which of those
directions, what it develops into will look back
on it and say, 'That was the original germ of
me.'

In *principle*, then, the real units of our imme-
diately-felt life are unlike the units that intellectualist logic holds to and makes its calcula-
tions with. They are not separate from their
own others, and you have to take them at
widely separated dates to find any two of them
that seem unblent. Then indeed they do appear separate even as their concepts are separate; a chasm yawns between them; but the
chasm itself is but an intellectualist fiction,
got by abstracting from the continuous sheet
of experiences with which the intermediary
time was filled. It is like the log carried first
by William and Henry, then by William,
Henry, and John, then by Henry and John,
then by John and Peter, and so on. All real
units of experience *overlap*. Let a row of equi-
distant dots on a sheet of paper symbolize the

concepts by which we intellectualize the world.
Let a ruler long enough to cover at least three
dots stand for our sensible experience. Then
the conceived changes of the sensible experience can be symbolized by sliding the ruler
along the line of dots. One concept after another will apply to it, one after another drop
away, but it will always cover at least two of
them, and no dots less than three will ever
adequately cover *it*. You falsify it if you treat
it conceptually, or by the law of dots.

What is true here of successive states must
also be true of simultaneous characters. They
also overlap each other with their being. My
present field of consciousness is a centre sur-
rounded by a fringe that shades insensibly into
a subconscious more. I use three separate
terms here to describe this fact; but I might as
well use three hundred, for the fact is all shades
and no boundaries. Which part of it properly
is in my consciousness, which out? If I name
what is out, it already has come in. The centre
works in one way while the margins work in
another, and presently overpower the centre

and are central themselves. What we conceptually identify ourselves with and say we are thinking of at any time is the centre; but our *full* self is the whole field, with all those indefinitely radiating subconscious possibilities of increase that we can only feel without conceiving, and can hardly begin to analyze. The collective and the distributive ways of being coexist here, for each part functions distinctly, makes connexion with its own peculiar region in the still wider rest of experience and tends to draw us into that line, and yet the whole is somehow felt as one pulse of our life, — not conceived so, but felt so.

In principle, then, as I said, intellectualism's edge is broken; it can only approximate to reality, and its logic is inapplicable to our inner life, which spurns its vetoes and mocks at its impossibilities. Every bit of us at every moment is part and parcel of a wider self, it quivers along various radii like the wind-rose on a compass, and the actual in it is continuously one with possibles not yet in our present sight.[8] And just as we are co-conscious with

our own momentary margin, may not we ourselves form the margin of some more really
central self in things which is co-conscious
with the whole of us? May not you and I be
confluent in a higher consciousness, and con-
fluently active there, tho we now know it not?

I am tiring myself and you, I know, by
vainly seeking to describe by concepts and
words what I say at the same time exceeds
either conceptualization or verbalization. As
long as one continues *talking*, intellectualism
remains in undisturbed possession of the field.
The return to life can't come about by talking.
It is an *act*; to make you return to life, I must
set an example for your imitation, I must
deafen you to talk, or to the importance of
talk, by showing you, as Bergson does, that the
concepts we talk with are made for purposes of
practice and not for purposes of insight. Or I
must *point*, point to the mere *that* of life, and
you by inner sympathy must fill out the *what*
for yourselves. The minds of some of you, I
know, will absolutely refuse to do so, refuse to
think in non-conceptualized terms. I myself

absolutely refused to do so for years together, even after I knew that the denial of manyness-in-oneness by intellectualism must be false, for the same reality does perform the most various functions at once. But I hoped ever for a revised intellectualist way round the difficulty, and it was only after reading Bergson that I saw that to continue using the intellectualist method was itself the fault. I saw that philosophy had been on a false scent ever since the days of Socrates and Plato, that an *intellectual* answer to the intellectualist's difficulties will never come, and that the real way out of them, far from consisting in the discovery of such an answer, consists in simply closing one's ears to the question. When conceptualism summons life to justify itself in conceptual terms, it is like a challenge addressed in a foreign language to some one who is absorbed in his own business; it is irrelevant to him altogether — he may let it lie unnoticed. I went thus through the 'inner catastrophe' of which I spoke in the last lecture; I had literally come to the end of my conceptual stock-in-trade, I was bankrupt intellectualistically, and had to change my base. No words of mine will probably convert you, for words can be the names only of concepts. But if any of you try sincerely and pertinaciously on your own separate accounts to intellectualize reality, you may be similarly driven to a change of front. I say no more: I must leave life to teach the lesson.

We have now reached a point of view from which the self-compounding of mind in its smaller and more accessible portions seems a certain fact, and in which the speculative assumption of a similar but wider compounding in remoter regions must be reckoned with as a legitimate hypothesis. The absolute is not the impossible being I once thought it. Mental facts do function both singly and together, at once, and we finite minds may simultaneously be co-conscious with one another in a superhuman intelligence. It is only the extravagant claims of coercive necessity on the absolute's part that have to be denied by *a priori* logic. As an hypothesis trying to make itself probable on analogical and inductive grounds, the absolute is entitled to a patient hearing. Which is as much as to say that our serious business from now onward lies with Fechner and his method, rather than with Hegel, Royce, or Bradley. Fechner treats the superhuman consciousness he so fervently believes in as an hypothesis only, which he then recommends by all the resources of induction and persuasion.

It is true that Fechner himself is an absolutist in his books, not actively but passively, if I may say so. He talks not only of the earth-soul and of the star-souls, but of an integrated soul of all things in the cosmos without exception, and this he calls God just as others call it the absolute. Nevertheless he *thinks* only of the subordinate superhuman souls, and content with having made his obeisance once for all to the august total soul of the cosmos, he leaves it in its lonely sublimity with no attempt to define its nature. Like the absolute, it is 'out of range,' and not an object for distincter vision. Psychologically, it seems to me that Fechner's God is a lazy postulate of his, rather than a part of his system positively thought

out. As we envelop our sight and hearing, so
the earth-soul envelops us, and the star-soul
the earth-soul, until — what? Envelopment
can't go on forever; it must have an *abschluss*,
a total envelope must terminate the series, so
God is the name that Fechner gives to this
last all-enveloper. But if nothing escapes this
all-enveloper, he is responsible for everything,
including evil, and all the paradoxes and difficulties which I found in the absolute at the
end of our third lecture recur undiminished.
Fechner tries sincerely to grapple with the
problem of evil, but he always solves it in
the leibnitzian fashion by making his God
non-absolute, placing him under conditions of
'metaphysical necessity' which even his omnipotence cannot violate. His will has to struggle with conditions not imposed on that will
by itself. He tolerates provisionally what he
has not created, and then with endless patience
tries to overcome it and live it down. He has,
in short, a history. Whenever Fechner tries
to represent him clearly, his God becomes the
ordinary God of theism, and ceases to be the

absolutely totalized all-enveloper.[9] In this shape, he represents the ideal element in things solely, and is our champion and our helper and we his helpers, against the bad parts of the universe.

Fechner was in fact too little of a metaphysician to care for perfect formal consistency in these abstract regions. He believed in God in the pluralistic manner, but partly from convention and partly from what I should call intellectual laziness, if laziness of any kind could be imputed to a Fechner, he let the usual monistic talk about him pass unchallenged. I propose to you that we should discuss the question of God without entangling ourselves in advance in the monistic assumption. Is it probable that there is any superhuman consciousness at all, in the first place? When that is settled, the further question whether its form be monistic or pluralistic is in order.

Before advancing to either question, however, and I shall have to deal with both but very briefly after what has been said already, let me finish our retrospective survey by one more remark about the curious logical situation of the absolutists. For what have they invoked the absolute except as a being the peculiar inner form of which shall enable it to overcome the contradictions with which intellectualism has found the finite many as such to be infected? The many-in-one character that, as we have seen, every smallest tract of finite experience offers, is considered by intellectualism to be fatal to the reality of finite experience. What can be distinguished, it tells us, is separate; and what is separate is unrelated, for a relation, being a ' between,' would bring only a twofold separation. Hegel, Royce, Bradley, and the Oxford absolutists in general seem to agree about this logical absurdity of manyness-in-oneness in the only places where it is empirically found. But see the curious tactics! Is the absurdity *reduced* in the absolute being whom they call in to relieve it? Quite otherwise, for that being shows it on an infinitely greater scale, and flaunts it in its very definition. The fact of its not being related to any outward environment, the fact that all relations are inside of itself, does n't save it, for Mr. Bradley's great argument against the finite is that *in* any given bit of it (a bit of sugar, for instance) the presence of a plurality of characters (whiteness and sweetness, for example) is self-contradictory; so that in the final end all that the absolute's name appears to stand for is the persistent claim of outraged human nature that reality *shall* not be called absurd. *Somewhere* there must be an aspect of it guiltless of self-contradiction. All we can see of the absolute, meanwhile, is guilty in the same way in which the finite is. Intellectualism sees what it calls the guilt, when comminuted in the finite object; but is too near-sighted to see it in the more enormous object. Yet the absolute's constitution, if imagined at all, has to be imagined after the analogy of some bit of finite experience. Take any *real* bit, suppress its environment and then magnify it to monstrosity, and you get identically the type of structure of the absolute. It is obvious that all your difficulties here remain and go with you. If the relative experience was inwardly absurd, the absolute experience is infinitely more so. Intellectualism, in short, strains off the gnat, but swallows the whole camel. But this polemic against the absolute is as odious to me as it is to you, so I will say no more about that being. It is only one of those wills of the wisp, those lights that do mislead the morn, that have so often impeded the clear progress of philosophy, so I will turn to the more general positive question of whether superhuman unities of consciousness should be considered as more probable or more improbable.

In a former lecture I went over some of the fechnerian reasons for their plausibility, or reasons that at least replied to our more obvious grounds of doubt concerning them. The numerous facts of divided or split human personality which the genius of certain medical men, as Janet, Freud, Prince, Sidis, and others, have unearthed were unknown in Fechner's time, and neither the phenomena of automatic writing and speech, nor of mediumship and 'possession' generally, had been recognized or studied as we now study them, so Fechner's

stock of analogies is scant compared with our
present one. He did the best with what he
had, however. For my own part I find in some
of these abnormal or supernormal facts the
strongest suggestions in favor of a superior co-
consciousness being possible. I doubt whether
we shall ever understand some of them without
using the very letter of Fechner's conception
of a great reservoir in which the memories of
earth's inhabitants are pooled and preserved,
and from which, when the threshold lowers or
the valve opens, information ordinarily shut
out leaks into the mind of exceptional individuals among us. But those regions of inquiry
are perhaps too spook-haunted to interest an
academic audience, and the only evidence I
feel it now decorous to bring to the support of
Fechner is drawn from ordinary religious experience. I think it may be asserted that there
are religious experiences of a specific nature,
not deducible by analogy or psychological
reasoning from our other sorts of experience. I think that they point with reasonable
probability to the continuity of our conscious-

ness with a wider spiritual environment from which the ordinary prudential man (who is the only man that scientific psychology, so called, takes cognizance of) is shut off. I shall begin my final lecture by referring to them again briefly.

VIII

CONCLUSIONS

LECTURE VIII

CONCLUSIONS

At the close of my last lecture I referred to
the existence of religious experiences of a specific nature. I must now explain just what I
mean by such a claim. Briefly, the facts I have
in mind may all be described as experiences
of an unexpected life succeeding upon death.
By this I don't mean immortality, or the death
of the body. I mean the deathlike termination
of certain mental processes within the individual's experience, processes that run to failure,
and in some individuals, at least, eventuate in
despair. Just as romantic love seems a comparatively recent literary invention, so these
experiences of a life that supervenes upon despair seem to have played no great part in
official theology till Luther's time; and possibly the best way to indicate their character
will be to point to a certain contrast between
the inner life of ourselves and of the ancient
Greeks and Romans.

Mr. Chesterton, I think, says somewhere,

that the Greeks and Romans, in all that concerned their moral life, were an extraordinarily solemn set of folks. The Athenians thought that the very gods must admire the rectitude of Phocion and Aristides; and those gentlemen themselves were apparently of much the same opinion. Cato's veracity was so impeccable that the extremest incredulity a Roman could express of anything was to say, 'I would not believe it even if Cato had told me.' Good was good, and bad was bad, for these people. Hypocrisy, which church-Christianity brought in, hardly existed; the naturalistic system held firm; its values showed no hollowness and brooked no irony. The individual, if virtuous enough, could meet all possible requirements. The pagan pride had never crumbled. Luther was the first moralist who broke with any effectiveness through the crust of all this naturalistic self-sufficiency, thinking (and possibly he was right) that Saint Paul had done it already. Religious experience of the lutheran type brings all our naturalistic standards to bankruptcy. You are strong only by being weak, it shows. You cannot live on pride or self-sufficingness. There is a light in which all the naturally founded and currently accepted distinctions, excellences, and safeguards of our characters appear as utter childishness. Sincerely to give up one's conceit or hope of being good in one's own right is the only door to the universe's deeper reaches.

These deeper reaches are familiar to evangelical Christianity and to what is nowadays becoming known as 'mind-cure' religion or 'new thought.' The phenomenon is that of new ranges of life succeeding on our most despairing moments. There are resources in us that naturalism with its literal and legal virtues never recks of, possibilities that take our breath away, of another kind of happiness and power, based on giving up our own will and letting something higher work for us, and these seem to show a world wider than either physics or philistine ethics can imagine. Here is a world in which all is well, in *spite* of certain forms of death, indeed *because* of certain forms of death — death of hope, death of strength, death of responsibility, of fear and worry, competency and desert, death of everything that paganism, naturalism, and legalism pin their faith on and tie their trust to.

Reason, operating on our other experiences, even our psychological experiences, would never have inferred these specifically religious experiences in advance of their actual coming. She could not suspect their existence, for they are discontinuous with the 'natural' experiences they succeed upon and invert their values. But as they actually come and are given, creation widens to the view of their recipients. They suggest that our natural experience, our strictly moralistic and prudential experience, may be only a fragment of real human experience. They soften nature's outlines and open out the strangest possibilities and perspectives.

This is why it seems to me that the logical understanding, working in abstraction from such specifically religious experiences, will always omit something, and fail to reach completely adequate conclusions. Death and failure, it will always say, *are* death and failure simply, and can nevermore be one with life; so religious experience, peculiarly so called, needs, in my opinion, to be carefully considered and interpreted by every one who aspires to reason out a more complete philosophy.

The sort of belief that religious experience of this type naturally engenders in those who have it is fully in accord with Fechner's theories. To quote words which I have used elsewhere, the believer finds that the tenderer parts of his personal life are continuous with a *more* of the same quality which is operative in the universe outside of him and which he can keep in working touch with, and in a fashion get on board of and save himself, when all his lower being has gone to pieces in the wreck. In a word, the believer is continuous, to his own consciousness, at any rate, with a wider self from which saving experiences flow in. Those who have such experiences distinctly enough and often enough to live in the light of them remain quite unmoved by criticism, from whatever quarter it may come, be it academic or scientific, or be it merely the voice of logical common sense. They have had their vision and they *know*—that is enough—that we inhabit an invisible spiritual environment from which help comes, our soul being mysteriously one with a larger soul whose instruments we are.

One may therefore plead, I think, that Fechner's ideas are not without direct empirical verification. There is at any rate one side of life which would be easily explicable if those ideas were true, but of which there appears no clear explanation so long as we assume either with naturalism that human consciousness is the highest consciousness there is, or with dualistic theism that there is a higher mind in the cosmos, but that it is discontinuous with our own. It has always been a matter of surprise with me that philosophers of the absolute should have shown so little interest in this department of life, and so seldom put its phenomena in evidence, even when it seemed obvious that personal experience of some kind must have made their confidence in their own vision so strong. The logician's bias has always been too much with them. They have preferred the thinner to the thicker method, dialectical abstraction being so much more dignified and academic than the confused and unwholesome facts of personal biography.

In spite of rationalism's disdain for the particular, the personal, and the unwholesome, the drift of all the evidence we have seems to me to sweep us very strongly towards the belief in some form of superhuman life with which we may, unknown to ourselves, be co-conscious. We may be in the universe as dogs and cats are in our libraries, seeing the books and hearing the conversation, but having no inkling of the meaning of it all. The intellectualist objections to this fall away when the authority of intellectualist logic is undermined by criticism, and then the positive empirical evidence remains. The analogies with ordinary psychology and with the facts of pathology, with those of psychical research, so called, and with those of religious experience, establish, when taken together, a decidedly *formidable* probability in favor of a general view of the world almost identical with Fechner's. The outlines of the superhuman consciousness thus made probable must remain, however, very vague, and the number of functionally distinct 'selves' it comports and carries has to be left entirely problematic. It may be polytheistically or it may be monotheistically conceived of. Fechner, with his distinct earth-soul functioning as our guardian angel, seems to me clearly polytheistic; but the word 'polytheism' usually gives offence, so perhaps it is better not to use it. Only one thing is certain, and that is the result of our criticism of the absolute: the only way to escape from the paradoxes and perplexities that a consistently thought-out monistic universe suffers from as from a species of auto-intoxication — the mystery of the 'fall' namely, of reality lapsing into appearance, truth into error, perfection into imperfection; of evil, in short; the mystery of universal determinism, of the block-universe eternal and without a history, etc.;—the only way of escape, I say, from all this is to be frankly pluralistic and assume that the superhuman consciousness, however vast it may be, has itself an external environment, and consequently is finite. Present day monism carefully repudiates complicity with spinozistic monism. In that, it explains, the many get dissolved in the one and lost, whereas in the improved idealistic form they get preserved in all their manyness as the one's eternal object. The absolute itself is thus represented by absolutists as having a pluralistic object. But if even the absolute has to have a pluralistic vision, why should we ourselves hesitate to be pluralists on our own sole account? Why should we envelop our many with the 'one' that brings so much poison in its train?

The line of least resistance, then, as it seems to me, both in theology and in philosophy, is to accept, along with the superhuman consciousness, the notion that it is not all-embracing, the notion, in other words, that there is a God, but that he is finite, either in power or in knowledge, or in both at once. These, I need hardly tell you, are the terms in which common men have usually carried on their active commerce with God; and the monistic perfections that make the notion of him so paradoxical practically and morally are the colder addition of remote professorial minds operating *in distans* upon conceptual substitutes for him alone.

Why cannot 'experience' and 'reason' meet on this common ground? Why cannot they compromise? May not the godlessness usually but needlessly associated with the philosophy of immediate experience give way to a theism now seen to follow directly from that experience more widely taken? and may not rationalism, satisfied with seeing her *a priori* proofs of God so effectively replaced by empirical evidence, abate something of her absolutist claims? Let God but have the least infinitesimal *other* of any kind beside him, and empiricism and rationalism might strike hands in a lasting treaty of peace. Both might then leave abstract thinness behind them, and seek together, as scientific men seek, by using all the analogies and data within reach, to build up the most probable approximate idea of what the divine consciousness concretely may be like. I venture to beg the younger

Oxford idealists to consider seriously this alternative. Few men are as qualified by their intellectual gifts to reap the harvests that seem certain to any one who, like Fechner and Bergson, will leave the thinner for the thicker path.

Compromise and mediation are inseparable from the pluralistic philosophy. Only monistic dogmatism can say of any of its hypotheses, 'It is either that or nothing; take it or leave it just as it stands.' The type of monism prevalent at Oxford has kept this steep and brittle attitude, partly through the proverbial academic preference for thin and elegant logical solutions, partly from a mistaken notion that the only solidly grounded basis for religion was along those lines. If Oxford men could be ignorant of anything, it might almost seem that they had remained ignorant of the great empirical movement towards a pluralistic panpsychic view of the universe, into which our own generation has been drawn, and which threatens to short-circuit their methods entirely and become their religious rival unless they are willing to make themselves its allies. Yet, wedded as they seem to be to the logical machinery and technical apparatus of absolutism, I cannot but believe that their fidelity to the religious ideal in general is deeper still. Especially do I find it hard to believe that the more clerical adherents of the school would hold so fast to its particular machinery if only they could be made to think that religion could be secured in some other way. Let empiricism once become associated with religion, as hitherto, through some strange misunderstanding, it has been associated with irreligion, and I believe that a new era of religion as well as of philosophy will be ready to begin. That great awakening of a new popular interest in philosophy, which is so striking a phenomenon at the present day in all countries, is undoubtedly due in part to religious demands. As the authority of past tradition tends more and more to crumble, men naturally turn a wistful ear to the authority of reason or to the evidence of present fact. They will assuredly not be disappointed if they open their minds to what the thicker and more radical empiricism has to say. I fully believe that such an empiricism is a more natural ally than dialectics ever were, or can be, of the religious life. It is true that superstitions and wild-growing over-beliefs of all sorts will undoubtedly begin to abound if the notion of higher consciousnesses enveloping ours, of fechnerian earth-souls and the like, grows orthodox and fashionable; still more will they superabound if science ever puts her approving stamp on the phenomena of which Frederic Myers so earnestly advocated the scientific recognition, the phenomena of psychic research so-called — and I myself firmly believe that most of these phenomena are rooted in reality. But ought one seriously to allow such a timid consideration as that to deter one from following the evident path of greatest religious promise? Since when, in this mixed world, was any good thing given us in purest outline and isolation? One of the chief characteristics of life is life's redundancy. The sole condition of our having anything, no matter what, is that we should have so much of it, that we are fortunate if we do not grow sick of the sight and sound of it altogether. Everything is smothered in the litter that is fated to accompany it. Without too much you cannot have enough, of anything. Lots of inferior books, lots of bad statues, lots of dull speeches, of tenth-rate men and women, as a condition of the few precious specimens in either kind being realized! The gold-dust comes to birth with the quartz-sand all around it, and this is as much a condition of religion as of any other excellent possession. There must be extrication; there must be competition for survival; but the clay matrix and the noble gem must first come into being unsifted. Once extricated, the gem can be examined separately, conceptualized, defined, and insulated. But this process of extrication cannot be short-circuited — or if it is, you get the thin inferior abstractions which we have seen, either the hollow unreal god of scholastic theology, or the unintelligible pantheistic monster, instead of the more living divine reality with which it appears certain that empirical methods tend to connect men in imagination.

VIII. CONCLUSIONS

Arrived at this point, I ask you to go back to my first lecture and remember, if you can, what I quoted there from your own Professor Jacks—what he said about the philosopher himself being taken up into the universe which he is accounting for. This is the fechnerian as well as the hegelian view, and thus our end rejoins harmoniously our beginning. Philosophies are intimate parts of the universe, they express something of its own thought of itself. A philosophy may indeed be a most momentous reaction of the universe upon itself. It may, as I said, possess and handle itself differently in consequence of us philosophers, with our theories, being here; it may trust itself or mistrust itself the more, and, by doing the one or the other, deserve more the trust or the mistrust. What mistrusts itself deserves mistrust.

This is the philosophy of humanism in the widest sense. Our philosophies swell the current of being, add their character to it. They are part of all that we have met, of all that makes us be. As a French philosopher says, 'Nous sommes du réel dans le réel.' Our

thoughts determine our acts, and our acts rede
termine the previous nature of the world.

Thus does foreignness get banished from
our world, and far more so when we take the
system of it pluralistically than when we take
it monistically. We are indeed internal parts
of God and not external creations, on any
possible reading of the panpsychic system.
Yet because God is not the absolute, but is
himself a part when the system is conceived
pluralistically, his functions can be taken as
not wholly dissimilar to those of the other
smaller parts,—as similar to our functions
consequently.

Having an environment, being in time, and
working out a history just like ourselves, he
escapes from the foreignness from all that is
human, of the static timeless perfect absolute.

Remember that one of our troubles with that
was its essential foreignness and monstrosity —
there really is no other word for it than that.
Its having the all-inclusive form gave to it an
essentially heterogeneous *nature* from our-

selves. And this great difference between absolutism and pluralism demands no difference in the universe's material content — it follows from a difference in the form alone. The all-form or monistic form makes the foreignness result, the each-form or pluralistic form leaves the intimacy undisturbed.

No matter what the content of the universe may be, if you only allow that it is *many* everywhere and always, that *nothing* real escapes from having an environment; so far from defeating its rationality, as the absolutists so unanimously pretend, you leave it in possession of the maximum amount of rationality practically attainable by our minds. Your relations with it, intellectual, emotional, and active, remain fluent and congruous with your own nature's chief demands.

It would be a pity if the word 'rationality' were allowed to give us trouble here. It is one of those eulogistic words that both sides claim — for almost no one is willing to advertise his philosophy as a system of irrationality. But like most of the words which people used eulogistically, the word 'rational' carries too many meanings. The most objective one is that of the older logic — the connexion between two things is rational when you can infer one from the other, mortal from Socrates, *e. g.;* and you can do that only when they have a quality in common. But this kind of rationality is just that logic of identity which all disciples of Hegel find insufficient. They supersede it by the higher rationality of negation and contradiction and make the notion vague again. Then you get the æsthetic or teleologic kinds of rationality, saying that whatever fits in any way, whatever is beautiful or good, whatever is purposive or gratifies desire, is rational in so far forth. Then again, according to Hegel, whatever is 'real' is rational. I myself said awhile ago that whatever lets loose any action which we are fond of exerting seems rational. It would be better to give up the word 'rational' altogether than to get into a merely verbal fight about who has the best right to keep it.

Perhaps the words 'foreignness' and 'intimacy,' which I put forward in my first lecture, express the contrast I insist on better than the words 'rationality' and 'irrationality'—let us stick to them, then. I now say that the notion of the 'one' breeds foreignness and that of the 'many' intimacy, for reasons which I have urged at only too great length, and with which, whether they convince you or not, I may suppose that you are now well acquainted. But what at bottom is meant by calling the universe many or by calling it one?

Pragmatically interpreted, pluralism or the doctrine that it is many means only that the sundry parts of reality *may be externally related*. Everything you can think of, however vast or inclusive, has on the pluralistic view a genuinely 'external' environment of some sort or amount. Things are 'with' one another in many ways, but nothing includes everything, or dominates over everything. The word 'and' trails along after every sentence. Something always escapes. 'Ever not quite' has to be said of the best attempts made anywhere in the universe at attaining all-inclusiveness. The pluralistic world is thus more like a federal republic than like an empire or a kingdom. However much may be collected, however much may report itself as present at any effective centre of consciousness or action, something else is self-governed and absent and unreduced to unity.

Monism, on the other hand, insists that when you come down to reality as such, to the reality of realities, everything is present to *everything* else in one vast instantaneous co-implicated completeness—nothing can in *any* sense, functional or substantial, be really absent from anything else, all things interpenetrate and telescope together in the great total conflux.

For pluralism, all that we are required to admit as the constitution of reality is what we ourselves find empirically realized in every minimum of finite life. Briefly it is this, that nothing real is absolutely simple, that every smallest bit of experience is a *multum in parvo* plurally related, that each relation is one aspect, character, or function, way of its being taken, or way of its taking something else; and that a bit of reality when actively engaged in one of these relations is not *by that very fact* engaged in all the other relations simultaneously. The relations are not *all* what the French call *solidaires* with one another. Without losing its identity a thing can either take up or drop another thing, like the log I spoke of, which by taking up new carriers and dropping old ones can travel anywhere with a light escort.

For monism, on the contrary, everything, whether we realize it or not, drags the whole universe along with itself and drops nothing. The log starts and arrives with all its carriers supporting it. If a thing were once disconnected, it could never be connected again, according to monism. The pragmatic difference between the two systems is thus a definite one. It is just thus, that if *a* is once out of sight of *b* or out of touch with it, or, more briefly, 'out' of it at all, then, according to monism, it must always remain so, they can never get together; whereas pluralism admits that on another occasion they may work together, or in some way be connected again. Monism allows for no

such things as 'other occasions' in reality —
in *real* or absolute reality, that is.

The difference I try to describe amounts,
you see, to nothing more than the difference
between what I formerly called the each-form
and the all-form of reality. Pluralism lets
things really exist in the each-form or distributively. Monism thinks that the all-form or col-
lective-unit form is the only form that is rational. The all-form allows of no taking up
and dropping of connexions, for in the all the
parts are essentially and eternally co-implicated.
In the each-form, on the contrary, a thing may
be connected by intermediary things, with a
thing with which it has no immediate or essential connexion. It is thus at all times in many
possible connexions which are not necessarily
actualized at the moment. They depend on
which actual path of intermediation it may
functionally strike into: the word 'or' names
a genuine reality. Thus, as I speak here, I may
look ahead *or* to the right *or* to the left, and in
either case the intervening space and air and
ether enable me to see the faces of a different

portion of this audience. My being here is independent of any one set of these faces.

If the each-form be the eternal form of reality no less than it is the form of temporal appearance, we still have a coherent world, and not an incarnate incoherence, as is charged by so many absolutists. Our 'multiverse' still makes a 'universe'; for every part, tho it may not be in actual or immediate connexion, is nevertheless in some possible or mediated connexion, with every other part however remote, through the fact that each part hangs together with its very next neighbors in inextricable interfusion. The type of union, it is true, is different here from the monistic type of *alleinheit*. It is not a universal co-implication, or integration of all things *durcheinander*. It is what I call the strung-along type, the type of continuity, contiguity, or concatenation. If you prefer greek words, you may call it the synechistic type. At all events, you see that it forms a definitely conceivable alternative to the through-and-through unity of all things at once, which is the type opposed to it by monism. You see also that it stands or falls with the notion I have taken such pains to defend, of the through-and-through union of adjacent minima of experience, of the confluence of every passing moment of concretely felt experience with its immediately next neighbors. The recognition of this fact of coalescence of next with next in concrete experience, so that all the insulating cuts we make there are artificial products of the conceptualizing faculty, is what distinguishes the empiricism which I call 'radical,' from the bugaboo empiricism of the traditional rationalist critics, which (rightly or wrongly) is accused of chopping up experience into atomistic sensations, incapable of union with one another until a purely intellectual principle has swooped down upon them from on high and folded them in its own conjunctive categories.

Here, then, you have the plain alternative, and the full mystery of the difference between pluralism and monism, as clearly as I can set it forth on this occasion. It packs up into a nutshell: — Is the manyness in oneness that indubitably characterizes the world we inhabit, a property only of the absolute whole of things, so that you must postulate that one-enormous-whole indivisibly as the *prius* of there being any many at all — in other words, start with the rationalistic block-universe, entire, unmitigated, and complete? — or can the finite elements have their own aboriginal forms of manyness in oneness, and where they have no immediate oneness still be continued into one another by intermediary terms—each one of these terms being one with its next neighbors, and yet the total 'oneness' never getting absolutely complete?

The alternative is definite. It seems to me, moreover, that the two horns of it make pragmatically different ethical appeals — at least they *may* do so, to certain individuals. But if you consider the pluralistic horn to be intrinsically irrational, self-contradictory, and absurd, I can now say no more in its defence. Having done what I could in my earlier lectures to break the edge of the intellectualistic *reductiones ad absurdum*, I must leave the issue in your hands. Whatever I may say, each of you will be sure to take pluralism or leave it, just as your own sense of rationality moves and inclines. The only thing I emphatically insist upon is that it is a fully co-ordinate hypothesis with monism. This world *may*, in the last resort, be a block-universe; but on the other hand it *may* be a universe only strung-along, not rounded in and closed. Reality *may* exist distributively just as it sensibly seems to, after all. On that possibility I do insist.

One's general vision of the probable usually decides such alternatives. They illustrate what I once wrote of as the 'will to believe.' In some of my lectures at Harvard I have spoken of what I call the 'faith-ladder,' as something quite different from the *sorites* of the logic-books, yet seeming to have an analogous form. I think you will quickly recognize in yourselves, as I describe it, the mental process to which I give this name.

A conception of the world arises in you somehow, no matter how. Is it true or not? you ask.

VIII. CONCLUSIONS

It *might* be true somewhere, you say, for it is not self-contradictory.

It *may* be true, you continue, even here and now.

It is *fit* to be true, it would be *well if it were true*, it *ought* to be true, you presently feel.

It *must* be true, something persuasive in you whispers next; and then — as a final result —

It shall be *held for true*, you decide; it *shall be* as if true, for *you*.

And your acting thus may in certain special cases be a means of making it securely true in the end.

Not one step in this process is logical, yet it is the way in which monists and pluralists alike espouse and hold fast to their visions. It is life exceeding logic, it is the practical reason for which the theoretic reason finds arguments after the conclusion is once there. In just this way do some of us hold to the unfinished pluralistic universe; in just this way do others hold to the timeless universe eternally complete.

Meanwhile the incompleteness of the pluralistic universe, thus assumed and held to as the most probable hypothesis, is also represented by the pluralistic philosophy as being self-reparative through us, as getting its disconnections remedied in part by our behavior. 'We use what we are and have, to know; and what we know, to be and have still more.'[1] Thus do philosophy and reality, theory and action, work in the same circle indefinitely.

I have now finished these poor lectures, and as you look back on them, they doubtless seem rambling and inconclusive enough. My only hope is that they may possibly have proved suggestive; and if indeed they have been suggestive of one point of method, I am almost willing to let all other suggestions go. That point is that *it is high time for the basis of discussion in these questions to be broadened and thickened up.* It is for that that I have brought in Fechner and Bergson, and descriptive psychology and religious experiences, and have ventured even to hint at psychical research and other wild beasts of the philosophic desert. Owing possibly to the fact that Plato and

VIII. CONCLUSIONS

Aristotle, with their intellectualism, are the basis of philosophic study here, the Oxford brand of transcendentalism seems to me to have confined itself too exclusively to thin logical considerations, that would hold good in all conceivable worlds, worlds of an empirical constitution entirely different from ours. It is as if the actual peculiarities of the world that is were entirely irrelevant to the content of truth. But they cannot be irrelevant; and the philosophy of the future must imitate the sciences in taking them more and more elaborately into account. I urge some of the younger members of this learned audience to lay this hint to heart. If you can do so effectively, making still more concrete advances upon the path which Fechner and Bergson have so enticingly opened up, if you can gather philosophic conclusions of any kind, monistic or pluralistic, from the *particulars of life*, I will say, as I now do say, with the cheerfullest of hearts, 'Ring out, ring out my mournful rhymes, but ring the fuller minstrel in.'

NOTES

NOTES

LECTURE I

Note 1, page 5. — Bailey: *op. cit.*, First Series, p. 52.

Note 2, page 11. — *Smaller Logic*, § 194.

Note 3, page 16. — *Exploratio philosophica*, Part I, 1865, pp. xxxviii, 130.

Note 4, page 20. — Hinneberg: *Die Kultur der Gegenwart : Systematische Philosophie.* Leipzig: Teubner, 1907.

LECTURE II

Note 1, page 50. — The difference is that the bad parts of this finite are eternal and essential for absolutists, whereas pluralists may hope that they will eventually get sloughed off and become as if they had not been.

Note 2, page 51. — Quoted by W. Wallace: *Lectures and Essays*, Oxford, 1898, p. 560.

Note 3, page 51. — *Logic*, tr. Wallace, 1874, p. 181.

Note 4, page 52. — *Ibid.*, p. 304.

Note 5, page 53. — *Contemporary Review*, December, 1907, vol. 92, p. 618.

Note 6, page 57. — *Metaphysic*, sec. 69 ff.

Note 7, page 62. — *The World and the Individual*, vol. i, pp. 131–132.

Note 8, page 67. — A good illustration of this is to be found in a controversy between Mr. Bradley and the present writer, in *Mind* for 1893, Mr. Bradley contending (if I understood him rightly) that 'resemblance' is an illegitimate category, because it admits of degrees, and that the only real relations in comparison are absolute identity and absolute non-comparability.

NOTES

Note 9, page 75. — *Studies in the Hegelian Dialectic*, p. 184.

Note 10, page 75. — *Appearance and Reality*, 1893, pp. 141–142.

Note 11, page 76. — Cf. *Elements of Metaphysics*, p. 88.

Note 12, page 77. — *Some Dogmas of Religion*, p. 184.

Note 13, page 80. — For a more detailed criticism of Mr. Bradley's intellectualism, see Appendix A.

LECTURE III

Note 1, page 94. — Hegel, *Smaller Logic*, pp. 184–185.

Note 2, page 95. — Cf. Hegel's fine vindication of this function of contradiction in his *Wissenschaft der Logik*, Bk. ii, sec. 1, chap. ii, C, Anmerkung 3.

Note 3, page 95. — *Hegel*, in *Blackwood's Philosophical Classics*, p. 162.

Note 4, page 95. — *Wissenschaft der Logik*, Bk. i, sec. 1, chap. ii, B, a.

Note 5, page 96. — Wallace's translation of the *Smaller Logic*, p. 128.

Note 6, page 101. — Joachim, *The Nature of Truth*, Oxford, 1906, pp. 22, 178. The argument in case the belief should be doubted would be the higher synthetic idea: if two truths were possible, the duality of that possibility would itself be the one truth that would unite them.

Note 7, page 115. — *The World and the Individual*, vol. ii, pp. 385, 386, 409.

Note 8, page 116. — The best *uninspired* argument (again not ironical!) which I know is that in Miss M. W. Calkins's excellent book, *The Persistent Problems of Philosophy*, Macmillan, 1902.

Note 9, page 117. — Cf. Dr. Fuller's excellent article, ' Ethical monism and the problem of evil,' in the *Harvard Journal of Theology*, vol. i, No. 2, April, 1908.

Note 10, page 120. — *Metaphysic*, sec. 79.

Note 11, page 121. — *Studies in the Hegelian Dialectic*, secs. 150, 153.

Note 12, page 121. — *The Nature of Truth*, 1906, pp. 170–171.

Note 13, page 121. — *Ibid.*, p. 179.

Note 14, page 123. — The psychological analogy that certain finite tracts of consciousness are composed of isolable parts added together, cannot be used by absolutists as proof that such parts are essential elements of all consciousness. Other finite fields of consciousness seem in point of fact not to be similarly resolvable into isolable parts.

Note 15, page 128. — Judging by the analogy of the relation which our central consciousness seems to bear to that of our spinal cord, lower ganglia, etc., it would seem natural to suppose that in whatever superhuman mental synthesis there may be, the neglect and elimination of certain contents of which we are conscious on the human level might be as characteristic a feature as is the combination and interweaving of other human contents.

LECTURE IV

Note 1, page 143. — *The Spirit of Modern Philosophy*, p. 227.

Note 2, page 165. — Fechner: *Über die Seelenfrage*, 1861, p. 170.

Note 3, page 168. — Fechner's latest summarizing of his views, *Die Tagesansicht gegenüber der Nachtansicht*, Leipzig, 1879, is now, I understand, in process of translation. His

NOTES

Little Book of Life after Death exists already in two American versions, one published by Little, Brown & Co., Boston, the other by the Open Court Co., Chicago.

Note 4, page 176. — Mr. Bradley ought to be to some degree exempted from my attack in these last pages. Compare especially what he says of non-human consciousness in his *Appearance and Reality*, pp. 269–272.

LECTURE V

Note 1, page 182. — Royce: *The Spirit of Modern Philosophy*, p. 379.

Note 2, page 184. — *The World and the Individual*, vol. ii, pp. 58–62.

Note 3, page 190. — I hold to it still as the best description of an enormous number of our higher fields of consciousness. They demonstrably do not *contain* the lower states that know the same objects. Of other fields, however this is not so true; so, 'n the *Psychological Review* for 1895, vol. ii, p. 105 (see especially pp. 119–120), I frankly withdrew, in principle, my former objection to talking of fields of consciousness being made of simpler 'parts,' leaving the facts to decide the question in each special case.

Note 4, page 194. — I abstract from the consciousness attached to the whole itself, if such consciousness be there.

LECTURE VI

Note 1, page 250. — For a more explicit vindication of the notion of activity, see Appendix B, where I try to defend its recognition as a definite form of immediate experience against its rationalistic critics.

NOTES

I subjoin here a few remarks destined to disarm some possible critics of Professor Bergson, who, to defend himself against misunderstandings of his meaning, ought to amplify and more fully explain his statement that concepts have a practical but not a theoretical use. Understood in one way, the thesis sounds indefensible, for by concepts we certainly increase our knowledge about things, and that seems a theoretical achievement, whatever practical achievements may follow in its train. Indeed, M. Bergson might seem to be easily refutable out of his own mouth. His philosophy pretends, if anything, to give a better insight into truth than rationalistic philosophies give: yet what is it in itself if not a conceptual system? Does its author not reason by concepts exclusively in his very attempt to show that they can give no insight?

To this particular objection, at any rate, it is easy to reply. In using concepts of his own to discredit the theoretic claims of concepts generally, Bergson does not contradict, but on the contrary emphatically illustrates his own view of their practical rôle, for they serve in his hands only to 'orient' us, to show us to what quarter we must *practically turn* if we wish to gain that completer insight into reality which he denies that they can give. He directs our hopes away from them and towards the despised sensible flux. *What he reaches by their means is thus only a new practical attitude.* He but restores, against the vetoes of intellectualist philosophy, our naturally cordial relations with sensible experience and common sense. This service is surely only practical; but it is a service for which we may be almost immeasurably grateful. To trust our senses again with a good philosophic conscience! — who ever conferred on us so valuable a freedom before?

By making certain distinctions and additions it seems easy to meet the other counts of the indictment. Concepts are realities of a new order, with particular relations between them. These relations are just as much directly perceived, when we compare our various concepts, as the distance between two sense-objects is perceived when we look at it. Conception is an operation which gives us material for new acts of perception, then; and when the results of these are written down, we get those bodies of 'mental truth' (as Locke called it) known as mathematics, logic, and *a priori* metaphysics. To know all this truth is a theoretic achievement, indeed, but it is a narrow one; for the relations between conceptual objects as such are only the static ones of bare comparison, as difference or sameness, congruity or contradiction, inclusion or exclusion. Nothing *happens* in the realm of concepts ; relations there are 'eternal' only. The theoretic gain fails so far, therefore, to touch even the outer hem of the real world, the world of causal and dynamic relations, of activity and history. To gain insight into all that moving life, Bergson is right in turning us away from conception and towards perception.

By combining concepts with percepts, *we can draw maps of the distribution* of other percepts in distant space and time. To know this distribution is of course a theoretic achievement, but the achievement is extremely limited, it cannot be effected without percepts, and even then what it yields is only static relations. From maps we learn positions only, and the position of a thing is but the slightest kind of truth about it; but, being indispensable for forming our plans of action, the conceptual map-making has the enormous practical importance on which Bergson so rightly insists.

But concepts, it will be said, do not only give us eternal truths of comparison and maps of the positions of things, they bring new *values* into life. In their mapping function they stand to perception in general in the same relation in which sight and hearing stand to touch — Spencer calls these higher senses only organs of anticipatory touch. But our eyes and ears also open to us worlds of independent glory: music and decorative art result, and an incredible enhancement of life's value follows. Even so does the conceptual world bring new ranges of value and of motivation to our life. Its maps not only serve us practically, but the mere mental possession of such vast pictures is of itself an inspiring good. New interests and incitements, and feelings of power, sublimity, and admiration are aroused.

Abstractness *per se* seems to have a touch of ideality. Royce's 'loyalty to loyalty' is an excellent example. 'Causes,' as anti-slavery, democracy, liberty, etc., dwindle when realized in their sordid particulars. The veritable ' cash-value' of the idea seems to cleave to it only in the abstract status. Truth at large, as Royce contends, in his *Philosophy of Loyalty*, appears another thing altogether from the true particulars in which it is best to believe. It transcends in value all those 'expediencies,' and is something to live for, whether expedient or inexpedient. Truth with a big T is a 'momentous issue'; truths in detail are 'poor scraps,' mere 'crumbling successes.' (*Op. cit.*, Lecture VII, especially § v.)

Is, now, such bringing into existence of a new *value* to be regarded as a theoretic achievement? The question is a nice one, for altho a value is in one sense an objective quality perceived, the essence of that quality is its relation to the will, and consists in its being a dynamogenic spur that makes our action different. So far as their value-creating function goes, it would thus appear that concepts connect themselves more with our active than with our theoretic life, so here again Bergson's formulation seems unobjectionable. Persons who have certain concepts are animated otherwise, pursue their own vital careers differently. It does n't necessarily follow that they understand other vital careers more intimately.

Again it may be said that we combine old concepts into new ones, conceiving thus such realities as the ether, God, souls, or what not, of which our sensible life alone would leave us altogether ignorant. This surely is an increase of our knowledge, and may well be called a theoretical achievement. Yet here again Bergson's criticisms hold good. Much as conception may tell us *about* such invisible objects, it sheds no ray of light into their interior. The completer, indeed, our definitions of ether-waves, atoms, Gods, or souls become, the less instead of the more intelligible do they appear to us. The learned in such things are consequently beginning more and more to ascribe a solely instrumental value to our concepts of them. Ether and molecules may be like co-ordinates and averages, only so many crutches by the help of which we practically perform the operation of getting about among our sensible experiences.

We see from these considerations how easily the question of whether the function of concepts is theoretical or practical may grow into a logomachy. It may be better from this point of view to refuse to recognize the alternative as a sharp one. The sole thing that is certain in the midst of it all is that Bergson is absolutely right in contending that the whole life of activity and change is inwardly impenetrable to conceptual treatment, and that it opens itself only to sympathetic apprehension at the hands of immediate feeling. All the *whats* as well as the *thats* of reality, relational as well as terminal, are in the end contents of immediate concrete perception. Yet the remoter unperceived *arrangements*, temporal, spatial, and logical, of these contents, are also something that we need to know as well for the pleasure of the knowing as for the practical help. We may call this need of arrangement a theoretic need or a practical need, according as we choose to lay the emphasis; but Bergson is accurately right when he limits conceptual knowledge to arrangement, and when he insists that arrangement is the mere skirt and skin of the whole of what we ought to know.

Note 2, page 266. — Gaston Rageot, *Revue Philosophique*, vol. lxiv, p. 85 (July, 1907).

Note 3, page 268. — I have myself talked in other ways as plausibly as I could, in my *Psychology*, and talked truly (as I believe) in certain selected cases; but for other cases the natural way invincibly comes back.

LECTURE VII

Note 1, page 278. — *Introduction to Hume*, 1874, p. 151.

Note 2, page 279. — *Ibid.*, pp. 16, 21, 36, *et passim*.

Note 3, page 279. — See, *inter alia*, the chapter on the 'Stream of Thought' in my own Psychologies; H. Cornelius, *Psychologie*, 1897, chaps. i and iii; G. H. Luquet, *Idées Générales de Psychologie*, 1906, *passim*.

Note 4, page 280. — Compare, as to all this, an article by the present writer, entitled 'A world of pure experience,' in the *Journal of Philosophy*, New York, vol. i, pp. 533, 561 (1905).

Note 5, page 280. — Green's attempt to discredit sensations by reminding us of their 'dumbness,' in that they do not come already *named*, as concepts may be said to do, only shows how intellectualism is dominated by verbality. The unnamed appears in Green as synonymous with the unreal.

Note 6, page 283. — *Philosophy of Reflection*, i, 248 ff.

NOTES

Note 7, page 284. — Most of this paragraph is extracted from an address of mine before the American Psychological Association, printed in the *Psychological Review*, vol. ii, p. 105. I take pleasure in the fact that already in 1895 I was so far advanced towards my present bergsonian position.

Note 8, page 289. — The conscious self of the moment, the central self, is probably determined to this privileged position by its functional connexion with the body's imminent or present acts. It is the present *acting* self. Tho the more that surrounds it may be 'subconscious' to us, yet if in its 'collective capacity' it also exerts an active function, it may be conscious in a wider way, conscious, as it were, over our heads.

On the relations of consciousness to action see Bergson's *Matière et Mémoire, passim*, especially chap. i. Compare also the hints in Münsterberg's *Grundzüge der Psychologie*, chap. xv; those in my own *Principles of Psychology*, vol. ii, pp. 581–592; and those in W. McDougall's *Physiological Psychology*, chap. vii.

Note 9, page 295. — Compare *Zend-Avesta*, 2d edition, vol. i, pp. 165 ff., 181, 206, 244 ff., etc.; *Die Tagesansicht*, etc., chap. v, § 6; and chap. xv.

LECTURE VIII

Note 1, page 330. — Blondel: *Annales de Philosophie Chrétienne*, June, 1906, p. 241.

APPENDIX

ON THE NOTION OF REALITY
AS CHANGING

APPENDIX

ON THE NOTION OF REALITY AS CHANGING

In my *Principles of Psychology* (vol. ii, p. 646) I gave the name of the 'axiom of skipped intermediaries and transferred relations' to a serial principle of which the foundation of logic, the *dictum de omni et nullo* (or, as I expressed it, the rule that what is of a kind is of that kind's kind), is the most familiar instance. More than the more is more than the less, equals of equals are equal, sames of the same are the same, the cause of a cause is the cause of its effects, are other examples of this serial law. Altho it applies infallibly and without restriction throughout certain abstract series, where the 'sames,' 'causes,' etc., spoken of, are 'pure,' and have no properties save their sameness, causality, etc., it cannot be applied offhand to concrete objects with numerous properties and relations, for it is hard to trace a straight line of sameness, causation, or whatever it may be, through a series of such objects without swerving into some 'respect' where the relation, as pursued originally, no longer holds: the objects have so many 'aspects' that we are constantly deflected from our original direction, and find, we know not why, that we are following something different from what we started with. Thus a cat is in a sense the same as a mouse-trap, and a mouse-trap the same as a bird-cage; but in no valuable or

347

easily intelligible sense is a cat the same as a bird-cage
Commodore Perry was in a sense the cause of the new
régime in Japan, and the new régime was the cause of
the russian Douma; but it would hardly profit us to
insist on holding to Perry as the cause of the Douma:
the terms have grown too remote to have any real or
practical relation to each other. In every series of real
terms, not only do the terms themselves and their associates and environments change, but we change, and
their *meaning* for us changes, so that new kinds of sameness and types of causation continually come into view
and appeal to our interest. Our earlier lines, having
grown irrelevant, are then dropped. The old terms can
no longer be substituted nor the relations 'transferred,'
because of so many new dimensions into which experience has opened. Instead of a straight line, it now follows a zigzag; and to keep it straight, one must do violence to its spontaneous development. Not that one
might not possibly, by careful seeking (tho I doubt
it), *find* some line in nature along which terms literally
the same, or causes causal in the same way, might be
serially strung without limit, if one's interest lay in such
finding. Within such lines our axioms might hold,
causes might cause their effect's effects, etc.; but such
lines themselves would, if found, only be partial members of a vast natural network, within the other lines of
which you could not say, in any sense that a wise man or

a sane man would ever think of, in any sense that would not be concretely *silly*, that the principle of skipt intermediaries still held good. In the *practical* world, the world whose significances we follow, sames of the same are certainly not sames of one another; and things constantly cause other things without being held responsible for everything of which those other things are causes.

Professor Bergson, believing as he does in a heraclitean 'devenir réel,' ought, if I rightly understand him, positively to deny that in the actual world the logical axioms hold good without qualification. Not only, according to him, do terms change, so that after a certain time the very elements of things are no longer what they were, but relations also change, so as no longer to obtain in the same identical way between the new things that have succeeded upon the old ones. If this were really so, then however indefinitely sames might still be substituted for sames in the logical world of nothing but pure sameness, in the world of real operations every line of sameness actually started and followed up would eventually give out, and cease to be traceable any farther. Sames of the same, in such a world, will not always (or rather, in a strict sense will never) be the same as one another, for in such a world there *is* no literal or ideal sameness among numerical differents. Nor in such a world will it be true that the cause of the cause is unreservedly the cause of the effect; for if we follow lines of real causation, instead of contenting ourselves with Hume's and Kant's eviscerated schematism, we find that remoter effects are seldom aimed at by causal intentions,[1] that no one kind of causal activity continues indefinitely, and that the principle of skipt intermediaries can be talked of only *in abstracto*.[2]

Volumes i, ii, and iii of the *Monist* (1890–1893) contain a number of articles by Mr. Charles S. Peirce, articles the originality of which has apparently prevented their making an immediate impression, but which, if I mistake not, will prove a gold-mine of ideas for thinkers of the coming generation. Mr. Peirce's views, tho reached so differently, are altogether congruous with Bergson's. Both philosophers believe that the appearance of novelty in things is genuine. To an observer standing outside of its generating causes, novelty can appear only as so much 'chance'; to one who stands inside it is the expression of 'free creative activity.' Peirce's 'tychism' is thus practically synonymous with Bergson's 'devenir réel.' The common objection to admitting novelties is that by jumping abruptly in, *ex nihilo*, they shatter the world's rational continuity. Peirce meets this objection by combining his tychism

---

[1] Compare the douma with what Perry aimed at.

[2] Compare above, Vol. I, Essay VI, as to what I mean here by 'real' causal activity.

with an express doctrine of 'synechism' or continuity, the two doctrines merging into the higher synthesis on which he bestows the name of 'agapasticism (*loc. cit.*, iii, 188), which means exactly the same thing as Bergson's 'évolution créatrice.' Novelty, as empirically found, does n't arrive by jumps and jolts, it leaks in insensibly, for adjacents in experience are always interfused, the smallest real datum being both a coming and a going, and even numerical distinctness being realized effectively only after a concrete interval has passed. The intervals also deflect us from the original paths of direction, and all the old identities at last give out, for the fatally continuous infiltration of otherness warps things out of every original rut. Just so, in a curve, the same direction is *never* followed, and the conception of it as a myriad-sided polygon falsifies it by supposing it to do so for however short a time. Peirce speaks of an ' infinitesimal' tendency to diversification. The mathematical notion of an infinitesimal contains, in truth, the whole paradox of the same and yet the nascent other, of an identity that won't *keep* except so far as it keeps *failing*, that won't *transfer*, any more than the serial relations in question transfer, when you apply them to reality instead of applying them to concepts alone.

A friend of mine has an idea, which illustrates on such a magnified scale the impossibility of tracing the same line through reality, that I will mention it here. He thinks that nothing more is needed to make history 'scientific' than to get the content of any two epochs (say the end of the thirteenth and the end of the nineteenth century) accurately defined, then accurately to define the direction of the change that led from the one epoch into the other, and finally to prolong the line of that direction into the future. So prolonging the line, he thinks, we ought to be able to define the actual state of things at any future date we please. We all feel the essential unreality of such a conception of 'history' as this; but if such a synechistic pluralism as Peirce, Bergson, and I believe in, be what really exists, every phenomenon of development, even the simplest, would prove equally rebellious to our science should the latter pretend to give us literally accurate instead of approximate, or statistically generalized, pictures of the development of reality.

I can give no further account of Mr. Peirce's ideas in this note, but I earnestly advise all students of Bergson to compare them with those of the french philosopher.

INDEXES

INDEX TO
ESSAYS IN RADICAL EMPIRICISM

355

INDEX

KNOWLEDGE: 4, 25, 56 ff., 68 ff., 87–88, 196 ff., 231. *See also* under COGNITIVE RELATION, OBJECTIVE REFERENCE.

LIFE: 87, 161.
LOCKE: 10.
LOTZE: 59, 75, 167.

MATERIALISM: 179, 232.
MILL, J. S.: x, 43, 76.
MILL, JAMES: 43.
MILLER, D.: 54.
MINDS, their Conterminousness: 76 ff., Essay IV.
MONISM: vii, 208.
MOORE, G. E.: 6–7.
MÜNSTERBERG, H.: 1, 18–20, 158.

NATORP, P.: 1, 7–8.
NATURALISM: 96.
NEO-KANTISM: 5–6.

OBJECTIVE REFERENCE: 67 ff.
OBJECTIVITY: 23 ff., 79.

PANPSYCHISM: 89, 188.
PARALLELISM: 210.
PERCEPTION: 11 ff., 17, 33, 65, 78, 82 ff., 197, 200, 211 ff.
PERRY, R. B.: 24.
PHYSICAL REALITY: 14, 22, 32, 124 ff., 139 ff., 149 ff., 154, 211 ff., 229.
PLURALISM: 89, 90, 110.
PRAGMATISM: iv, x, xi–xii, 11, 72, 97 ff., 156, 159, 176.
PRIMARY QUALITIES: 147.
PRINCE, M.: 88.
PRINGLE-PATTISON, A. S.: 109.
PSYCHOLOGY: 206, 209 ff.
PURE EXPERIENCE: 4, 23, 26–27,

35, Essay II, 74, 90, 93 ff., 96, 121, 123, 134, 135, 138, 139, 160, 193, 200, 226 ff.

RADICAL EMPIRICISM: iv–v, vii, ix–xiii, 41 ff., 47, 48, 69, 76, 89, 91, 107, 109, 121, 148, 156, 159, 182.
RATIONALISM: 41, 96 ff.
REALISM: 16, 40, 76, 82 ff.
REHMKE, J.: 1.
RELATIONS: x, 16, 25, 42 ff., 71, 81, Essay III, 148. *See also* under CONJUNCTIVE and DISJUNCTIVE.
RELIGION: xiii, 194.
RENOUVIER: 184–185.
REPRESENTATION: 61, 196 ff., 212 ff. *See also* under SUBSTITUTION.
ROYCE, J.: 21, 158, 186–187, 195.

SANTAYANA, G.: 143, 218.
SCHILLER, F. C. S.: 109, 191, 204.
SCHUBERT-SOLDERN, R. v.: 2.
SCHUPPE, W.: 1.
SECONDARY QUALITIES: 146, 219.
SELF: 45, 46, 94, 128 ff.
SENSATION: 30, 201.
SIDIS, B.: 144.
SPACE: 30–31, 84, 94, 110, 114.
SPENCER, H.: 144.
SPINOZA: 208.
SPIR, A.: 106.
STOUT, G. F.: 109, 158.
STRONG, C. A.: 54, 88, 89, 188.
SUBJECTIVITY: 23 ff.
SUBSTITUTION: 62 ff., 104, 201.

TAINE: 20, 62.
TAYLOR, A. E.: 111.
TELEOLOGY: 179.

356

INDEX

INDEX TO
A PLURALISTIC UNIVERSE

INDEX

his God; and religious experience, 308.

FERRIER, Jas., 13.

Finite experience, 39, 48, 182, 192–193.

Finiteness, of God, 111, 124, 294.

Foreignness, 31.

German manner of philosophizing, 17.

GOD, 24 f., 111, 124, 193, 240, 294.

GREEN, T. H., 6, 24, 137, 278.

HALDANE, R. B., 138.

HEGEL, Lecture III, *passim*, 11, 85, 207, 211, 219, 296. His vision, 88, 98 f., 104; his use of double negation, 102; his vicious intellectualism 106; Haldane on, 138; McTaggart on, 140; Royce on, 143.

HODGSON, S. H., 282.

Horse, 265.

HUME, 19, 267.

Idealism, 36. See Absolutism.

Identity, 93.

Immortality, Fechner's view of, 171.

'Independent' beings, 55, 58.

Indeterminism, 77.

Infinity, 229.

Influence, 258.

Intellect, its function is practical, 247 f., 252.

Intellectualism, vicious, 60, 218.

Intellectualist logic, 216, 259, 261.

Intellectualist method, 291.

Interaction, 56.

Intimacy, 31.

Irrationality, 81; of the absolute, 117–129.

JACKS, L, P., 35.

JOACHIM, H., 121, 141.

JONES, H., 52.

KANT, 19, 199, 238, 240.

LEIBNITZ, 119.

Life, 235, 253.

Log, 323.

Logic, 92, 211; intellectualist, 217, 242.

LOTZE, 55, 120.

LUTHER, 304.

McTAGGART, 51, 74 f., 120, 140 f., 183.

Manyness in oneness, 322. See Compounding.

Mental chemistry, 185.

MILL, J. S., 242, 260.

Mind, dust theory, 189.

Mind, the eternal, 137. See Absolute.

Monism, 36, 117, 125, 201, 313, 321 f.; Fechner's, 153. See Absolutism.

Monomaniacs, 78.

Motion, 233, 238, 254; Zeno on, 228.

MYERS, F. W. H., 315.

Nature, 21, 286.

Negation, 93 f.; double, 102.

Newton, 260.

INDEX

1972